Your Food: Whose Choice?

Edited by the
National Consumer Council

LONDON: HMSO

© Crown copyright 1992
First published 1992
Applications for reproduction should be made to HMSO

ISBN 0 11 701577 6

 **HMSO**

HMSO publications are available from:

HMSO Publications Centre
(Mail, fax and telephone orders only)
PO Box 276, London, SW8 5DT
Telephone orders 071-873 9090
General enquiries 071-873 0011
(queuing system in operation for both numbers)
Fax orders 071-873 8200

HMSO Bookshops
49 High Holborn, London, WC1V 6HB
(counter service only)
071-873 0011 Fax 071-873 8200
258 Broad Street, Birmingham, B1 2HE
021-643 3740 Fax 021-643 6510
Southey House, 33 Wine Street, Bristol, BS1 2BQ
0272 264306 Fax 0272 294515
9-21 Princess Street, Manchester, M60 8AS
061-834 7201 Fax 061-833 0634
16 Arthur Street, Belfast, BT1 4GD
0232 238451 Fax 0232 235401
71 Lothian Road, Edinburgh, EH3 9AZ
031-228 4181 Fax 031-229 2734

HMSO's Accredited Agents
(see Yellow Pages)

and through good booksellers

Contents

iii

Chapter 6

From High Street to Hypermarket

Food retailing in the 1990s

by Spencer Henson

One-stop, once-a-week shopping for food has become the norm for many of us. Superstore prices are lower - and the quality often better - than in the corner shop. But the power of a handful of companies over the price, quality and range of the food we buy and their effect on the economics of local shops are hotly debated. This chapter reviews the effects of these trends on consumer choice.

Chapter 7

Food Quality

What does it mean?

by Ann Foster and Sandra Macrae

What does 'quality' mean to retailers and producers? And does it match their customers' own standards for a quality product? This chapter charts the latest initiatives by industry, government, the European Commission and consumer organisations to find some common ground when it comes to defining quality in food.

Chapter 8

Freedom of Choice

Principles and practice

by Roger Straughan

Freedom of choice is a key consumer principle. But should consumers be free to choose food that might harm them? Should some processes be banned on ethical grounds? Can there ever be too much choice? How much information do consumers need about food? This chapter sketches the philosophical background to the principle of consumer choice and the practical issues it raises.

Chapter 9

Food Law and Regulation

Is the consumer voice heard?

by David Jukes

Every country imposes some legal controls on the ingredients, processing and labelling of food, in the interests of its citizens' health - and consumer confidence. This chapter outlines how food laws and regulations are now made - at UK, European and worldwide levels - and highlights some issues of consumer concern.

Chapter 10

Science at the Supermarket

What's on the menu tomorrow?

by Lucy Harris

Genetic modification and other biotechnological techniques are driving major advances in food and agriculture. They also raise anxieties about long-term safety and about the economics and ethics of food production. This chapter is both a layperson's guide to the latest food products and processes and a review of their implications for consumers.

About the National Consumer Council

The NCC was set up by government in 1975 to give a vigorous and independent voice to consumers in the United Kingdom. We research and campaign on behalf of the consumers of goods and services of all kinds.

Food safety, regulation and supply have always been high on the Council's agenda. This book is our first major review of another vital concern - the influences affecting consumers' *choices* in food.

Chapters 2 to 10 were commissioned from individual experts whose findings and views are personal to them. We are extremely grateful to these authors for their contributions. The summary chapter that opens the book was written by Beti Wyn Thomas (senior policy and development officer, NCC), with advice from Robin Simpson (deputy director, NCC).

The entire project was overseen by the Council's food policy committee, chaired by Jill Moore OBE. The other members of the committee were Anthony Burton OBE, Pat Cooper, Mary McAnally, Lady Anne McCollum, Helen Millar, Jean Varnam OBE and Alan White. The chapters were originally commissioned by Ann Foster, then NCC's food policy adviser, now director of the Scottish Consumer Council, and prepared for publication by NCC staff - Beti Wyn Thomas, Liz Dunbar, Joanne Stone, Rita O'Rourke and Eldorna Mapp.

The members of the National Consumer Council (mid-1992) are Lady Wilcox (Chairman), Ann Scully (Vice-chairman), Beata Brookes, Kumar Bhattacharyya, Anthony Burton OBE, Philip Circus, Noel Hunter, Paul Fairest, Jennifer Francis, John Hughes, Deirdre Hutton, George Jones, John Mitchell, Mary McAnally, Lady Anne McCollum, Jill Moore OBE, Jean Varnam OBE and Martin Wolf.

The National Consumer Council is as much concerned with public and professional services - and how they are regulated - as with shopping and other high street issues. We publish a wide range of policy papers and reports on consumer issues. Most of them are on sale from the Council's office: please send for a publications catalogue.

National Consumer Council,
20 Grosvenor Gardens,
London SW1W ODH
Telephone: 071-730 3469 Fax: 071-730 0191

About the contributors

Ann Foster (chapter 7) is Director of the Scottish Consumer Council

Lucy Harris (chapter 10) is a policy and development officer with the National Consumer Council

Spencer Henson (chapter 6) is a lecturer in food economics, University of Reading

David Jukes (chapter 9) is a lecturer in the department of food science and technology, University of Reading

Suzi Leather (chapter 5) is a freelance researcher and a member of the Ministry of Agriculture, Fisheries and Food Consumer Panel

Jeanette Longfield (chapter 4) was formerly with the Coronary Prevention Group

Sandra Macrae (chapter 7) is a consultant with MacKay Consultants Ltd, Stirling

David J. Mela (chapter 2) is a research scientist in the consumer sciences department, AFRC Institute of Food Research, Reading

Peter J. Rogers (chapter 2) is a research scientist in the consumer sciences department, AFRC Institute of Food Research, Reading

Richard Shepherd (chapter 3) is a research scientist in the consumer sciences department, AFRC Institute of Food Research, Reading

Paul Sparks (chapter 3) is a research scientist in the consumer sciences department, AFRC Institute of Food Research, Reading

Roger Straughan (chapter 8) is Reader in the faculty of education and community studies, University of Reading

Chapter 1
Food, Choice and the Consumer
Summary and recommendations by
the National Consumer Council

Choice is important to consumers – and when it comes to food, it could
be argued that UK consumers now have more choice than ever before.
One glance along the check-out counters of a large supermarket on a
Saturday morning demonstrates the wide range of choices that face
many families every week.

But what brings consumers to this check-out or to that corner shop?
What makes us choose this brand of breakfast cereal or that pound of
apples? How far does the television commercial or the package label
affect our decisions? How important is price? How much do shoppers
know about the effects of modern biotechnology, of international food
law, of food production and retailing? And what part do consumers
play in the decisions that directly affect the preparation, content,
range and availability of the food on high street shelves?

Any single decision about choosing or eating food is the result of a
whole jigsaw of conscious and subconscious influences, no one of which
on its own can be said to be the over-riding influence. The National
Consumer Council wanted to examine each piece in the jigsaw more
closely, as a way of improving consumer information and
understanding, helping people to make more informed decisions and
improving consumers' input into the decisions taken in the food supply
chain on their behalf.

We therefore commissioned these nine chapters, each focusing on one
of the important factors that contribute to people's everyday food
decisions – from family heredity to family income, from TV
commercials to EC directives, from supermarket competition to super-
strain gene technology. The authors all have wide knowledge and
expertise in their fields, and the chapters – and the views expressed in
them – are personal ones. But they all raise a number of issues
important to consumers, and in this first chapter we draw on the ideas
and evidence in the rest of the book to suggest further research and
recommend official action that could give all consumers a more robust
and informed role in the choices they make about food.

In assessing the way any goods or services are provided, the National
Consumer Council uses a number of criteria against which to measure
how well they perform from the consumer's point of view. Choice is one
of them. Others cover such points as safety, access, price, information,
redress, and consumer representation. When it comes to food,
consumers are naturally interested in all these criteria but they all
presuppose one fundamental right:

1

- that consumers should have access to *a secure supply of staple foods*.

The question of access is basic. The degree to which other factors are important, and how they interact with each other, will depend on the individual making the decision. In general, though, we can say that:

- *the price of food* is important to consumers. It affects their ability to exercise choice in the market place. Every family spends over ten per cent of its income on food, and food price trends have a major impact on everyone's standard of living. For families on low incomes who spend a larger proportion of their incomes on food, prices become even more important;

- consumers expect their food to meet high *quality standards* – to be of the variety, content, composition, nutritional value, taste, freshness and appearance they want;

- consumers want to be confident that the food they buy and eat is *safe*. This covers both legal regulation and, in the 1990s, issues such as the use of additives, veterinary drug residues, pesticide residues and the incidence of microbiological contamination;

- in order to make informed choices about their purchases and diet, consumers need *clear, consistent and reliable information*. This helps them in decisions about quality and value (including nutritional value) for money and in making valid comparisons;

- consumers need to know that their views are being taken into account when decisions affecting their food are made. There must be effective *representation of consumer views* to government and industry, with strong consumer representation on the main committees concerned with advice, policy, priorities and strategy on agriculture and food – both in the UK and Europe;

and lastly,

- consumers should have *access to a wide choice of food*, including fresh food. They should be in a position to follow official dietary and nutrition advice and they should not be barred from a safe, healthy diet by low income.

These basic consumer criteria inform this introductory chapter and the recommendations we make in it.

1.1 Do we like what we eat or eat what we like?

We start with human basics. Is what we eat largely governed by our biological make-up – our genes? We obviously have innate preferences. There is not much doubt, for example, that babies prefer sweet to bitter tastes. But hereditary biases can be changed and, as we grow older, we learn to like – and dislike – other foods.

In chapter 2, David Mela and Peter Rogers suggest that the human body is still programmed with a tendency to over-eat – to eat and store food today against a shortage tomorrow. In the western world today, there is rarely a serious scarcity of food. So this biological safety mechanism, a hangover from our more primitive environment, tends to encourage obesity.

The research studies they outline make depressing reading for the millions of people who diet. In tests that introduced reduced-fat products and artificial sweeteners into people's normal diets without their knowledge, the volunteers compensated very quickly by eating more of the higher calorie food. More importantly, when the higher-fat, higher-sugar items were re-introduced into their diet, the subjects did not make comparable reductions; they over-ate by large amounts. This was the body working on its own. Without information about what we are eating, our biological make-up can take over.

David Mela and Peter Rogers assert that fat and sweetener substitutes by themselves are unlikely to reduce total energy intake, although as part of a conscious, controlled diet, they may make a useful contribution.

Recommendation 1

Further research is needed into the effects of low-fat and reduced-sugar diets. We need to understand more about the relationship between the individual's intellectual decision to control food intake and the body's natural balancing act.

1.2 Cultural and social imprints

As well as biological influences on our choice in foods, there is another layer of personal influences – our cultural, social and psychological backgrounds. Simple geography is a major influence although, in a country like the UK, territorial boundaries become more and more blurred with the opening up of trade barriers, increased travel, the introduction of new cuisines and the round-the-year availability of foods which were once only seasonal. Social influences are also strong.

3

In chapter 3, Richard Shepherd and Paul Sparks review the effects of culture, family, economic and social status, self-image and identity. (Later chapters examine some of these more fully, especially the impact of low incomes and advertising on choices.) Many women will recognise one study's conclusion that husbands change their eating habits when they get married more than their wives do.

The effect of the family needs further study, especially as changes in family eating patterns obviously affect the shopping basket. For example, families are less likely to eat together nowadays. And more and more households consist of only one person – in 1990 this was 26 per cent of all households. How far have the rise in ownership of freezers and micro-waves and the introduction of 'convenience foods' and ready-prepared meals encouraged, or been affected by, these trends?

1.3 Do we eat what we're told to?

(a) Food advertising

'What shall we eat tonight?' The answer can often hinge on an impulse to try a new recipe or ingredient or to see whether the product behind an advertising campaign stands up to expectations.

What are the facts behind these influences? Are consumers readily convinced by the advertising campaigns of the food industry? Do they all rush to buy the ready-made meal believing it will give them the freedom to 'live their lives more fully' or the full-of-fibre breakfast cereal because it is 'the sensible option'? Or do they use the information offered by advertisers to make rational, informed choices?

Jeanette Longfield in chapter 4 delves into the facts behind the £500 million a year spent by food companies on advertising. Food companies rank high in the top twenty list of spenders on all types of advertising – with advertisements for coffee, a cola drink, crisps, tea, breakfast cereals, margarine, soup and a chocolate bar taking thirteen of the top twenty places.

But research also suggests that, where television advertising is concerned, viewers in fact tend to use the commercial breaks to go out to the kitchen or to channel-hop. And, as consumers of advertising, we also believe that we personally are rarely influenced by advertising campaigns – at the same time believing that they do have a powerful influence on *other people's* choices.

So who *does* advertising affect? Any parent watching independent television during children's programmes will know how targeted the advertising at those times is. It has been shown that during one week of television broadcasts for children, over half the commercials were for food and soft drinks (eight times higher than any other category, including toys).

This might not necessarily be a cause for concern. More often than not, children are able to distinguish between the programmes and the advertisements; any influence from advertising can be 'controlled' by the parents who make the purchasing decisions; and indeed the Independent Television Commission's code of advertising standards and practice does cover children and misleading advertising and all advertisements concerning food and health.

But it has been shown, too, that some children cannot discriminate between programmes and advertisements. Others will not recognise the purpose of television commercials – to *sell* items to the viewer. More generally, the claim by the Incorporated Society of British Advertisers – that advertising to children helps provide them with 'useful information about products they are interested in and increases their ability to make informed choices' (1) – presupposes that the children are being offered comparable information about different brands within the same product range and that they are capable of differentiating them. The reality is that children are likely to become attached to products because of their attachment to a cartoon or other character, to songs and jingles, and to the overall impact of a particular advertisement.

The influence of children on adults' food purchases is also often underestimated. The industry claims that advertising can make food more interesting to children, especially the fussy eaters. This would make sense if the advertisements targeted at children were for particularly nutritional foods.

But the 1990 survey quoted by Jeanette Longfield suggests that, in ten hours' viewing, about 75 per cent of the 92 commercials for food and drink were for products high in fat, sugar or both. During Saturday morning viewing, the percentage for fatty and/or sugary foods rose to 85 per cent. In one four-hour period, the same sweetened breakfast cereal was advertised eight times, sometimes twice in the same break. It is no wonder that parents say that children's influence on the weekly shop is more likely to be in the biscuits, soft drinks, puddings, breakfast cereals, crisps and fast food lines. Parents' attempts to raise the nutritional value of the family diet often go out of the window in

5

an effort to persuade their children to eat anything. Arguably it is the adults, the actual purchasers of the products, at whom the advertising should be directed.

Recommendation 2

We recommend that the Independent Television Commission update its guidance on the advertising of foods, particularly food with high sugar and/or fat content, targeted at children. We urge the relevant committees of the Independent Television Commission to develop guidance on the frequency of such commercials and to consider whether such advertising should be directed at children at all.

(b) Classroom resources

A related issue, which the National Consumer Council has examined in some detail, is business-sponsored education material. Advertisements for children are at least monitored. Material for use in the classroom is not. Yet teachers depend more and more in their day-to-day work on leaflets, posters, videos and so on produced or paid for by business and industry.

We take the view that it is in everyone's interest to establish and maintain trust in the quality and integrity of these classroom resources. In 1988, with the help of representatives of business, consumer interests, teachers' associations and local education authorities, the National Consumer Council published guidelines to help business sponsors in the production of educational material and to help educationalists assess their suitability for use with schoolchildren (2). While the guidelines have no enforcement mechanism, they were an attempt to encourage sponsors to regulate the promotional side of their educational activities. Our guidelines appear to have gained wide acceptance among both sponsors and educationalists.

However, a new issue now requires further and urgent attention. The publication of official guidelines on healthy eating has called into question the activities of commercial sponsors when it comes to health and nutrition education. For example, attempts by government health workers to encourage young people to reduce their intake of sugar and some kinds of fat are being combated by sponsored education materials, carefully and expertly prepared to meet the demands of the new curriculum but which subtly promote such products in young minds. This has led to another initiative, to develop an 'accreditation scheme' to regulate and vet health- and food-related education materials (3). The scheme would be voluntary and independent of the producers of the material, with some government funding.

While recognising that the practicalities need careful work, the National Consumer Council endorses this idea. It may be necessary to start with a pilot study which would involve setting guidelines; this would seem to be particularly appropriate for government funding.

Recommendation 3

The National Consumer Council endorses the proposal for a voluntary 'accreditation scheme' for education materials, and urges the Department for Education, the Department of Health and the Ministry of Agriculture, Fisheries and Food to give financial support to its development.

1.4 Healthy eating – at what cost?

The whole problem of advertising and promotion directed at children is exacerbated when a family is shopping on a low fixed budget. The quote from one mother, reported in chapter 4, will ring true with many parents:

> 'They tend to want you to spend money you haven't got ... you have a set amount that you want to spend, and if you've got children with you they can exasperate you into buying things that you don't really want to get.'

This can mean parents buying brands that their children urge them to buy and, with more serious implications, not buying foods that are the basis of a healthy diet.

As Suzi Leather says in chapter 5, it is possible to eat a healthy, balanced diet on very little money – by cooking all meals from raw ingredients and relying on vegetable protein. Some people do so. But a more typical average diet among lower-income groups will be high in manufactured foods – a consequence not of ignorance but of lack of choice, lack of transport, lack of storage and lack of money. A family without a car or access to public transport is much more dependent on small local shops where the range of fresh produce is smaller and the prices higher than in an out-of-town supermarket. They often have less storage, fridge and freezer facilities and may be concerned to save money on power for cooking. And their priority may be to ensure that all the family (including the fussiest) eats *something* rather than aiming to provide healthier food that might be refused (and in a house where there is less likelihood of there being anything else to eat).

This raises a number of crucial issues. First, do we know enough, individually, about what constitutes a healthy diet? And do we, as a society, know enough about the cost of healthy eating and the ability of low-income families to afford to choose healthier food?

(a) What do people understand by 'healthy food'?

Most EC countries now issue dietary guidelines to the public. In the northern European context, this usually means advising people to eat less fat, salt and sugar and to eat more fibre, fruit, vegetables, white meat, fish, and starchy staples such as pasta, bread, rice or potatoes. As a result of this kind of information – produced and distributed by governments, health and consumer organisations, retailers and trade organisations – people by and large are increasingly aware of the links between diet and disease.

There have been major publicity campaigns on diet and health. These often concentrate on translating scientific jargon, like the official 'percentage nutrient recommendations', into simpler and more straightforward guidelines that people will understand – such as 'cut down on fat' and 'grill rather than fry'. Booklets like the one produced by the Healthy Eating Campaign, *Eat Well, Live Well* which describes in plain language what the current dietary exhortations mean in terms of day-to-day foods, are very welcome.

The general message is certainly getting across – but often the detail is being lost. Many of us know something about cholesterol, saturated fats, fibre, salt, sugar and so on without really understanding their place in our diets, and how – and whether – to control intakes. In this context, the National Consumer Council welcomes the work of the Coronary Prevention Group, funded by the Ministry of Agriculture, Fisheries and Food, in making nutritional information on packages more accessible and meaningful to consumers (4). A clearer method of labelling food by describing its nutrient content as high, medium or low will make it simpler for people to make healthy choices.

Recommendation 4

The Ministry of Agriculture, Fisheries and Food should undertake further research into the popular conceptions and misconceptions about healthy foods/diets so that information and advice can be better targeted. In particular, much clearer guidance on, for example, sugar, fibre and fat levels is needed.

(Specific recommendations about labelling appear later in this chapter.)

(b) Too poor to make a healthy choice?

But where does this leave people who are shopping on a low income? Attempts have been made in recent years to define a healthy diet more precisely and also to quantify its cost (some of the calculations are described in chapter 5). The results suggest two broad conclusions. People on lower incomes are less likely to 'eat well' and they are less likely to be able to afford a 'healthy diet'.

Work by the Family Budget Unit at York University has gone some of the way to produce realistic food budgets for various family types. Based on actual patterns of food purchasing and using data from the *National Food Survey*, the Unit has devised a 'modest but adequate' diet that meets the recommended intakes of all nutrients and the official guidelines for healthy eating. The Family Budget Unit's report concluded:

'it is unlikely that households at the lowest levels of income would be able to purchase a healthy diet which allows a range of food choice commensurate with the notion of "modest but adequate".' (5)

The Ministry of Agriculture, Fisheries and Food has also tried to cost a healthy diet. It suggested that, in early 1992, a 'healthy diet' cost on average £11.71 per person per week. MAFF also managed to construct a diet that would meet the government's nutritional requirements and only cost £10 per person per week.

However, Suzi Leather (chapter 5) argues that in order to eat healthily for £10 per person per week, low-income groups would have to cut out meat almost entirely, more than double their consumption of tinned fruit, frozen vegetables and breakfast cereals and eat five times more wholemeal bread and more white bread, often without even the thinnest spread of butter or margarine. Added to which, these are the people who will experience difficulties in travelling to shops where goods can be purchased most cheaply and in storing, preparing and cooking food.

Given the increasing official emphasis on the need for a healthy diet, consumers need much more practical guidance on what this means. Ways need to be found to enable families on low incomes to buy the various components of a healthy diet.

One way forward would be for the government to address some of the immediate problems through the benefits system. However, the Department of Social Security argues that income support levels are not calculated to cover specific amounts for specific items, according to evidence from chapter 5. The allowance for food is not separately costed – 'claimants, like most people, are free to spend their money in any way they choose' (6).

Recommendation 5

The Department of Social Security should review benefit levels to take account of the actual purchasing power of family budgets. In particular, decisions on benefit levels should be informed by the link between their incomes, their food purchases and their needs in terms of a healthy diet.

The effect of a low income on a child's diet also warrants comment. Research suggests that generally speaking children do eat unhealthily, with particularly high levels of fat and sugar. Suzi Leather notes how much cheaper it is to buy the nutrients children need in a diet high in fats and sugar. To get sufficient dietary energy (calories), sweets and biscuits are much cheaper than fruit.

A further problem is school meals. The uptake is shrinking. Some local education authorities provide them only for children who are eligible for free meals. The nutritional guidelines for them have been abolished (under the Education Act 1980). The nutritional and financial implications of these moves need review. The National Consumer Council welcomes the initiatives that encourage parents and children to monitor local provision, like the School Meals Campaign, and the work of organisations like the British Nutrition Foundation which is closely involved with the Ministry of Agriculture, Fisheries and Food in the preparation of educational packs for 5 to 7-year-olds.

Recommendation 6

To improve children's nutrition, and especially the nutrition of children in low-income families, the Department for Education, the Department of Health and the Ministry of Agriculture, Fisheries and Food should review the provision of school meals, taking into account the need to reinstate nutritional guidelines.

I.5 Where can I buy my food?

Supermarkets are in the business of making money: their bread and butter is the consumer's weekly shopping basket. All the evidence suggests that being able to make large food purchases at supermarkets benefits the consumer in a number of ways – price, quality and choice. But are the supermarkets offering all that we would wish them to?

The competition for custom has become fierce. Supermarkets vie with each other to provide car parking, banking facilities, in-store pharmacies, coffee shops, dry cleaners and hairdressing, on top of the 'traditional' foods and household goods. However, this is just in the large multiple chains. The total number of retail outlets has fallen in recent years while the size of individual outlets has increased.

This reflects the change in the structure of ownership. 'National' operators now control large numbers of stores. There has also been a cut in the total number of multiple retailers, as a result of takeovers and mergers. The result is that over half of UK food purchases are now made in two per cent of food shops.

Food stores are increasingly located outside town centres. In chapter 6, Spencer Henson describes how this trend has gone along with changes in people's shopping patterns. A once-a-week food shopping trip, by car, is now the norm. As the Chairman of Safeway plc said (on Channel 4's *Food File* programme), these big stores are 'best placed to develop quality foods, hygienic foods, wide ranges and to achieve real efficiencies which are reflected in their prices'. And the author's own surveys reported in chapter 6, confirm the relatively lower prices in these larger stores.

But while it is exactly these advantages that attract many consumers, there are others who find these stores inaccessible. At the same time, the number of small supermarkets and independent stores has dropped, leaving food-shopping gaps in the high street. Lower-income families, elderly and disabled people are often physically and financially less mobile and may have to pay more for the same basket of goods and to choose from a smaller range of goods (although this may be offset by the arrival in UK high streets of discount chains from the continent).

This raises the issue of supermarket pricing policies. Among other factors, it is the discounts available to the major multiples from their suppliers that enables them to offer products at very much lower prices than other types of food store, often lower than the manufacturers' list prices. While consumers may have benefited from these discounts, so too have the retailers, argues Spencer Henson. The power of the major chains when it comes to contracts and prices has worked to the detriment of the local, independent retail sector and hence to consumers who have lost access to – and choice of – this type of outlet.

Local planning decisions also have a bearing on these developments. There is need for further research into how far the planning process can make a contribution to decisions about the siting and distribution of food stores.

However, the large supermarkets now offer a much wider choice of goods and services than was traditionally associated with grocery shops. The size, cleanliness and comfort of the large outlets, their extra facilities, their opening hours and wide range of products are now important features in the marketing strategies of the big retailers, both in competition with each other and with the independent sector. This is undoubtedly a result of the emphasis consumers themselves place on quality, choice and convenience in their choice of food and where they buy it.

Other reviews of the operations of the major food retailers have concluded that, although there has been a concentration in ownership, this has not operated to the detriment of the consumer. Spencer Henson's chapter does not dispute this broad conclusion, although he does point to the dangers of some consumers - the less well-off - being bypassed. His chapter investigates in detail both the ever-increasing degree of concentration and the rising financial returns to food retailers.

Recommendation 7

Given the growing concentration of ownership in food retailing and its growing returns, we recommend that the competition authorities monitor the sector closely, to ensure that consumers are not exploited.

1.6 Food prices and agricultural policy

The retail sector clearly influences price - a major factor in consumer choice. However, food shops are at the end of a long supply chain which starts, often, with farmers via processors, manufacturers and distributors. The first link in that chain, agriculture, has been examined by the National Consumer Council in the past. Our 1988 report *Consumers and the Common Agricultural Policy* described our policy in full and, although events have moved on, our analysis still stands.

The European Commission's common agricultural policy, by operating a price support scheme, in effect levies a regressive tax on food. This is unfair. As Suzi Leather points out in chapter 5, low-income families spend a higher than average proportion of their income on food.

Indeed, according to some calculations, to eat a healthy diet, many families on income support would have to spend more than half their income on food. European Community prices are usually three to four times higher than world prices for sugar, three times for butter, twice for wheat and one-and-a-half times for beef. It is estimated that the CAP puts up consumers' food bills by between five and ten per cent. This bears especially hard on poor families.

The system does not even succeed in its stated aim of helping the small family farm. Support through high prices is wasteful, given that the poorer small farmers produce least and therefore gain least. It is estimated that eighty per cent of EC support to farmers goes to twenty per cent of farmers, generally the wealthiest. This is an inevitable consequence of the price support system.

Our view has long been that the common agricultural policy should be reformed. Its social objectives should be met by shifting expenditure away from price support (paid for by all food consumers) towards direct assistance to those farmers who need it (paid for by taxpayers). This would be less regressive and more transparent. Prices could then be allowed to move towards world levels – that is, downwards. Reducing price support may not recoup the full extra costs to consumers immediately. It is attenuated through the food chain. But, especially combined with the monitoring of the retail sector we have called for (recommendation 7), some effects should certainly work their way through in due course.

The agreement reached by the Council of European agriculture ministers in May 1992 to reduce some support prices is a welcome step in the right direction (although some sectors are still to be reformed). The question is: to what extent will these reductions benefit consumers? We are concerned about the set-aside quota measures which accompany the agreement. These will restrict supply and could prevent the full benefit of the cuts feeding through to consumers. The overall thrust of the agreement, however, allowing EC agriculture to become more market-oriented, is welcome.

Recommendation 8

We reiterate our view that the European Commission's common agricultural policy needs reform to bring pricing more into line with consumer demand, by moving prices closer to world levels. Social objectives should be decoupled from pricing policy and should be paid for directly, through taxation. The 1992 agreement is a step in this direction.

1.7 Judging by the label

Underlying any discussion about food and about how consumers are to judge whether their purchase lives up to their expectations is the basic issue of information. Labelling – and packaging in its widest sense – are vital in communicating information about food products.

Labelling can cover a vast amount of information. There are ingredient and nutritional contents; marketing claims; quality assurance scheme labels; country of origin marks; and of course the name and description of the product, plus details of storage and cooking. Much of this helps consumers with their choices.

Currently, all foodstuffs on sale in the UK (except for fresh fruit and vegetables, carbonated water, vinegar, cheese, butter, fermented milk and cream, and products of a single ingredient) have to list their ingredients, in descending order of weight. Some producers offer extra information, giving the percentage of one or more of the main ingredients. Usually, though, it is difficult to differentiate between like products just from their labels, beyond a vague notion that one pasta dish may contain more tomato and the other more pasta. Without more specific information, how can the shopper decide which product offers the better value?

Consumer organisations have long called for a fuller declaration of ingredients on labels, following the move away from specific composition and ingredient standards (seen by the European Commission as a potential barrier to trade). Fuller information on labels has yet to be accepted. Proposed amendments to the labelling directive on 'quantitative ingredient declarations' (known as QUID) go some way down this road but will require percentages to be given only for ingredients that are mentioned in the name or labelling of a product or that are essential characterising ingredients. This does not go far enough. Faced with an increasing choice of food products which often look alike but are not the same, consumers need the protection of clear, full and accurate label information. This will enable them to make their own choices according to their own priorities.

Recommendation 9

We recommend that the amendments to the European Commission's 1979 labelling directive, which introduced quantitative ingredient declarations (QUID), should insist on full percentage declarations of all main ingredients.

The same argument holds for nutritional labelling. Only with full information can consumers differentiate between products and judge their pros and cons for themselves. We do not doubt that, for many consumers, nutritional information is still difficult to translate into meaningful practice and we have already suggested (recommendation 4) that research and publicity are essential to improving public understanding. But at least when the information is given on some items, as it is now, more and more people start to use it in their purchasing decisions – if only to look at the levels of fat per serving.

Recommendation 10

We urge the European Commission to amend the directive on nutrition labelling and introduce full and compulsory nutrition labelling on food.

Linked closely to this same issue is the vexed question of 'health' or 'nutritional' claims on foodpacks and labels. Consumers must not be misled into choosing one product over another by claims that cannot be substantiated.

In the absence of speedy progress from the EC on this question, the food safety directorate at the UK Ministry of Agriculture, Fisheries and Food released for consultation its own draft regulations on nutritional claims early in 1992. Any move to regulate claims on food labels is to be welcomed. 'Health' messages have to be rigorously controlled. Consumers must be protected from claims that do more to sell the product than to promote public health. We shall monitor progress.

1.8 Choosing a 'quality' product

Increasingly, there is a new dimension to labelling – the quality mark. In order to differentiate between products, various parts of the food industry now run quality assurance schemes (for example, Farm Assured Scotch Livestock) and Food From Britain, supported by the Ministry of Agriculture, Fisheries and Food, has set up its own quality certification scheme. All these schemes have their own 'marks' or stamps, which appear on the packaging and often include the word 'quality'. But what does quality mean in this context? And what do consumers understand by the word?

Quality in food, as in any product, is difficult to define precisely. What is an important component of quality to one consumer may be unimportant to another. Perceptions are highly subjective.

For example it could be argued that the direct link between producers and large retailers, as for fresh fruit and vegetables, has benefited consumers in terms of the quality of produce available to them. Retailers insist on uniformity in their fresh produce. Contracts are agreed which specify the requirements in terms of size, shape, colour and so on. But does this offer consumers a *quality* product – that is, a product distinct from or superior to another product?

The four-tier model (in chapter 7 by Ann Foster and Sandra Macrae) gives one interesting 'hierarchy' of consumer priorities when it comes to quality. As each quality level is reached, consumer requirements expand to encompass an increasingly sophisticated set of needs. As the hierarchy moves from the basic inner circle of 'safety' to the outer one of 'ethics' (in the way food is produced), consumers may find they are paying a price premium.

So do the symbols and marks suggesting 'quality' produce help consumers decide which products to buy? And are they truly a guarantee of 'better' foods?

The answers seem to be – maybe. Consumers are fairly confused about the quality symbols that currently appear on food, although symbols that include straightforward statements are apparently used by shoppers as a guide to their purchases. A small-scale Consumers' Association study in 1990 (see chapter 7) suggested that shoppers could not distinguish between symbols that denote an 'official' scheme and those that are purely a design or marketing feature. None of the participants in the group discussions, for example, recognised the official status of the Food From Britain symbol and few said that it would influence their decision to buy a product.

In more recent research in Scotland, consumers were asked what they would expect from a proposed quality scheme for meat. The responses reveal a perception of quality that puts heavy emphasis on food safety, animal welfare and more natural methods of food production. Similarly, when asked what a label saying that the produce was 'quality assured' should mean, the respondents confirmed the importance of food safety, product superiority and animal welfare.

So consumers' perceptions of quality now go well beyond the freshness, appearance and colour of a food. They want to be able to delve further back into the food chain, to be reassured that steps have been taken to produce food in ways that they approve. This means that consumers themselves must make an effort to understand what is being offered to them, by reading leaflets and seeking information. But it also suggests that the industry should note the concerns of consumers and consult them when quality schemes are at the planning stage. Shoppers need to be convinced that quality schemes are more than a marketing tool. It is essential to their credibility, for example, that standards are independently monitored and inspected and that there are tangible and enforceable sanctions for breaches of standards.

Recommendation 11

Before launching any food quality scheme, the industry should undertake careful research into consumer requirements and involve all interested parties in developing standards for the scheme. An independent body should be set up to oversee each scheme and to ensure that inspections and sanctions are enforceable.

On a simpler level, it would be to the benefit of the industry - and certainly of consumers - if the rash of labels and symbols and marks were rationalised. There is a limit to the amount of information consumers can read and take in when they go shopping. Fewer, more identifiable quality marks, which guarantee higher standards than the legal minimum and which meet the qualities defined by the third and fourth tier of the 'hierarchy' model in chapter 7, should be the aim.

1.9 Just how much freedom of choice?

We have said that people's buying and eating decisions are based on a jigsaw of influences and that clear, accurate information is an essential linking piece in freedom of choice. But in chapter 8, Roger Straughan asks us to pause and ask: do consumers actually want to be left to take all the decisions? Indeed, should they? What exactly is freedom of choice? Should there be limits? If so, what are they?

Freedom of choice in food is never an absolute freedom, of course. There are some inevitable limits - the money in your purse, the problem of not being able to get to where 'better' choices can be made, the availability of goods, market forces, and so on. It is also obvious that many choices about our food are made so regularly and so automatically that they are second nature and are not perceived as choices at all. More and more, though, consumers are making conscious judgements – for example on health, ethical, political or religious grounds – and it is right that each of us should be free to make such decisions for ourselves, without paternalistic regulation.

But what about safety? Few people would insist on freedom of choice when it comes to contaminated food – and one of the key tenets of the National Consumer Council's food charter is that consumers must be able to enjoy food without anxiety (7). Food on public sale must continue to meet high standards of safety.

However, Roger Straughan tackles the question: how safe is safe? No product can ever be entirely risk-free. And when a risk has been identified, does it follow that the food should be automatically removed from the market place? Many consumers like the taste of unpasteurised milk and cheese. These carry a known safety risk. Should the sale of unpasteurised milk be banned, or is it fairer to tell consumers of the risks and let them make their own decision? In that particular debate, the National Consumer Council came out in favour of continued sales of unpasteurised milk, so long as it also carries the 'green top' as a warning to consumers. But the balance of the decision can often be a fine one.

All food safety risks should be minimised by the use of raw materials that meet high standards and by hygienic production processes. Often, though, consumers will wish to assess the balance of risks and benefits for themselves, and they can only do this if they are in full possession of the relevant facts. As Roger Straughan concludes, there should always be a presumption that consumer choice needs extending, not reducing.

1.10 Food law: is the consumer voice heard?

How much information to provide about food, and how, are questions that have exercised the minds of legislators of late. And indeed casting its shadow over much of the discussion in this book is the long arm of the law. Food regulations decided at national, European and, increasingly, at international levels affect nearly all the choices we are able to make.

Over the years, food laws have been made that have certainly had consumer protection at their heart. They have nevertheless been made with little input from consumers and with little investigation into their needs and concerns. The United Kingdom government is currently working on new regulations within the European

Community and – at worldwide level – within GATT (the general agreement on tariffs and trade) and the Codex Alimentarius Commission. How are consumers' views being identified and expressed within these international bodies?

David Jukes, in chapter 9, describes the various layers of decision making and how the voice of consumers increasingly influences governments' actions. Within the UK, for example, moves to appoint consumer or lay members to the committees that advise the government on food policy and practice are welcome. Further openness in the committees' and the food ministry's dealings with consumer representatives should be encouraged. But the perception, from outside, is of a close liaison between the Ministry of Agriculture, Fisheries and Food and the food producers and farmers. Consumers need to be reassured that their views are heard with equal seriousness and given equal weight with the 'other side'.

Recommendation 12

We remain concerned about responsibility for food safety. We want to see an agency independent of the Ministry of Agriculture, Fisheries and Food to deal with food safety, food standards, food science and nutrition, with prime responsibility for regulation, inspection, enforcement and consumer protection (8). Consumer representation on the agency would be essential, with as much emphasis as possible on open decision making.

As David Jukes points out, however, UK legislation is often now the final stage in a process started in the European Community. The member states implement the details of European directives. Consumer and other non-governmental organisations in this country know what that entails – consultation about the detail of regulations, implementation, enforcement, redress, provision of information to the public and so on. As far as it goes, the UK system does allow for some consultation on the decisions that will affect consumers' choices.

But nowadays the implementation procedures within other member states of the EC can also directly affect the UK consumer. We need to know how each state is interpreting details of EC directives – or at least to know that someone is collating such information. We do not.

One great problem of the consumer movement over the years has been its inability to make any significant impact on decision making in Brussels, despite recent efforts by the Commission's Consumer Policy Service. The traditional imbalance in power between producer and industry interests on the one hand and the consumer interest on the other has been perpetuated in the institutions of Europe. The National Consumer Council's earlier work on the common agricultural policy (9) and on EC food and nutrition policy (10) examined the shortcomings of the system in detail.

Decisions about the food we eat are being taken at more and more remote levels. Consumers need to have confidence that these structures have taken their views into account - through adequately resourced consumer representation, appropriate consumer consultation and a more informed understanding of consumer needs. We must not allow obsessive secrecy to work against the consumer interest.

Recommendation 13

The National Consumer Council has supported and continues to support the setting up of a European Food Agency that is independent of the European Commission. We need a central body to which producers and consumers can turn with confidence.

The key functions of a European Food Agency would be in:

● formulating a Community food and nutrition policy;

● collating food consumption and nutrition status data;

● undertaking a food quality audit;

● co-ordinating the implementation of framework directives;

● acting in an advisory and conciliation role;

● being responsible for the Community inspection service;

● housing the database of details of all legislation;

● reviewing the role of advisory committees;

● ensuring that consumers play a more active role.

Chapter 9 also describes the role of the international food standards body, called the Codex Alimentarius Commission. This was set up thirty years ago by the World Health Organisation and the Food and Agriculture Organisation to ensure fair practices in food and to promote co-ordination of food standards work internationally. The Commission is likely to assume greater importance in future years and consumer organisations must be ready to play their part in the important decisions that will be taken. The National Consumer

Council was pleased when the International Organisation of Consumers Unions (IOCU) was given observer status at general (non-expert) Codex committees. Further improvements are needed, however, and in 1991 IOCU made a series of recommendations (11). We recommend that these are adopted.

Recommendation 14

We recommend that the Codex Alimentarius Commission make the following reforms:

- *appoint independent experts to act as consumer advocates to its expert committees, to promote and protect the interests of consumers in discussions that require specialist technical knowledge;*

- *address consumer concerns, by establishing a new tier of advisory committees composed of representatives of consumers, industry and government in equal proportions;*

- *support consumer participation by addressing the problem of funding;*

- *improve access to information by adopting a full 'freedom of information' charter and publishing the reports of the proposed advisory committees.*

In addition IOCU recommended that national governments should inform and consult consumer groups before Codex meetings and publish reports of the position their country representatives have taken at the meetings.

Based on these recommendations, a 1991 conference on food standards organised by the Food and Agriculture Organisation and the World Health Organisation agreed a recommendation aimed at increasing consumer participation in the work of the Codex Commission at national level:

'Governments should be encouraged to consider setting up a regular consultative procedure (eg. in a national Codex advisory group) in which the representative views of consumers are given equal consideration with the views of producers, industry and trade.'

This was later endorsed by the Codex Alimentarius Commission.

The invitation (in mid-1992) from the Ministry of Agriculture, Fisheries and Food – as the UK Codex contact point – to consumer organisations, industry and enforcement authorities to nominate members to a national Codex consultative committee is a very welcome step.

1.11 Science and food – what does the future hold?

We are already looking at the future. Many scientific developments once thought to be in the realms of science fiction are now a reality. Consumers will increasingly be faced with choices in food that call for all the analytic and balancing skills we have described so far in this chapter.

The last chapter in our book, by Lucy Harris, is an insight into the so-called 'novel foods and processes' now beginning to come on to the market and the developments we may expect as a consequence of biotechnology, including gene manipulation. Has 'low fat' become 'no fat'? When is a mushroom not a mushroom? How are consumers going to be able to choose between 'natural' and 'engineered' foods? Will we know enough about the processes to be able to take the ethical and nutritional decisions involved?

Lucy Harris acknowledges that the food choices open to consumers may be increased. But what does 'food' mean in this context and who controls the entry of new forms of food into the food chain?

The definition of 'novel foods' is important: they are 'foods or food ingredients which have not hitherto been used for human consumption to a significant extent in the United Kingdom and/or which have been produced by extensively modified or entirely new food production processes' (12). No novel food should be offered for sale in the UK before it has been cleared by the Advisory Committee on Novel Foods and Processes. This committee assesses the adequacy of the toxicological and nutritional tests carried out by the company developing the product. The committee's 'decision-tree' approach to safety assessment identifies the necessary studies according to perceived risk. This approach has been welcomed by consumer organisations.

We can already buy products in the supermarket that are the result of, for example, genetically-modified enzymes in cheese production, a new fructose syrup developed for use in diabetic and diet foods, calorie-reduced fat substitutes, and mycoprotein (Quorn); and the process of irradiation is now permitted.

A potential weakness of the present UK system, however, is that the safety assessments are not compulsory. A company that develops a new food does not have to notify the Advisory Committee on Novel Foods and Processes nor submit the product for clearance. While we have no reason to suppose that products are being marketed to consumers without prior clearance or indeed that companies would wish to mislead consumers, the National Consumer Council has argued in the past that the assessment scheme should have statutory backing. The Food Safety Act 1990 does now give the Minister the power to make notification compulsory.

Under the proposed European Commission regulation on novel foods, safety assessments would become compulsory and notification or authorisation of all novel products would be required. This is welcome; the National Consumer Council will be pressing for the adoption of such a mandatory assessment procedure. Until it is adopted, however, the voluntary system for submitting novel foods and processes in the UK to the Advisory Committee on Novel Foods and Processes needs to be closely monitored.

The regulations governing the labelling of new products come under the remit of the government's Food Advisory Committee. In 1990 the committee issued interim guidelines on the labelling of genetically-modified products. It suggested four different categories of products, two of which would have to be labelled, namely:

- novel foods of genetically-modified organisms which differ from conventional products; and

- food derived from an organism which has been modified to contain one or more genes from sources outside its own species.

The guidelines suggested that these foods should be labelled (13):

(contains) products of gene technology.

But what will a label like that mean to the shopper? A Europe-wide survey in 1991, reported in Lucy Harris' chapter, suggests that public understanding of biotechnology is very low; indeed only one in five respondents felt capable of answering the questions (14). A second study in the Netherlands in the same year found that the amount and type of information influenced the level of acceptance of the product (15). Where foods were presented as new products, but with no reference to genetic engineering, they were rated positively; if it was revealed that they had been made using genetic engineering, the acceptance level was lower.

However, the complexity and amount of information that might be needed to win consumer confidence in, and acceptance of, these products suggests that labelling is not the only answer. Much wider public discussion about the advantages (or otherwise) of these scientific processes is needed before consumers will be able to use any labelling information constructively. Biotechnology raises important ethical questions. We cannot expect these to be addressed by labelling regulations, nor can food labels become the sole source of information for consumers on this important issue.

We welcome the setting up of the European Commission's group of advisers on bio-ethics, which will consider the implications of biotechnological developments. This move could play a significant part in bringing non-scientists into the discussions. But the group is remote from consumers. How will its members know what the concerns and anxieties of consumers are? Will they be able to discuss issues openly and will members be encouraged to seek views from different groups at national level? The need to encourage a better informed dialogue between 'experts' and 'non-experts' suggests that ways should be found to increase consumer representatives' involvement in the important decisions that are being taken on our behalf.

Recommendation 15

We recommend that the Ministry of Agriculture, Fisheries and Food consider setting up an independent committee of representatives of interested bodies whose remit would be to consider the ethical questions of biotechnological developments in food from the consumer point of view. Guidance from this committee should inform the work of the Advisory Committee on Novel Foods and Processes in the UK and the group of advisers on bio-ethics in the EC.

1.12 Your food: your choice?

In this chapter we have focused on some of the key issues for UK consumers when it comes to exercising – and strengthening – their choices in food and, where appropriate, we have made recommendations for reform. These are the National Consumer Council's views. The authors of the remaining nine chapters also suggest their own pointers for change. We hope the whole book will encourage and inform debates about food production, retailing and regulation throughout the 1990s and help individual consumers to make more effective choices for themselves.

References to chapter 1

1. Incorporated Society of British Advertisers, *Advertising, Food and Health*, ISBA, 1991.

2. National Consumer Council, *Guidelines for Business Sponsors of Educational Material*, NCC, 1988.

3. Coronary Prevention Group, *Health Education Resources Concerning Food and Health: a consultative document*, CPG, 1991.

4. Coronary Prevention Group, *Nutrition Banding*, CPG's proposed scheme for nutrition labelling, 1992.

5. Michael Nelson and Anne-Marie B. Mayer, *Establishing a Food Budget for Three Family Types*, Family Budget Unit, University of York, 1991.

6. Correspondence between Department of Social Security and author of chapter 5, 1991.

7. National Consumer Council, *A Food Charter for Consumers*, NCC, 1989.

8. National Consumer Council, *The Future of Food Regulation: a discussion document*, NCC, 1989.

9. National Consumer Council, *Consumers and the Common Agricultural Policy*, HMSO, 1988.

10. National Consumer Council, 'EC Food and Nutrition Policy', an unpublished report commissioned by the Consumer Policy Service of the European Commission, 1990.

11. International Organisation of Consumers Unions, *Consumer Participation in Setting International Food Standards*, IOCU, The Hague, March 1991.

12. Advisory Committee on Novel Foods and Processes, *Guidelines on the Assessment of Novel Foods and Processes,* HMSO, 1991.

13. Food Advisory Committee, *Guidelines for the Labelling of Foods Produced Using Genetic Modification*, Ministry of Agriculture, Fisheries and Food, 1990.

14. Commission of the European Communities, *Highlights of the Preliminary Results of the Spring 1991 Eurobarometer,* DGXII, Concertation Unit for Biotechnology in Europe, 1991.

15. A.M. Hamstra, *Biotechnology in Foodstuffs: towards a model of consumer acceptance*, SWOKA, The Netherlands, 1991.

Chapter 2

Biology and the Senses

Do you eat what you like or like what you eat?
by Peter J. Rogers and David J. Mela

*Underlying almost every other influence on what we eat, and how much,
is the basic one of human biology. We seem to be born with a fondness
for sugar, but not for whisky, coffee or cabbage. Why? The human body
defends itself against losing weight better than it does against putting
on weight. Why? This chapter examines the important influence of taste,
smell, appetite and other physical mechanisms on what we eat, in light
of the latest biological evidence.*

2.1 Biology's balancing act

(a) What do humans need from food?

For omnivorous animals like ourselves, the key biological priorities
are:

- to select a diet that meets our nutritional requirements;
- to avoid eating harmful substances; and
- to exploit resources efficiently.

The first two of these priorities have been called the 'omnivore's
paradox' (1). We have to balance the need to find sustenance from
among a large number of food sources, no one of which can provide all
the necessary nutrients in the right amounts, with the need to avoid
eating toxins.

The biological mechanisms that meet these needs have evolved over
millions of years through the relatively slow process of natural
selection. So some human traits seem to conflict with more recent
social, cultural and economic developments.

In times of plenty, for instance, over-eating and the storage of energy
as body fat provide a buffer against subsequent food shortages.
Accordingly, the appetite control system seems to respond readily to an
under-supply of energy, but to be rather tolerant of over-supply - or
over-eating. As a result there is more resistance to weight loss than
weight gain. If the availability of food is never, or only rarely, limited,
this biological 'safety mechanism' in fact tends to encourage obesity -
now a major public health concern in many industrialised societies.

(b) How does the body balance energy and nutrition?

Some researchers have suggested that we eat or avoid specific
nutrients because of some innate biological mechanisms. However,
except for salt, water and total energy intake (the hunger for calories),
this idea remains controversial.

26

But there is little doubt that physiological *changes* in the body can affect food preferences. The craving for carbohydrates – called 'hunger riot' – following large doses of insulin and the powerful urge to eat salty foods that accompanies adrenocortical insufficiency (which causes too much salt to be lost from the body) are two examples of the influence of extreme physiological events.

However, the body can also tolerate fairly wide fluctuations in different nutrients without great harm being done. To a large extent, the body's need for precise, short-term control of nutrients is avoided by sophisticated buffering mechanisms. These include absorption (of selected minerals, for instance), storage, metabolic transformation, and excretion. The kidneys, for instance, closely regulate the conservation and excretion of sodium and water. The proportions of protein, carbohydrate and fat that people eat vary widely, but metabolic pathways enable each of them to be used for energy production or, when consumed in excess, to be converted to body fat for storage.

A concept that has dominated much of the thinking about the biological mechanisms of appetite control is called 'homeostatic behaviour'. The basic idea is that animals behave in certain ways simply in response to chemical or other internal signals. For example, eating might be triggered when the circulating metabolic fuels fall below a critical level. But this view generally fails to take ecology into account. In most natural habitats food supplies are unpredictable. Accordingly evolution has made physiological adaptations which allow for the *anticipation* of needs and the optimal *exploitation* of the resources available. We have already mentioned one example – storing energy in the form of body fat, which is taken to extremes in hibernating animals.

Recent research suggests that the human appetite is also adapted in this way. In one study the calorie content of some foods was reduced without the subjects' knowledge (2). The subjects lived continuously in a residential laboratory. By substituting reduced-fat products and artificial sweeteners, their energy intake from this group of food items was cut by 500 kilocalories per day. But within one to three days the subjects were compensating completely for the reduction by eating more of the other (non-calorie-manipulated) items. Subsequently, when they only had access to the regular items during a final three-day period, the subjects failed to compensate for the increase in calories and over-ate by a significant amount.

A similar result came from another study (3). Subjects were provided with lunches containing two-thirds *less* energy than their customary lunches (which had been established during a baseline period). Again calorie values were secretly cut by the use of reduced-fat products and a low-calorie sweetener. Then the subjects had a period of lunches with two-thirds *more* energy than usual. During the two weeks when the subjects got the low-calorie lunch, their daily energy intake (recorded in diet diaries) did not differ from the baseline level: in other words, they ate more to compensate. But in the two weeks of the high-calorie lunch, their daily energy intake rose significantly.

2.2 Sensory mechanisms: the effects of taste and smell

(a) The three sensory systems

Human perceptions of 'flavour' in foods largely come from combinations of sensations in three separate sensory systems – gustation (taste), olfaction (smell), and the trigeminal system (sometimes called the 'common chemical sense').

Table 2.1: The sensory systems involved in flavour perception

Sensory system	The sensations mediated
gustatory	*taste*: sweet, sour, salty, bitter, others ('umami'? See below)
olfactory	*odour* (aroma, volatile flavour): an unlimited number?
trigeminal (or 'common chemical sense')	*tactile, thermal, pain/ irritation*

Taste sensations come from the interaction of water-soluble compounds ('tastants') with specialised cells inside the oral cavity, particularly on the surface of the tongue.

The classic view is that taste is limited to mixtures of four basic qualities – sweet, sour, salty and bitter. This is supported by a number of lines of evidence but is not fully resolved. For example, the savoury quality associated with some flavour enhancers, such as monosodium glutamate, is generally accepted as a fifth basic taste (called 'umami') in Japanese science and culture. Other research suggests that the 'basic' tastes may simply be easily recognised points in a continuum, or the result of limitations in language or cultural exposure.

Sensations of smell come from the interaction of small volatile 'odourants', carried in the air we breathe, with a small area of sensory tissue in the top of the nasal cavity just under the brain. Unlike the limited repertoire of tastes, the number of unique odours that humans can discern seems to be unlimited. Indeed, it is clearly their odours (or aromas or 'volatile flavours') that makes most individual foods recognisably unique. Despite numerous attempts to organise the world of smells – like tastes – into limited categories, no single odour classification scheme has ever received general endorsement. People invariably describe odours in terms of familiar, specific sources like 'popcorn', 'rose' or 'vomit'.

The sense of smell does not involve anything tactile. Nothing solid touches the olfactory receptor region and there is no sensation to indicate the specific site of origin. But we do feel foods and their tastes on our tongue – hence the natural, but false, inclination to refer sensations of food-related aromas to the mouth and confuse the terms 'taste', 'smell' and 'flavour'.

In fact it is easy to demonstrate the different contributions of taste and smell to flavour. With the nose pinched shut, the flavours of chicken and beef broths or patés are more or less indistinguishable. Their tastes (salty and 'umami') are nearly identical; it is their odours which are different. Pinching the nose largely stops the flow of air carrying the unique aromas of foods from the oral cavity to the olfactory receptor areas. Although people with colds often complain of a loss of 'taste', it is in fact only their ability to smell that has been temporarily lost. Indeed, in most cases where people report a loss of their sense of 'taste', it is usual to find that their perception of the basic tastes (sweet, sour, salt and bitter) is intact, and that their altered perception of food is due to their inability to detect or recognise food odours.

A third sensory system, called *the trigeminal system*, mediates various sensations – tactile (touch), thermal (heat/cold), nociceptive (pain) and proprioceptive (muscle/joint position) – on the surfaces of the lips, mouth and nasal cavity. Although often described as taste or smell, experiences such as the 'burn' from hot peppers and ethanol, the 'cooling' from menthol and wintergreen, or the irritation from bleach and other vapours in fact rely chiefly on this distinct system.

The system may have a protective function, by generating irritation in response to many harmful chemicals. It is therefore also known as the 'common chemical sense'. Reflex responses to stimulants of this system include sneezing, salivation, sweating, crying, flushing and momentary interruption of breathing.

29

(b) Innate sensory likes and dislikes

Unlike the koala bear which appears to be programmed to enjoy a diet consisting almost solely of eucalyptus leaves, humans are not born with innate preferences for specific food items. It is apparent, though, that they do have some innate taste – and perhaps odour – preferences. Sweet tastes appear to be readily accepted at birth. Bitter and possibly sour tastes are rejected. The ability to detect or respond to salt appears to develop between four to six months after birth (when babies seem to like it).

A likely explanation for this small core of in-built sensory likes and dislikes is that it directs humans towards safe sources of energy and nutrients and away from harmful ones. In nature, bitter tastes tend to go along with the presence of toxins (like alkaloids in plants), and sweet tastes normally signal a safe and ready source of energy in the form of sugar. Even more significantly, the near universal enthusiasm for sweetness may be important in the infant's early acceptance of the mother's sweet-tasting milk.

The powerful effect of sweet taste on infant behaviour has been demonstrated in recent studies by Blass and his colleagues (4). In one experiment two- and three-day-old babies were given 2 millilitres either of plain water or of 12 per cent sucrose solution to drink, immediately before their heels were lanced (for blood samples). The babies given the sucrose cried far less and for a shorter time in response to the blood collection. Similar studies on rats indicate that this analgesic or calming property of a sweet taste is probably governed by endogenous opiate systems (the same brain systems activated by drugs like morphine). Blass interprets the effects as part of the biological basis of the mother-infant bonding process.

It is often assumed that people all receive similar sensory sensations, and differ only in their individual responses. This is not so. One well-tested difference is sensitivity to the taste of a class of bitter chemicals, one of which is phenylthiocarbamide (PTC). People with high sensitivity to taste – 'tasters' – perceive weak concentrations of PTC as intensely bitter; 'non-tasters' perceive no taste at all except at very high levels. The proportion of 'tasters' has been found to vary from sixty to almost one hundred per cent among different racial and ethnic groups. 'Tasters' also seem to perceive common compounds such as caffeine, saccharin and sucrose differently from 'non-tasters'.

Table 2.2: The ability to taste PTC among selected population groups

Population	Percentage of PTC 'tasters'
northern European	69%
Spanish and Portuguese	76%
Japanese	93%
black African	97%
Brazilian Indian	99%

Source: A.C. Allison and B.S. Blumberg, 'Ability to taste PTC among Alaskan eskimos and other populations', *Human Biology*, 31, pp. 352-9.

In addition, anosmias (the inability to smell a particular compound) have been shown for a number of odours.

Table 2.3: The percentage of people unable to detect specific odours

The source of the smell	Its characteristic odour	Estimated % of humans unable to detect the odour
iodocresol	medicinal	90%
androstenone	urinous/sweaty	45-50%
isobuteraldehyde	malty	36%
1,8-cineole	camphoraceous	33%
omega-pentadecalactone	musky	10%
trimethylamine	fishy	6%
isovaleric acid	sweaty	3%

Source: see reference 5, at the end of the chapter.

So the percentage of the population not able to smell a given odour ranges from three per cent for the sweaty odour of isovaleric acid to about ninety per cent for the medicinal odour of iodocresol (5). The latter was discovered during the development of a commercial cake mix. A small percentage of taste panellists consistently reported a strong 'off' flavour, to the great consternation of the technical flavour experts who were all unable to smell – were anosmic to – the offending ingredient.

The range of factors affecting perceptions of different compounds can be complicated, but researchers believe that sensitivity to PTC and several others is largely genetic.

Androstenone, a steroid compound found in the secretions of many mammals, gives an outstanding example of this complexity in individual variation. Androstenone is perceived as offensively sweaty or urine-like by about thirty-five per cent of adults, subtle and perhaps

31

somewhat pleasant by about fifteen per cent, and not detected at all by the remaining fifty per cent. Perceptions of its pleasantness may also vary with the stage of the menstrual cycle and the ability to detect it at all may be lost during puberty, particularly among males. Moreover about half of the anosmic group can become sensitive to the smell with repeated exposure. So genetics, age, hormones and experience all interact to determine the actual ability to sense this compound, not just the perceived quality or liking of it.

This individual variation clearly extends to the sensory stimuli in foods, and may form one underlying basis for differences in people's perceptions and selection of particular foods.

(c) Learned preferences and aversions

Humans and other animals have the ability to recognise and learn about the consequences – metabolic, physiological and psychological – of eating specific foods (for a review of the field, see (6)). These learned responses are very powerful. They can overcome innate preferences and, certainly in the case of aversions, can last a lifetime.

A prompt and persistent aversion to the specific sensory qualities of a food often develops after a negative outcome, particularly nausea and stomach upsets. A large proportion (up to 65 per cent) of people report at least one strong food aversion. Most seem to be acquired during childhood which of course is when many foods are tried for the first time and when sickness with gastro-intestinal symptoms are particularly common. Some aversions which develop in childhood still persist fifty years later. We go on disliking the food long after the initial incident is forgotten and often despite the knowledge that it is known to be safe to eat or did not cause the illness. So food aversion learning is a powerful phenomenon and can account for the idiosyncratic avoidance of particular foods.

Similarly it now appears that our preferences can be fostered by pairing a specific sensory quality with a positive outcome, although technical difficulties make this difficult to demonstrate experimentally.

This type of learning probably plays a very fundamental role in the development of food choice. The sensation of the food (that is, our perception of its flavour) is probably not altered, but our liking – or dislike – for its flavour, texture and so on is. So, for example, a learned aversion gives the food a 'nasty taste' and not simply the perception that it is dangerous. It is likely that the rewarding psycho-biological effects of products like coffee and whisky explain why adults come to like tastes they dislike as children. There is no known specific mechanism in the body to explain the human predilection for the sensory properties of fat in foods; the evidence suggests that we like fat for its association with metabolic properties, especially the energy content (7).

The very significant role of *learned* responses in food preferences is well supported by animal research, though not yet by definitive studies on humans. The psychological effects of eating particular foods on subsequent food liking also await further research. But there is an obvious biological advantage in a capacity to modify our likes and dislikes for a food according to the benefit we derive from consuming it, and it is likely that such learned influences play an important role in guiding choice. The ability of healthy humans to detect, to recognise, to select or to avoid particular tastes and smells may help to ensure the intake of a wide diversity of safe foods and so reduce the likelihood of any single nutrient deficiency.

(d) The social factor

Social contacts and settings can have a marked influence on food preference and consumption; this is discussed more fully in chapter 3. Here we simply highlight the clear biological basis for the social transmission of food preferences, evident from studies on animals. Young rats, for example, readily acquire the same food preferences as adult members of their social group. They seem to do this by watching adults at the feeding site, by chemical cues left at the feeding site and by flavour cues in maternal milk. Smells also seem to play a role. Although similar mechanisms have not been definitively established in humans, they remain realistic possibilities. New-born babies, for example, quickly learn to respond to specific odours from their mothers.

2.3 Sensory versus biological influences

(a) During a meal: the short-term effects

Does food begin to taste unpleasant as we come near to the end of a meal, or do we stop eating because of feelings of fullness in the stomach?

A number of studies have shown that in the course of one meal, human eating is variously stimulated and inhibited. Negative feedback during a meal seems to depend on the accumulation of food in the stomach and its entry into the upper small intestine. This generates a complex sequence of neural and hormonal signals which, along with the effects of absorbed nutrients, inhibits eating and produces a feeling of 'fullness'. The positive feedback effect probably comes from sensory - mainly smell and taste - contact with food. This stimulation of eating by eating is well known both subjectively (*l'appetit vient en mangeant* or appetite comes with eating) and from objective studies. Furthermore, the strength of the positive effect depends on the quality of the sensory stimuli - that is, the palatability of the food.

Research also shows that eating a food can lead to a temporary decrease in our liking for it. This is true even where the choice is among foods that differ only in their shape or colour. This mechanism may increase the variety of food we consume - and so increase the likelihood of a nutritionally adequate diet. Variety may literally be the spice of life. We do not know how this biological mechanism works. It may depend on decreases in a food's sensory qualities during eating. Or sensory variety may re-stimulate preference. It may simply be attributable to a general tendency to alternate choices, a behaviour we share with other animals.

The disagreement among researchers arises because of the difficulty of interpreting subjective ratings of pleasantness, and in particular because of the failure to distinguish between the pleasantness of the 'taste' of food in the mouth (influenced by palatability) and the pleasantness of eating or ingesting that food (influenced by palatability and by feelings of hunger and fullness). During a meal, people report that hunger declines and fullness increases; but their ratings of the pleasantness of the 'taste' of what they eat remains relatively unchanged (8). So the pleasantness of the taste of a food is determined largely by innate bias and by learning, and probably does not change in the short term.

(b) Eating for life: long-term control

It has been known for many years that most animals, when offered a choice of single or mixed nutrient sources, will select a diet compatible with normal growth and health.

Recent studies suggest that while our sensory mechanisms allow recognition of different nutrient sources, it is what happens *after* we have eaten them that eventually dictates what we choose next time. Indeed, these shifts in food selection are often accompanied by changes in sensory preferences, and this may be largely explained by learned preference mechanisms.

34

2.4 Can the system be fooled?
Fat substitutes and high intensity sweeteners

The expanding production of low-energy substitutes is almost solely a response to consumers' anxieties about eating excessive fat, sugar and energy. The safety and function of most of these new ingredients and processes are of course scrutinised by industrial and government bodies. But there is very little study of their nutritional implications.

What is the practical effect of substitutes in reducing fat or sugar intake or in maintaining the right energy intake? While the sensory systems may be fooled, at least in the short term, how do the biological regulatory systems respond?

We have seen that sensory assessments of food and eating play a central role in signalling nutritional benefit. However, very low-energy fat and sweetener substitutes markedly alter the natural relationships between the sensory and physiological effects of foods. As we have seen, normal, healthy humans with access to food supplies generally compensate well for dilutions of food energy (9). They eat more. So fat and sweetener substitutes, by themselves, are unlikely to reduce total energy intake. This is not to say that they cannot be useful to people consciously trying to control their intake. Eating fat substitutes does seem to lead to a slight fall in the percentage of energy derived from fat.

But there is still very little information to tell us how ordinary consumers respond to reduced-fat or reduced-sugar versions of foods. Most of the research has been conducted on fairly small numbers of people for a few days at most, within a laboratory or clinic, and often by providing subjects with fixed meals or a limited selection of food. Many of the laboratory studies may also lack validity because the dietary changes were concealed from the test subjects. There might be even more compensation for a reduction in energy from food if the subjects know about it.

It is widely recognised that consumer perceptions of foods can be strongly influenced by label information, though little is known about how this affects what they eat. There is some evidence that compensation for reduced-energy foods may go further – or even go too far – when subjects are informed about it, for instance by conventional packaging labels and advertising claims.

2.5 Conclusion

Do we eat what we like or like what we eat? The short answer is – both.

It is clear that although food liking is influenced by innate factors, it is also modified by our reactions to food. In particular, through a powerful form of learning, our preferences for foods change according to their beneficial or harmful effects. Our views of flavours are derived from combinations of sensations; and individual variations in the perception of those sensations also help to explain why different people choose different foods.

References to chapter 2

1. P. Rozin, 'The significance of learning mechanisms in food selection: some biology, psychology and sociology of science', in *Learning Mechanisms in Food Selection*, edited by L.M. Barker and others, Baylor University Press, Houston, Texas, 1977, pp. 557-589.

2. R.N. Foltin, M.W. Fischman, C.S. Emurian and J.J. Rachlinski, 'Compensation for caloric dilution in humans given unrestricted access to food in a residential laboratory', in *Appetite*, 10, 1988, pp. 13-24.

3. R.D. Mattes, C.B. Pierce and M.I. Friedman, 'Daily caloric intake of normal-weight adults: response to changes in dietary energy density of a luncheon meal', in *American Journal of Clinical Nutrition*, 46, 1988, pp. 886-892.

4. E.M. Blass, 'Suckling: opioid and nonopioid processes in mother-infant bonding', in *Chemical Senses Volume 4: Appetite and Nutrition*, edited by M.I. Friedman and others, Marcel Dekker, New York, 1991, pp. 283-302.

5. J.N. Labows and C.J. Wysocki, 'Individual differences in odor perception', *Perfumer and Flavorist*, 9, 1984, pp. 21-26.

6. P. Rozin, 'The role of learning in the acquisition of food preferences by humans', in *Handbook of the Psychophysiology of Human Eating*, edited by R. Shepherd, Wiley, 1989, pp. 205-227.

7. D.J. Mela, 'The basis of dietary fat preferences', *Trends in Food Science & Technology*, 1, 1990, pp. 31-73.

8. P.J. Rogers and J.E. Blundell, 'Psychobiological bases of food choice', *Why We Eat What We Eat*, edited by M. Ashwell, British Nutrition Foundation Nutrition Bulletin 15 (suppl.1), 1990, pp. 21-40.

9. P.J. Rogers and J.E. Blundell, 'Evaluation of the influence of intense sweeteners on the short-term control of appetite and caloric intake: a psychobiological approach', in *Progress in Sweeteners*, edited by T.H. Grenby, Elsevier Applied Science, 1989, pp. 267-289.

Chapter 3
Culture, Identity and Psychology
Eating what the others eat
by Richard Shepherd and Paul Sparks

Some of the influences on people's diets – like climate or poverty or even human biology – can be relatively simple to identify and measure. It is not difficult to explain, for instance, why people in the UK ate less fat and sugar during the second world war. But what about the effects of culture, class, religion, family or personal values? As this chapter shows, these are less easy to quantify. And the answer often depends on the question you ask.

How do we start to unravel the cultural, social and psychological influences on people's eating habits? On the next page is just one of many models of the various influences – and it highlights the problem of measuring the likely effect of any one of them. (The different models are discussed in detail by R. Shepherd (1).)

So this chapter can do no more than touch on some of the strands in a complex web. No one strand on its own can explain why A chooses that breakfast cereal, why B is a vegetarian or why C likes peanut butter and mayonnaise sandwiches. Their preferences in food, as in other things, have multiple, interlocking causes. But we outline the chief avenues of current research. If you have an appetite for more, the publications listed under 'References' at the end will give you wider and deeper reading.

3.1 Consumers and their cultures

Culture is one of the most obvious influences on food preferences and choice. People from different cultures make very different choices from each other, even where the cultural variation is otherwise relatively small – for instance within northern Europe.

(a) Geography and culture

Some of the distinctions have become blurred, though, especially this century. Increased travel lets people try more exotic foods. Emigration often brings diversification and the adoption of foreign foods into a national cuisine. It is now more practicable to transport food over long distances and, although this often means getting the same foods cheaper or out of season (Spanish-grown tomatoes in the UK, say), it also gives greater access to foods that cannot be grown locally at all.

Figure 3.1: One model of the factors that influence preferences in food

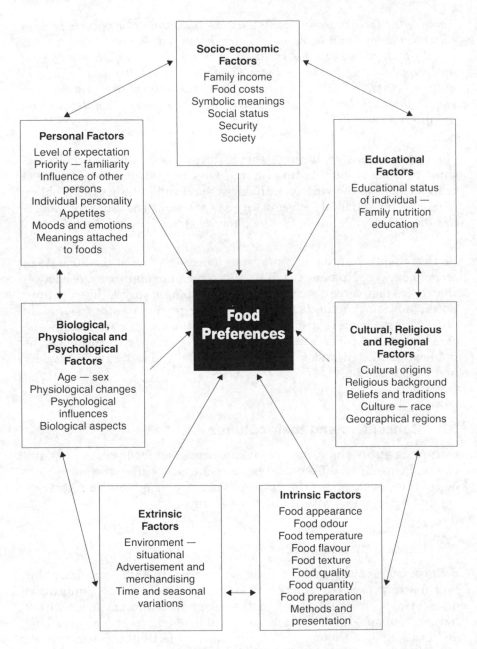

Source: M.A. Khan, 'Evaluation of food selection patterns and preferences', *CRC Critical Reviews: Food Science and Nutrition*, 15, 1981, pp. 129-53.

The influence of 'outside' cuisines on western consumption habits in fact goes back a long way. Eastern influences via the spice trade were well established during the time of the Roman empire. Pasta is thought to have originated from China and only reached Italy in the fifteenth century. In England, the Norman influence on English food and cooking was strong, if only for the upper classes at first.

Western foods and eating habits have also been exported. In west Africa, for example, a number of plant varieties (like tomatoes, maize, groundnuts) were introduced from America. Then canning methods were established, getting round many problems of seasonal supply and permitting food to travel greater distances. Today some types of food have expanded worldwide. McDonald's hamburgers and Coca Cola are commonly seen as typical of western, and particularly north American, food and carry with them strong associations with western culture.

(b) Nutrition and ritual

Anthropologists have studied various practices and rituals surrounding food preparation and how these are linked to the development of a nutritional diet. One example is the evolution of crop cultivation.

Many plants have natural defences against predators in the form of chemicals that are toxic to the animals and insects likely to eat them. While animals may develop a natural immunity to these toxins, this is likely to be specific to particular toxins and to rely on chance biological evolution. In cultivating plants, it might be possible by selective breeding to get rid of the natural toxins. However, the people cultivating the plants would then simply be in competition with all the other potential predators.

A more efficient system is to transform the raw plant material into food through some form of processing - cooking, fermentation, peeling and so on. If these processes are effective in removing the toxins, the humans have an advantage; they can eat the food derived from the plants while other animals and insects cannot. Modern food science and technology systematically use this kind of procedure, of course. But in traditional cultures, it is more likely to be developed in a hit-and-miss way and with no means of passing on the processing knowledge scientifically. Many rituals surrounding food preparation are therefore, in effect, a method of passing on information and skills.

The rituals in the preparation of 'blue corn' by the Hopi north American native population is an example, investigated by S.H. Katz (2). Although maize has been an important crop of north and central America for a long time, raw maize has serious nutritional shortcomings. When it is a staple of the diet, it can lead to pellagra, a disease associated with niacin deficiency. If the maize is treated with alkali, however, this releases niacin and improves the amino acid balance. Many north and central American natives use maize to make some form of tortilla or bread, first treating the maize with alkali, usually in the form of lime. Any excess lime is usually washed off. The Hopi tribe had little access to water, and would not have been able to wash off the excess lime. They have therefore developed elaborate rituals for producing corn in the right shade of blue to reflect the correct alkalinity of the bread. The ritual can incorporate training: a young woman will leave her best tortilla outside the house of the man she wants to marry, for instance - if he eats and likes the bread, he agrees to be her husband.

While people from a society like this would not describe these methods in terms of the production of nutritionally better bread and while the rituals have great symbolic meaning for them, the benefits of the production process and its establishment into unquestioned rituals give that tribe an advantage.

When European explorers came to America they took away with them the seeds for maize. But they did not take the traditions of preparation, nor did they have scientific understanding of how the raw materials should be processed. It was introduced as a crop to Spain but then abandoned, probably because of the development of pellagra. European traders also introduced the maize into Africa where it is still widely grown. Pellagra in Africa was common until recently and there is still a higher incidence in those African societies where consumption of maize is higher. No equivalent cultural traditions have developed in Africa to treat the maize with alkali.

In addition to 'biocultural' studies like these, social anthropology tries to understand cultural influences on food patterns from other perspectives (see (3) for a cogent account of the contributions of academic sociology and social anthropology). One approach is to treat eating habits and practices as indicative of wider social structures and relationships - for example, different castes in India have different food consumption practices. Some researchers describe food practices as 'expressing' or 'symbolising' social relationships, although this terminology has been criticised as ambiguous. 'Functionalist' theorists would argue that people's choices and decisions about food have a more 'purposive' element, for example to reinforce social differences and maintain the status quo. Certainly, there is a large body of thinking within the social sciences in support of the notion that people's choices often affirm or bolster what they see as their distinctive cultural, social or personal qualities.

In our own culture, too, rituals and traditions surround food. However, it is far more difficult to strip away the surface of our own rituals in order to understand their underlying reasons and motivations. They often 'just seem natural' or they are 'what we have always done'.

3.2 Social influences: class, families and fashions

The distinction between cultural and social influences is not entirely clear cut. We have used the 'cultural' heading to discuss comparisons *between* cultures; under the 'social influences' heading we look at the special factors operating *within* a culture.

(a) Broader social influences

'Sensory, symbolic, and structural dimensions notwithstanding, the overriding considerations in dietary constructions seem to be economic.' (4)

Income has a clear influence on the foods people choose: this is examined in detail in chapter 5. However, the relationship is not simply one of 'less money, less nutrition'. While income certainly puts restraints on choice, different social groups also develop their own preferences and tastes.

'Taste classifies, and it classifies the classifier', wrote Bourdieu (5). Not only are different social groups associated with certain tastes (in food and otherwise) but knowledge of these associations may lead to particular choices *because of* the value of being classified as a member of that group. So choice is influenced by the symbolic value of particular foods. Meat is often associated with masculinity, fish sometimes with femininity – the division may be to do with the degree of bloodiness and the degree of delicacy with which it is eaten. Meat-eating may also be associated with establishing or emphasising status.

Class divisions may also be marked by differences in food choice. People may hope to affirm an identity or image by selecting particular foods, perhaps influenced by advertising. This US teenager had strong perceptions about a canned drink:

'The true American should drink Pepsi. Just look at the can and you can plainly see the colours – red, white and blue. I am certainly a true red, white, and blue American. That's how I like to think of myself after drinking Pepsi.' (Quoted in (6).)

No reference here to sensory or nutritional benefits.

So to understand food choice we need to take into account both the obvious influences, such as the perceived sensory and health benefits, and the less tangible influences, like self-image and social classification.

(b) The family effect

The family unit is likely to play a major role in determining our choice of foods, although there has been little directly relevant research work.

One study found that husbands had little input into food selection or preparation, although they were more involved the older the couples became. Another study, of newly married couples, concluded that husbands changed their eating habits on marrying more than wives did, although there were differences between types of foods in these compromises. On the other hand, there is some evidence of men's control over the constituents of family diets, even though women do most of the shopping.

There has been little research so far on the interactions between family members in decision making, the influence of family members on each other's choices or changes in the social function of family meals as a result of new technology – like microwave ovens and freezers.

Similarities within families can of course also result from genetic inheritance. A question that often arises in this context is: how much influence do social and learning factors have when compared with genetic factors? In fact, genetic differences seem to account for very little (see (7) for a discussion). Most of the differences between people in preferences and choices seem to be related to learning, and this takes place within a social context.

Many would argue that preferences in foods must start with the family. It is here that the child first comes into contact with food, learns what is appropriate and develops idiosyncratic likes and dislikes. But although there are relationships between the preferences of children and those of their parents, surprisingly these tend to be no stronger than between the preferences of the child and a neighbouring child's parent. They seem to represent general cultural norms rather than accounting for differences between families within the same culture. There does seem to be a greater similarity among the preferences of brothers and sisters than between parents and children.

(c) Food preferences in children

Chapter 2 looks at the human body's in-built influence on food preferences, pointing out, for example, that the more we eat a food the more we like it. But food is seldom presented to children in a neutral way. Leann Birch has carried out extensive work, looking at how preferences and choices in food develop in children and emphasising the social context in which the learning takes place (8).

One clear influence is peer pressure. Ask a pre-school child – Sam – to rank different vegetables – 'which do you like best, which least?' It emerges that Sam likes carrots less than peas. If we then put Sam at a table with other children who prefer carrots and offer Sam a choice, he will tend to choose carrots. After a few days his ranking of preference also changes, with carrots now ranked more highly.

Birch's work has also explored the use of foods as rewards, with some interesting conclusions. Here food can be used in two ways. The food itself can be a reward – 'you can have a biscuit if you tidy your toys', or its consumption can be rewarded – 'eat up your greens and you can watch TV'. Often eating one food will be rewarded with another highly preferred one – 'you can only have pudding if you eat your greens'.

In one study, a teacher offered as a reward a snack about which the children were neutral; the offer increased the children's liking for the snack. When the reward for eating a neutral food was being allowed to play, consumption of the food increased; but when the reward – the playtime – was subsequently removed, liking for the food fell to *below* its initial level. So rewarding consumption of the food made the child like it less.

One explanation of this is in terms of a psychological theory of self-perception. If the children eat the food then they think they like it, unless they can see an external reason for eating it. In the playtime reward case, there is an external reason: 'I'm only doing this so that I can do something I want to'. Where the food acts as a reward, the opposite is true and the child thinks: 'I must like this food because I am eating it without any external force and I am even doing other things in order to earn it'.

Do parents use these techniques for increasing their children's liking for some foods? In a small survey of north American parents, the two most popular techniques they mentioned as inducements to get their children to eat a particular food were helping with its preparation and adults displaying how much they liked the food. No parent spontaneously said they used the food as a reward although a number said they rewarded *consumption* of a food. So their actions are contrary to the research findings. One problem with implementing the research findings is that it was based on foods about which children were initially neutral, not food they highly disliked; it is less likely to be successful if the reward for an action is a highly disliked food, since the child will see this as nonsensical at a very early age.

However there are many instances where learning appears to overcome initially highly disliked foods and flavours, such as the bitter taste of coffee or the burn of chilli pepper. Chilli is widely consumed in many cultures and the development of this preference has been researched by Rozin (7). With chilli it might also be important that the initial mouth burn is unpleasant: people may develop a liking for chilli as a form of thrill-seeking and there have been suggestions that the brain produces opiates which increase the pleasure of such experiences. Other explanations relate to the context in which the learning takes place and the acquisition of more adult tastes and identity.

Although many of a child's learned preferences are a progress towards adult preferences, food also offers a means for rebellion. Research on older children has shown a sub-culture of preferred sweets, with names, colours and taste sensations differentiating them from 'ordinary' sweets and foods. It suggested that the sweets represent rebellion against the adult world. The ability to share and swop them also emphasised their social element.

3.3 Psychological influences

The first thing to note about the psychological influences on food choice is that they take place within a particular social and cultural milieu. Some psychological explanations may therefore be limited to one social context; others may be more universally applicable.

(a) Social, moral and rational?

There has been a good deal of research into how food choice is related to people's psychology – their beliefs, attitudes and intentions.

Generally, the findings set people's beliefs about their food consumption in a framework that incorporates their other values and attitudes, social pressure from others and their perceptions of control over their choices. More recently, emphasis has been placed on the importance of moral, or ethical, influences on food choice and on the issues of *image* and *identity* mentioned earlier.

This line of research tends to characterise people as carefully weighing up all the costs and benefits of their choices in a very *rational* way, although it does sometimes try to incorporate the assessment of more impulsive or emotional factors. Chapter 8 discusses in more detail the principles and practice of freedom of choice.

(b) Why do we want variety?

People's preferences are obviously not so fixed that they only ever choose one type of food – their favourite – or even one brand within a product type.

What makes an individual regularly switch between brands? No one really knows, and much of the research goes on the assumption that variation will occur at random, rather than trying to explain it. A consumer may buy a variety of brands for use in different situations or by other people; some products may not always be available; people may be making a long-term change in their buying behaviour (such as switching to low-fat milk for health reasons); or buying different products to avoid monotony (and it may be that some types of people seek more variety than others). Other research has argued that there are two definite types of brand-switching: one rooted in dissatisfaction with an existing brand, the other in increasing novelty just for the sake of variety.

Some research assumes that consumers' choices are conditional on what they have eaten previously. This work is related to the notion of 'sensory specific satiety' which suggests that the pleasantness of the taste of a food decreases after eating it (9), although the interpretation of this research has been criticised (see chapter 2). Such a mechanism would, however, make sense biologically, since the best strategy to achieve a balanced nutritional diet is to eat many different foods. So although buying a different brand may not make nutritional sense, it may have developed from some underlying biological cause.

(c) Eating disorders

The cause and treatment of eating disorders like anorexia nervosa, bulimia and obesity represent a major challenge to psychology.

The study of these forms of behaviour also offers the potential for greater understanding of normal eating in the wider population.

Bulimia involves eating large amounts of foods followed by self-induced vomiting. It usually occurs in slightly older women, generally of normal weight but who often have a history of anorexia.

Anorexia nervosa is the clinical condition characterised by excessive dieting, and an obsession with thinness and with food. There is controversy about the incidence of anorexia and whether it is increasing. It is mainly a disorder of young females, with a higher incidence in occupational groups where body weight is seen as critically important (ballet dancers, for instance).

It is not clear what causes anorexia and although sufferers may display a number of physiological and psychological abnormalities, it is usually unclear how far these bring about the disorder or are the result of under-eating. A common assumption is that at least part of the cause is the cultural ideal of thinness in females, which for many is unattainable. Although average weights are increasing in most western countries, studies of data from Miss America Pageant finalists and *Playboy* magazine models reveal that their body shapes have got thinner over several decades. In so far as these models in any way represent the 'ideal form', the consequence is that some women are likely to be dissatisfied about their weight.

3.4 Issues in the 1990s

Even within one culture and certainly in one person, our food choices vary over time. While patterns of choice over a whole population may shift only slowly, there can be rapid changes at the individual level. This final section touches on some of those trends.

One major shift in attitudes during the 1970s and 1980s in the west was the one away from concern about price to concern about quality and health. Market research shows that many people are trying to eat healthily, although they often also have misconceptions about what this means – for instance, the belief that polyunsaturate-rich margarines have less fat than butter.

The *National Health Survey*, reviewing trends from 1985 to 1990, concluded that there had been a shift in emphasis from concern over specific ingredients to concern with the diet as a whole (10). People's ratings of the healthiness of meat declined, and over the years of the survey a fairly constant 45 per cent of women reported having cut down on meat consumption (although only 2 or 3 per cent reported themselves as vegetarian). The healthiness ratings for low-fat spread increased over the five years, those for butter and hard margarine declined. The main components of healthy foods are seen as vitamins, fibre, protein and freshness, along with a low amount of fat. Additives seem to be a declining concern.

Another recent and fast-growing development is concern with the environment and the emergence of the 'green consumer'. Green consumers are more likely to be in social groups ABC1, 25 to 44 years old, to have children and to be in employment. 'Organic' foods are the best established of the so-called environmentally-friendly food products. The prices of these can be forty to one hundred per cent higher than for 'non- organic' food. In 1989 organic vegetables had only 1.5 per cent of market share and organic fruit less than 1 per cent. It remains to be seen whether this is a trend that will extend to other social and cultural groups.

Food safety has been a third major issue in the UK over the past few years, prompted by the scares associated with microbiological problems such as salmonella and listeria, disease like BSE in animals, chemical contamination through accidents in production, and criminal tampering with packaged foods. The public may feel they have little control over food safety issues like these (and there is evidence to suggest that people are complacent about their own personal susceptibility to diet-related risks). But safety will undoubtedly remain of basic importance to consumer confidence in the food industry.

The social and psychological influences on food choices outlined in this chapter complement rather than compete with each other; they all need to be taken into account for a fuller understanding of individual decisions. But there are also other influences, as the rest of this book describes, which suggest the need for inter-disciplinary research and collaboration to improve our understanding of this complex web of actions and reactions.

References to chapter 3

1. R. Shepherd, 'Factors influencing food preferences and choice', in *Handbook of the Psychophysiology of Human Eating*, edited by R. Shepherd, Wiley, 1989, pp. 3-24.

2. S.H. Katz, 'Biocultural evolution of cuisine: the Hopi Indian blue corn tradition', in *Handbook of the Psychophysiology of Human Eating*, edited by R. Shepherd, Wiley, 1989, pp. 115-140.

3. A. Murcott, 'Sociological and social anthropological approaches to food and eating', in *World Review of Nutrition and Dietetics*, 55, edited by G.H. Bourne, Karger, Basel, 1989, pp. 1-40.

4. E. Messer, 'Anthropological perspectives on diet', *Annual Review of Anthropology*, 13, 1984, pp. 205-49.

5. P. Bourdieu, *Distinction: A Social Critique of the Judgement of Taste*, Routledge and Kegan Paul, 1984.

6. J. O'Shaughnessy and M.B. Holbrook, 'Understanding consumer behaviour: the linguistic turn in marketing research', *Journal of the Market Research Society*, 30, 1988, pp. 197-223.

7. P. Rozin, 'The role of learning in the acquisition of food preferences by humans', in *Handbook of the Psychophysiology of Human Eating*, edited by R. Shepherd, Wiley, 1989, pp. 205-27.

8. L.L. Birch, 'Developmental aspects of eating', in *Handbook of the Psychophysiology of Human Eating*, edited by R. Shepherd, Wiley, 1989, pp. 179-203.

9. B.J. Rolls and M. Hetherington, 'The role of variety in eating and body weight regulation', in *Handbook of the Psychophysiology of Human Eating*, edited by R. Shepherd, Wiley, 1989, pp. 57-84.

10. Jones Rhodes Associates, *National Health Survey*, JRA, Nottingham, 1990.

Chapter 4
Advertising and Labelling
How much influence?
by Jeanette Longfield

Information is essential to choice. People need full, reliable, relevant information about the products on the supermarket shelves before they decide which ones are right for them. Much of this information comes from the food industry itself – in television, radio, magazine and poster advertising and on food labels and packages. How useful and reliable is that information? How much does it influence consumers, and especially young consumers? And how effective are the legal and self-regulatory controls on food advertising and labelling that are supposed to protect us from misleading information?

Study after study has shown that people believe advertising to be a powerful influence on consumer choice. Interestingly though, the studies also show that these same respondents do not believe that advertising influences *their own* choices (1). It may be appealing to believe that in a world of gullible people, we alone remain rational and objective. This chapter may undermine that comfortable idea.

4.1 Advertising: is size everything?

The sheer size of the food advertising industry ought to tell us something. Food companies would not spend approximately £500 million a year on advertising unless they were reasonably confident of a fair return on their investment (2). And they must be more than reasonably satisfied with that return because the amount they spend has increased by 30 per cent over the last ten years (3). Advertising expenditure on all products and services, not just food, increased by an average of 3.8 per cent per year between 1977 and 1987, a rate of growth that easily outstrips the average growth rate of the UK economy as a whole (4). As a proportion of our gross national product, advertising accounts for some 1.4 per cent of the total, one of the highest in Europe and three times as high as Portugal and Greece (5).

About one-third of food advertising expenditure in this country goes on television advertising. And food and soft drinks advertising takes up more TV time that any other product category (6). Quite right too, you might think. Everyone eats, there are thousands of different food products, so it makes sense that food is advertised more heavily than any other product. But the amount spent on advertising different types of foods is not related to their nutritional value or how important they are in the national diet. In the world of food advertising expenditure (or 'adspend', in the jargon), some products are more equal than others.

At £100 million a year, confectionery is the most heavily advertised food category. Mars bars alone accounted for £4 million. Other high spenders include coffee (around £15 million between the two leading brands), fast food (almost £20 million for McDonalds), and soft drinks (for example, for every £8 of sales, Lucozade spends £1 on advertising) (7).

In short, of the top twenty spenders on advertising of all kinds, thirteen of the places are occupied by food products; coffee (1st and 3rd place), a cola drink, crisps, tea (7th and 16th), breakfast cereals (8th, 10th, 17th and 18th), margarine, soup and a chocolate bar. Given this rather unhealthy list, it is perhaps surprising to learn that advertisements for foods claiming some kind of health benefit have increased by some eighty per cent over the last ten years (8).

There are several possible reasons for this apparent conundrum. First, the claims may be made for food products outside the top twenty. Secondly, the rate of increase in the number of adverts making a health claim may be large but the absolute numbers and the amount spent is still small. Third, health claims are also made in those advertising media that make up the other two-thirds of food 'adspend' – newspapers, magazines, posters, leaflets, radio and so on.

However, less is known about the effectiveness of these advertising channels. Although most advertisers, in whatever medium, will carry out research to try to assess the effectiveness of their campaigns, most of their results are confidential. Few want to admit their campaign was a failure or, conversely, reveal the secret of their success. The difference with television advertising is that, since it is such a costly and sometimes controversial sector of advertising, it has been studied more intensively by independent researchers, and it is largely their findings which are used below.

4.2 Food labels: a Cinderella sector?

Commercial secrecy also surrounds the labelling and packaging of food. In the course of researching this chapter, we selected a small number of manufacturers at random and asked them for details of the success, or otherwise, of a recent change in the labelling of their products. Some refused to give any information, others replied in the vaguest terms and only a minority were happy to give the size of the sales increase.

Again, this is understandable. The food market is highly competitive and the last fact you would want to reveal to your rivals is how, by changing the labelling and packaging of your product, you were able to steal a march.

Advertising has been taken seriously for far longer than packaging and label design. Even after the 'designer boom' of the 1980s, one design industry representative still felt some thirty years behind the advertising sector in terms of status and research (9). Nonetheless, the packaging industry (including materials) is worth an estimated £6 billion per year (10) and in 1988 the top 135 design companies had a turnover of £265 million (11).

Of course, not all design and packaging relates to food and it has not proved possible to uncover design and packaging figures for this sector on its own. This is partly due to the fact that, for some purposes, the industry itself treats labelling and advertising as part of a whole. Together, the labelling (including the packaging) and advertising of any product, including food, make up part of the *image* of that product, and it is the image which sells. Labelling or advertising treated separately, or communicating inconsistent messages, would work less effectively. Imagine, for example, advertisements for luxury chocolates which came in a plain, brown paper bag, or a loaf of bread which came bedecked with satin ribbons?

United Kingdom and European Community law also recognise the inextricable link between labelling and advertising and the main food legislation covers both simultaneously. (North American food law is not constructed in this way so it is possible for a US food advertisement to claim something which is not permissible on the food label and vice versa. Health and consumer groups in the US are campaigning hard to remove this anomaly.)

The process of creating the single market has also completely altered the basis of consumer protection for food products. As David Jukes explains in chapter 9, food law in this and other EC countries used to be based largely on compositional standards which specified, sometimes very precisely, the content of particular foods and food products. To avoid the consumer being deceived and sometimes poisoned by brickdust in cocoa powder, for instance, or chalk in flour, governments established minimum standards and those found debasing foods were prosecuted.

The problem, in terms of creating a single EC market, is that one country's debasement is another country's special recipe. The British

51

sausage would not be a sausage for Britons unless it contained a certain amount of cereal. To a German, however, whose sausage was traditionally one hundred per cent meat, the British sausage would be an abomination. The EC's first attempt to solve this problem was to try to create common compositional standards which all member states would accept, an effort that was doomed to failure. Now, instead of trying to agree a 'Euro-recipe' for every food product, the EC operates on the principle that whatever is legal in one member state can be sold anywhere in the EC, provided the product carries the same basic information on the label.

So the information on a food label is now vital in allowing consumers to choose between foods, particularly those which to the naked eye appear identical. It is no longer possible, say, for a German consumer to rely on the centuries-old law on the purity of German beer when choosing what to drink. Any beer can now be sold in Germany and discerning drinkers must scrutinise the label to be sure the bottle contains all the ingredients they expect. Thus labelling, once merely an eye-catching aspect of the product image, is now also an essential element in consumer protection and choice.

Unfortunately, as we shall see below, EC labelling and advertising law is not yet complete and consumers are to some extent in limbo. While the protection afforded by compositional standards is all but abandoned, the free choice afforded by comprehensive (and comprehensible) labelling has not yet been fully introduced.

4.3 The resistant consumer?

Every year around ten thousand new food products are launched on to the European market (12). Only one in ten will survive for twelve months while a paltry one in twenty are still on the market after two years. Surely this is ample proof that the European consumer is a tough nut to crack and not the feeble victim of every ploy by the food marketer?

Only a proportion of these new products will be heavily advertised with lavish design budgets for the label and packaging, but it shows that consumers will not accept uncritically any food product put on the market. And even those new food products that are advertised on television will find a far from captive audience.

Studies have demonstrated convincingly that viewers take the advertising break as the cue for making a cup of tea (power consumption suddenly surges), going to the toilet (water pressure drops) or making a phone call. Talking, cooking, housework, eating, reading, playing and wandering around the room are just some of the activities that have been recorded by researchers looking at people's viewing habits (13). Much of this research was done before remote control units and videos were widespread. Nowadays advertisers live in fear of being 'zapped'. Viewers, particularly men and young people, will simply fast-forward over ads in the programme they have recorded and, if watching in real time, will channel hop during the commercial breaks (14).

There appears to be no comparable research for printed advertising nor for radio but some psychological theories suggest that human beings do not normally pay much attention to detail, operating instead on a complex filtering system. This is borne out by research on food labelling, some of which indicates that consumers rarely read ingredients lists or nutrition information (15).

This is not to say that consumers ignore everything that appears in a food label or advert. Evidence suggests that people take notice of simple messages, particularly ones that confirm what they already believe, or want to believe (16). In other words, advertising and labelling may not change consumer food choice, it may simply reassure us that the choice we have already made is the right one (17).

Given the wide range of other influences on food choice described in this book, some of which are very powerful, this view of advertising and labelling is quite logical. On the other hand, can we really believe that the food and soft drinks industry spend £500 million on TV advertising just to entertain us? Or that food labels have no more significance than wallpaper?

4.4 Information or persuasion?

While consumers reject thousands of new food products every year, it is worth remembering that hundreds are accepted. Some are entirely novel, like Pot Noodles and Quorn. Others are variations on a theme. The 'instant chocolate' drinks market, for example, is simply a new way of preparing a traditional product - although such seemingly trivial changes may mean more than they seem. 'Drinking chocolate' is one of the few food products which still has a compositional standard - a legal minimum for the amount of cocoa powder in the mix. By renaming the product an 'instant chocolate drink', manufacturers no longer had to comply with this compositional standard and the levels of cocoa in the product fell. The market for them grew from nothing and stands at around £40 million today (18).

Clearly this rate of growth would not be possible without advertising and labelling. Consumers need to know that the product exists and, since it involves a new method of preparation, they also need information on the label about what to do with the product once bought.

But some products also need a new image. To stay with the same example, hot chocolate used to conjure up images of frosty weather, warm slippers and families round the hearth – not at all the image a producer wants for year-round sales to single professionals. So, along with the factual information about this new product's existence and what to do with it, the advertising includes glamorous female models choosing frocks in penthouses. An interview with a packaging designer working for Sainsbury's was clear about the importance of a product's appearance:

> 'Revamps on pack design have often caused sales to shoot up by startling amounts.' (19).

Indeed, although figures are not available, those working in the field complain that more is spent on researching a new logo or graphic than on the product's container (20).

Changing the image through advertising and labelling can also help an existing product break out of a narrow market into the mainstream. Yoghurt, muesli, wholemeal bread and low-fat milk were all once the province of a small health-conscious sub- section of the population. Today all these products can be bought in any branch of the major supermarket chains. Advertising and labelling can, therefore, do rather more than reinforce existing spending patterns. They can help to push at the boundaries of what consumers believe they want to eat.

This is not to say that the food industry alone can change the eating habits of a nation. The apparent trend towards healthier eating owes at least some debt to the years of campaigning by health and consumer groups (among others) on the scientific evidence linking food and health. Cheap package holidays must also take some credit for the explosion of British interest in food from around the world and our willingness to try Italian (-based) sauces, French (-style) ready meals and (packet) paella.

At the same time, tradition has not been abandoned. We all feel a certain nostalgia when the gentleman talks about his 'exceedingly good cakes' while simultaneously assuming that the cakes in question are produced in a large, modern factory. The mixture, in advertising and on labels, between the traditional and the novel can seem confused and confusing. How can advertising and labelling both reinforce consumers' existing choices and at the same time encourage new ones?

Enter the brand name. An estimated eighty per cent of advertising is for branded goods. It aims to protect or expand the existing market share (21). And it works. In the depths of the 1991 recession, the advertising industry began to lose some of its coyness about the extent of its influence. As company after company cut back or even eliminated its advertising budget, the advertising industry produced figures to win back customers. Although these statistics cover all industries and services, not just food, they show that in the 1981/2 recession the companies that maintained or increased their adspend had 81 per cent higher sales over the next two years compared to those companies which cut their advertising budgets. Over the subsequent five years the comparison is even more stark; sales were 215 per cent higher for the advertising companies (22).

Similar figures were produced to show the effects of an ITV strike in 1979. The survey covered twenty-six product categories, ten of which were food or soft drinks; it concluded that, for every £1 not spent on TV ads because of the strike, some £2.80 was lost in sales (23).

Appeal to brand loyalty is therefore a powerful mechanism for influencing consumer choice. It appeals to existing beliefs (that a particular brand is good), caters to the human disregard for detail (recognise the brand name, don't bother with the tiresome, small writing on the back), and yet allows novelty and change (same brand, new product).

But does the power of the brand name mean that food advertising and labelling is largely irrelevant in shaping the nutritional balance of consumers' diets? If advertisers are merely competing for their share of the market, it makes no nutritional difference if consumers choose brand x or brand y. This would be true if the size of the market for food products remained the same, but it does not.

Carbonated soft drinks, ice-cream and breakfast cereals are just three examples of how, in the past forty years or so, an entirely new market has been created and has expanded beyond recognition. Manufacturers competing vigorously for increasing sales can all win if the market is expanding, and there is always a new generation of consumers to be won over.

Brand loyalty is not the only emotion aroused by advertising and labelling. Snobbery (those sophisticated after-dinner mints), sentimentality (happy cows in green fields for dairy products) and, of course, sex (the crumbly chocolate bar and, more recently, ice-cream) are just a few of the non-factual messages we get from advertising and labelling. These tactics, together with their own statistics, make the industry's occasional claims to be the neutral purveyors of 'information' ring rather hollow. The mask of objectivity slips most easily in the trade magazines that consumers rarely see. When talking about the problems of designing for countries other than the UK, one British design group said:

> '... the answer is not to appeal to the rational in people but to the subconscious desires, needs and wants that lurk in all of us ... and of which we are barely aware.' (24)

Some advertisers and label designers are adept at leaping on the bandwagon. Given public concern about additives and E numbers, one enterprising manufacturer of an orange squash introduced the flash 'additive free' on the front of the bottle. The recipe had not been changed at all but sales increased dramatically almost overnight.

Sometimes, though, the bandwagon rolls backwards. Poultry producers developed a process for increasing the moistness of the meat. It involved injecting the carcasses with polyphosphates, which increases the amount of water retained when the carcasses are drenched. True, it kept the chicken meat moist but it also had the side-effect of increasing the weight of the chicken. New regulations were then introduced by the EC to make producers reveal the polyphosphate treatment on the label. However, consumers never got the chance to exercise their choice over the newly labelled products. Fearful of consumer reaction, supermarkets simply changed their policy and refused to stock chicken carcasses treated with polyphosphates.

In some respects, none of this is surprising or even particularly reprehensible. We know that advertisers play on our emotions to cajole us into buying their products. Perhaps we even enjoy it? We laugh at the humour, marvel at the technical wizardry and appreciate the sheer beauty of some advertising. We are, after all, grown adults with the capacity to discriminate and the power to choose. But this is not true of all consumers.

4.5 Children: the advertisers' dream

There is evidence that young children cannot recognise the difference between programmes and advertisements on television (25). One study found that three-quarters of four-year-olds could not discriminate between programmes and adverts (26). As many as 20 per cent of ten-year-olds could not see the distinction either. How can children protect themselves against the influence of advertising when they are unaware of its existence? Even when children do know a commercial when they see one, the same study showed that only 15 per cent knew what they were for – that is, to sell something.

Advertisers are well aware of children's vulnerability and some target their advertising and labelling at children quite deliberately. It was reported in 1986, for example, that some £150 to £200 million was being spent on advertising children's products (27) and whereas around a third of total adspend goes on TV, this rises to ninety per cent for children's products (28).

Although we might expect most of these TV ads to be for toys, most of them, except around Christmas, are for food and soft drinks. In 1990 one survey showed that just over half of all advertisements during a week of children's television were for food and soft drinks, eight times higher than any other category including toys (29).

These food adverts, and their labels, often make use of cartoon characters which are either already familiar to children or specially designed to appeal to them. The Simpsons, Teenage Mutant Hero Turtles, Muppets and Real Ghostbusters are some of the famous media 'personalities' used to sell food and soft drinks to children. Tony the Tiger, the Honey Monster and the Munch Bunch are among the characters specially developed for a particular product to appeal to children. Songs and jingles are also effective, as one mother in a survey noted;

> '... my daughter will sing Honey Nut Loops, and she'll say, I want that...'
> (30)

Children's affection for and loyalty to certain characters and their enjoyment of songs and jingles sells products. It is hard to avoid the conclusion that some advertisers are playing, in a calculated manner, on children's confusion between programmes and advertising. Even if this is not their intention, it is certainly the result.

Research shows that food and soft drink ads are children's favourites, with those for confectionery being mentioned most often (31). (More worrying, though beyond the remit of this book, is the fact that by far the most popular commercial among 8 to 18-year-olds in one study was for a lager (32).)

Although they may not realise that these are advertisements at all or that their intention is to sell, children are particularly brand conscious. Some children as young as four demonstrate brand loyalty and one study showed that children were three times more likely to remember brand adverts than adults, needing to see less advertising than adults to produce the same response (33).

Given this influence on children, it is not surprising to learn that one survey of television advertising found that 85 per cent of children had asked a parent to buy them something they had seen advertised on TV. Some two-thirds of children claimed that they got what they asked for and, given the 'pester-power' of children, this is perhaps predictable. Certainly, mothers of young children questioned in another survey felt the power of advertising through their children (34):

> '"Mine don't even ask", said one, "they just pick it up and put it in the trolley".' (35).

The pressure can be particularly difficult for families on a low income:

> 'They tend to want you to spend money you haven't got ... you have a set amount that you want to spend, and if you've got children with you they can exasperate you into buying things that you don't really want to get.'

(In chapter 5 Suzi Leather discusses the effect of low income on diet.)

Although parents often feel they ought to resist, the certainty of knowing that the purchase won't be wasted is a powerful motivator:

> 'They advertise chocolate biscuits and things within children's programmes, and they always have a cartoon or song that goes with it, and they say, can you get those, and I must admit it I always do because I know they'll be eaten.'

And after all the aggravation of being pestered by children to buy a product, parents can find that children are disappointed when it does not live up to the attractive advertising and labelling:

> '... they're potatoes in batter shaped like letters. They're expensive and there's not many in the packet ... and you can never spell the word that they say on the front.' (36)

But perhaps the most worrying aspect of the influence of food advertising on children's TV is the *type* of food it encourages parents and children to buy. The 1990 survey showed that in just over ten hours viewing there were ninety-two ads for food and drink, an average of nearly ten an hour. The vast majority of these (around three-quarters) were for products high in fat, sugar or both, like sugary breakfast cereals, sweets, crisps, fast food and soft drinks. On Saturday morning TV, the percentage of commercials for fatty and/or sugary foods rose to 85 per cent. In just four hours on the Saturday morning there were eight advertisements for the same highly sweetened breakfast cereal and more than once they appeared twice in the same commercial break (37).

These foods are precisely the ones which children should be eating less frequently. But chapter 2 suggests that babies have a natural affinity for sweet foods. Perhaps the commercials simply reinforce what children would choose anyway? Perhaps health education has failed and children are simply not aware of the healthy eating message? Recent research suggests that this is not the case. When asked, children were found to be aware that particular foods – such as fruit, vegetables and salads – were better for them and that others – crisps, chocolate, sweets, sausages, cakes, biscuits, cola drinks – were less healthy. Despite this, children, like many adults, do not choose the foods which they know to be better for them (38).

The final defence against this barrage of advertising for fatty, sugary foods could be that children only eat them as occasional treats. They may ask for these products every day but this may not mean that they eat them every day.

Unfortunately it seems that they do. Fatty and sugary snack foods such as biscuits, crisps, confectionery and cakes now account for a third of children's energy (calorie) intakes (39).

Fat accounts for some 40 per cent of children's energy, significantly above the 35 per cent recommended by the UK government and way beyond the 30 per cent limit suggested by the World Health Organisation. Non-milk extrinsic sugars (or refined sugars) make up 17 per cent of the average UK child's diet, way beyond the recommended limit of 10 per cent, and fibre, vitamin and mineral intakes are low (40). The most common diet-related disorder among children is probably tooth decay which, though declining, still affected about half of five-year-olds in the early 1980s (41). More recent figures suggest that each child has an average 1.5 decayed, missing or filled teeth. With almost a fifth of a child's energy intake coming from sugar it will be a long time before tooth decay is a rarity.

With a diet high in fat and low in fibre, vitamins and minerals, many children are storing up serious health problems for the future. Coronary heart disease, some cancers and stroke are some of the diseases which have been linked to such a diet. The patterns of consumption established in childhood may well be maintained in adulthood. (Chapters 2 and 3 look in some detail at the biological and cultural effects of childhood eating patterns and chapter 5 outlines the links between diet and disease.) Surely, then, there should be more controls over the labelling and advertising of food to protect children from being persuaded to buy products which could damage their health?

4.6 Legal, decent, honest and truthful

There are in fact several layers of protection, from law through to government guidelines and advertising industry codes of practice. They exist to protect all consumers (and food manufacturers themselves) from unfair competition. On the face of it, the rules governing the labelling and advertising of food seem tough and comprehensive.

The main EC directive on food labelling and advertising was agreed as far back as 1979 and was translated into UK law in the food labelling regulations of 1984. With a small number of exceptions, these stipulate that all food labels must carry the following information:

● the name;

● a complete list of ingredients, including additives, in descending order of weight;

● an indication of how long the food will last plus any special storage conditions;

● instructions for use;

● the weight;

● the place of origin; and

● the name and address of the manufacturer or packer.

Nutrition information will soon be given in one of two standard formats. Regulations govern some types of nutrition and health claims, including any statement on the label or in advertising concerning energy (calories), protein, vitamins, minerals, slimming, diabetic foods, polyunsaturated fats and cholesterol. In addition, no food label or advertisement can claim to prevent or treat any disease.

The European Commission's 1984 directive on misleading advertising requires member states to give legal protection to the public against false and deceptive advertising of all products, including food. In this country, this led to the Director General of Fair Trading being given statutory power, under the control of misleading advertising regulations 1988, to intervene to protect the public against such advertising (though this power does not extend to broadcast advertising). The EC's directive on cross-frontier television also affects advertising, limiting it to 15 per cent of daily transmission time and specifying where and how often commercial breaks can interrupt programmes.

Finally, the UK's Broadcasting Act 1990 permits, among other things, new advertising opportunities in the form of programme sponsorship. However, news and current affairs programmes cannot be sponsored and limits are set on the credits given during programmes which are sponsored – 15 seconds at the beginning of the programme and 10 seconds at the end and going into the commercial breaks.

The UK laws on food labelling and advertising are mainly the responsibility of the Ministry of Agriculture, Fisheries and Food (MAFF) and are enforced by trading standards and environmental health officers. These local authority officers have the power to take samples of food and have them analysed and also visit the manufacturer's premises and inspect all aspects of the manufacturing process.

4.7 Flaws in the laws

This raft of law and regulation looks like a belt and braces operation. But closer examination reveals significant flaws.

Take something as seemingly straightforward as the name of the product – 'strawberry flavour yoghurt' for example. This product could legally contain no strawberries at all. A 'strawberry flavoured yoghurt', on the other hand, must derive most of its strawberry flavour from real strawberries or a flavouring essence derived from real strawberries. If you forget which is which, scrutinise the small print in the ingredients list; if the real ingredient is not there, you can be sure the flavour is the imitation version.

Even the ingredients list, though, is not a fail-safe guide. If you see a particular kind of meat listed, you might assume that this is the kind of meat you would buy in a butcher's shop. Not so. 'Meat' can include all parts of the animal (not just the muscle), and can also include mechanically recovered meat (particles of flesh removed from the carcase by high pressure hosing which can strip every last shred of meat and gristle from bones). The resulting paste can be treated and incorporated into food under the label 'meat'.

Another problem with the ingredients list is that, even though items must be listed in weight order with the weightiest ingredient first, there is currently no way of knowing precisely how much of each ingredient is present. Without quantitative ingredients declarations (or QUID, as it is known), it is possible to buy a packet of, say, fish fingers which lists fish as the first ingredient but which contains less than fifty per cent fish. Assuming consumers prefer to buy fish rather than breadcrumbs and water (the other main ingredients), this vagueness on the ingredients list makes it impossible for consumers to choose the best value for money and impossible for high quality manufacturers to protect themselves against less scrupulous competitors.

Moving on to the weight of the food, problems arise with products as ordinary as ice-cream. It is legal to label ice-cream by volume rather than weight, but some manufacturers increase the amount of air in the product, particularly in the 'economy' varieties. Of course, without some air ice-cream would not be ice-cream (it would be a kind of ice-cream lolly). But some manufacturers add far more air than others and if you want to compare one ice-cream with another on value-for-money terms, there is no way of knowing which contains the most. One trading standards officer estimated that British consumers were spending some £20 million a year on something which they thought was ice-cream but was in fact fresh air (42).

As for nutrition information, although standard formats are being introduced, they will not be compulsory. A recent survey showed that a quarter of labelled foods carried no nutrition information at all and only three per cent gave all the nutrition information consumers need to choose a healthy product (43). Health and consumer groups do not believe that the new rules, agreed by the EC in 1991, will make much difference to this unsatisfactory situation. Manufacturers will still be able to give no nutrition information at all or give only the bare minimum which would not include saturated fat, fibre, sugar or sodium (salt) – key details for choosing a healthy diet.

The only circumstance in which nutrition labelling will be compulsory is if the product makes a nutrition *claim*. But since the least nutritious foods are highly unlikely to make such a claim, this means that the foods consumers may like to have most information about will carry none.

At the time of writing (mid-1992) most nutrition claims are not regulated. The UK government has proposals but it is being held back by the EC which has yet to produce any. Meanwhile, some food manufacturers are having a field day. 'Low fat', for example, can mean genuinely low in fat, or less fat than similar products, or even slightly less fat than the same product used to contain which may have been very high or very low. Food companies can also highlight the positive attributes of their product – say with a high fibre claim on a breakfast cereal – and conceal the negative aspects, by not giving information about sugar in the nutrition label and listing it under several different headings in the ingredients list (44).

Claims such as 'natural', 'wholesome', 'full of goodness' and so on are also unregulated. EC rules are in preparation and UK government guidelines already exist for some of these types of claims. Indeed these guidelines can be used as the basis for a prosecution but it is all too easy for clever phrasing on the label to avoid complying with government advice. 'Natural', for example, is covered by the guidelines but 'naturally the best' would not be.

Some food manufacturers sail close to the wind, even where there is legislation. Despite the prohibition on foods claiming to treat or prevent a disease, some food manufacturers label and advertise their products in such a way that consumers may be led to believe that their hearts will benefit – and not in the romantic sense.

Given the regulations covering food labelling and advertising, how are these misleading practices possible?

4.8 David v. Goliath

Even the most carefully worded legislation rarely closes every possible loophole, hence the use of test cases. Unfortunately, government guidelines do not encourage trading standards and environmental health officers to take test cases to court. According to the Director of Public Prosecutions guidelines, there must be a 'realistic prospect of a conviction' before recourse to the courts. This is understandable. No one would want taxpayers' money to be spent on a stream of court cases which had no chance of success. But without some possibility of clarifying conflicting interpretations, food law enforcement officers are left with grey areas of law which are very difficult to enforce.

Even when an environmental health or trading standards officer *is* confident that a case is 'realistic', the legal fight is not exactly equal.

The modest resources of a local authority may end up being pitted against those of a multinational food conglomerate. A large food company can draw on the best team of lawyers their money can buy and on the testimony of international experts. Local authority officers have to employ the legal counsel they can afford and, although they too can call on expert testimony, must also rely on spontaneous complaints by members of the public.

In 1990 a little over 1,800 complaints were made about advertisements on TV and radio and just over 9,000 about printed adverts. Of the top ten product categories for complaints about printed adverts, none was for food or drink. No data is available for complaints about food labelling. Without evidence of expressed consumer concern, a magistrate or judge may well conclude that consumers are not concerned.

Finally, food law enforcement officers may be hampered by insufficiently sensitive analytical techniques. The meat content of a product, for example, is determined by measuring the levels of nitrogen in the product. However, nitrogen levels can be artificially inflated by the addition of blood and rind powder and milk and bone protein. A producer of a meat product could illegally label it with a higher percentage of meat than it actually contains, but avoid prosecution because the debasement is impossible to detect. Recent powers to inspect food manufacturers' premises will help to detect any such practices by UK firms: the illegal additives would be found on site. For products imported from the EC, however, UK enforcement officers must rely on the effectiveness of inspection systems in countries as diverse as Greece and Germany.

So the law to protect consumers against misleading food labelling and advertising is vague in parts, incomplete in others and very difficult to enforce.

4.9 Industry guidelines: safety net or fig leaf?

There exists an additional layer of protection for consumers: codes of practice. The system operates as follows.

(a) Broadcast advertising

Following the introduction of the Broadcasting Act in 1991, the Independent Television Commission (ITC) replaced the Independent Broadcasting Authority (IBA) as the keeper of standards in television advertising. The ITC has drawn up, and now monitors, the code of advertising standards and practice and investigates complaints about TV advertising. The code contains sections on the protection of children against misleading advertising and on adverts concerning food and health.

The Independent Television Commission has access to advice from a medical advisory panel and, until the new franchises come into operation in January 1993, all new adverts are viewed by the ITC a week or so before they are broadcast. In addition, pre-vetting of scripts is done by the Independent Television Association, representing the TV companies themselves. In this way, they can - and do - stop commercials from appearing and suggest changes. However, this means that advertisements are being scrutinised by the very companies whose livelihood depends on advertising revenue. After the introduction of the new franchises in 1993, the Commission will no longer be involved in any pre-clearance; it will concentrate on responding to complaints. The Independent Television Association's role will become even more important.

It is only possible for consumers to complain about a TV advert after it has been shown. If the Independent Television Commission agrees with the complainant(s) that an advert does breach the code, it will take several weeks, perhaps longer, to reach that decision. Television advertising campaigns rarely last more than a few weeks. It is more than likely that the campaign will be over by the time the ITC has deliberated. No fines are levied and no corrective advertising or apology is required from an advertiser in breach of the code.

It is arguable that the ITC interprets its own code somewhat narrowly. The code specifically forbids ads that encourage children to eat frequently throughout the day. In 1991, health groups complained about a long-running commercial for a chocolate bar on the grounds that it encouraged children to eat between meals. Although the ITC issued guidance to the advertiser, it turned down the complaint (45).

If the Independent Television Commission does not agree that an advertisement has breached the code, there is no appeal mechanism. The chair of the Commission is appointed by the Home Office and the opinion of the ITC is viewed as being final.

As for the ITC's medical advisory panel, it .as recently been reduced from twelve to six people. Even at full strength this panel rarely met and it has no representatives of consumer organisations or health groups. In any case, the panel has a purely advisory function and the ITC is not obliged to accept its members' opinions.

Radio advertising is regulated by a system that parallels TV advertising and has similar weaknesses.

(b) Non-broadcast advertising

Most other advertising in newspapers, magazines (except for food and drink advertisements in professional journals), leaflets, cinemas and on posters is the domain of the Committee of Advertising Practice and the Advertising Standards Authority.

The Committee of Advertising Practice (CAP) is composed of around twenty representatives mostly of advertising trade associations and drew up the British code of advertising practice (BCAP). The first edition of the code was published in 1961 and the current version, the eighth, dates from December 1988. Many of its provisions closely resemble the ITC code and the BCAP also contains sections on the protection of children and on health and nutrition claims. There is an associated code covering the specialised area of sales promotions.

Members of the Committee of Advertising Practice and others may submit their adverts to a sub-committee and/or to a sub- group of the CAP's copy panel for advice on whether or not it contravenes the British code of advertising practice. Until 1992 the CAP also investigated complaints about advertising covered by the BCAP which were made by commercial bodies against a rival.

The Advertising Standards Authority (ASA) oversees the work of the Committee of Advertising Practice and the operation of the code, and investigates complaints by the public about non-broadcast advertising. The chair of the ASA council, together with a majority of the members, should be independent of the advertising business.

The Advertising Standards Authority is funded by a levy on all display advertising. This permits a modest amount of market research as well as a system of monitoring types of advertising currently causing concern. Any conclusions resulting from a monitoring review which are agreed by the ASA council are reported in the ASA's monthly reports, together with the results of investigations into complaints.

The Advertising Standards Authority maintains that it is independent of the advertising industry as a whole and the Committee of Advertising Practice in particular. Indeed, it was set up by the CAP to be an independent watchdog.

However, the CAP and the ASA share the same building and the same paid staff service the committees of both bodies. It is difficult to see how the committee of twelve volunteers which comprises the ASA can 'oversee' the work of the CAP and the BCAP, using only the staff and facilities provided by the CAP.

The ASA relies on free advertising space provided by the members of the CAP to publicise its own existence and work. The value of this free advertising was £2.6 million in 1990 and compared with £500,000 of the ASA's own funds spent on publicity (46).

Like the Independent Television Commission's medical advisory panel, the CAP's panel with responsibility for health and nutrition issues has no representatives of consumer or health groups. Again like the ITC, the Advertising Standards Authority can only investigate complaints after the advertising has already appeared although, with some 100 million ads published every year, a pre-vetting system has never been suggested as a viable option (although one exists for tobacco advertisements). Instead, the Advertising Standards Authority supplements the complaints it receives with its system of monitoring and review.

One recent review concerned mail order health products in which slimming aids and dietary supplements featured prominently. The section of the British code of advertising practice which deals with slimming products runs to seven pages, second only to the guidance on health claims at seven-and-a-half pages. Despite this detailed guidance, the ASA found many ads contravening the code, with little or no substantiation for quite outrageous claims. Of a total of 128 ads for mail order health products sampled in one month, only 38 per cent were acceptable under the code (47). Faced with a serious breach of major sections of the code, the ASA suggested that New Year resolutions were the order of the day!

In fact, apart from issuing case reports, exhortations to improve are almost all the ASA can do to encourage compliance with the code. Enforcement relies on newspapers, magazines and other publishers refusing to accept advertisements which contravene the code. Thus, as with TV ads, those whose income depends on advertising are asked to sit in judgement on its standards.

As with TV advertising, even if a complaint is upheld there are no fines and no powers to compel corrective advertising or apologies. And although the issue of timing is less critical than for TV ads – since printed advertisements usually have a longer lifespan – complaints may take months to adjudicate. The process may be particularly lengthy if the advert falls within an area currently being monitored by the ASA and the final opinion may have to wait until the conclusion of that review.

In the meantime the advertiser can continue to reap the benefits of misleading advertising. Indeed, it is possible for advertisers to repeat a breach of the code in exactly the same or similar form several times before the weapon of last resort is invoked. The ultimate sanction is to ask the Office of Fair Trading to take out an injunction against a recalcitrant advertiser. Since the power to use injunctions came into force in June 1988 it has been used three times (48).

Like the Independent Television Commission, the ASA is open to the charge of taking a narrow approach to the terms of its own code. In 1991, for instance, dentists, local health authorities and members of the public complained about a national press advertisement as implying that refined sugar was as natural as the sugar in, say, fruit. The ASA turned down this complaint (although it did caution the advertiser about other parts of the same advertisement) (49).

4.10 A less regulated future

If enforcing law and encouraging compliance with codes is difficult now, it may be worse in future. Mindful of criticisms of misleading labelling and advertising, food companies may already be looking towards different – and as yet unregulated – methods of persuading adults and children to buy their products.

Product placement is already booming in the USA. It works as follows: a snack manufacturer pays a TV programme producer to put the snack in the hands of one or more of the characters in the show. The result is several seconds of advertising with no controls.

It couldn't happen here? It already has. A popular soap has featured several prominent shots of a savoury snack. A prime- time series has shown a particular brand of lager being, variously, drunk or carried about in crates. Films are also candidates for product placement and manufacturers often demand some editorial control to make sure that their product is shown in the most favourable way.

Sponsorship of televised events also seems to be increasing. The London Marathon, the English football team for the 1990 World Cup and the 1992 Olympic Games have all been recipients of food company sponsorship. The food products in question were high in sugar or fat or both. It is surely not coincidental that events associated with the peak of human fitness and health were chosen by these companies.

Finally, the Broadcasting Act 1990 allows, for the first time in Britain, direct commercial sponsorship of any independent television programme except news and current affairs. When food and soft drinks companies begin to sponsor children's programmes, how easy will it be for children to distinguish between the programme and the advert, and for adults to work out which came first; the sponsored programme or the product?

The author would like to acknowledge the contribution to this chapter of Sue Dibb, Mike Rayner, David Walker and Jack Winkler. Their advice, comments and ideas have been invaluable. Grateful thanks are also due for the research assistance of Caroline Mulvihill and Jane Saunders.

References to chapter 4

1. J. Lannon, 'How people choose food: the role of advertising and packaging', *The Food Consumer*, 1986.

2. *Media Register*, 1991.

3. W. Eccleshare, 'The role of advertising in food choice', J. Walter Thompson lecture, 1991.

4. J. Capel, 'The global advertising marketplace', paper included in *Advertising in a Recession: IPA Information Pack,* 1991/07.

5. J. Capel, see reference 4.

6. Euromonitor, *Children as Consumers: marketing and markets for the under 16s*, Euromonitor Publications Ltd, 1988.

7. Neilson, 'Checkout 1990/12', published in *The Food Magazine* 1991/4.

8. W. Eccleshare, see reference 3.

9. *Checkout*, 05, 1990, pp. 71-72.

10. *Checkout*, see reference 9.

11. *Marketing*, 7, 27, 1989, pp. 33-51.

12. Rt Hon. Sir Leon Brittan, 'Advertise and be damned? What 1992 means for advertising', opening address at the Forum Europe and the European Advertising Tripartite (EAT) conference, *Advertising in Europe: Freedom to Choose, Freedom to Trade*, Brussels, 1991.

13. F. Buttle, paper in the *International Journal of Advertising*, 10, 2, 1991, pp.98-99.

14. F. Buttle, see reference 13.

15. J. Lannon, see reference 1.

16. F. Buttle, see reference 13.

17. W. Eccleshare, see reference 3.

18. *Supermarketing*, 10, 5, 1990, p. 12.

19. *Marketing*, 2, 15, 1990, p. 30.

20. *Marketing*, 3, 29, 1990, p. 22.

21. J. Capel, see reference 4.

22. J. Capel, see reference 4.

23. A. Roberts, 'The 1979 ITV strike: its effects on sales', paper included in *Advertising in a Recession. IPA Information Pack*, 1991/7.

24. *Marketing*, 4, 26, 1990, p. 49

25. Ward, Reale and Levinson, 'Children's perceptions, explanations and judgements of television advertising; a further exploration', in E.A. Rubinstein and others, *Television and Social Behaviour*, US Government Printing Office, Washington DC, 1972, p. 4.

26. P. Zuckerman, and L. Gianinno, 'Measuring children's response to television advertising', in *Television Advertising and Children*, edited by J. Esserman, 1987.

27. Advertising Association, 1986.

28. Euromonitor, see reference 6.

29. Food Commission, 'Sweet persuasion', *The Food Magazine*, 4, 1990.

30. Mintel, *Children – The Influencing Factor*, Mintel special report, 1991.

31. B. Greenberg, S. Fazal and M. Wober, *Children's Views on Advertising*, Independent Broadcasting Authority, 1986.

32. P. Meller, 'Carling sets trend for youth ads', *Marketing*, 1990.

33. Millward Brown, quoted in P. Gullen (J. Walter Thompson), 'How Children Use Media', Marketing Week Seminar, *Advertising and Marketing to Children*; and *Marketing*, vol. 4, no. 26, 1991, p. 49.

34. B. Greenberg and others, see reference 31.

35. Mintel, see reference 30.

36. Leatherhead Food Research Association, *Children's Eating Habits: An In-Depth Study of the Attitudes and Behaviour of Children aged 6-11*, 1991, p.7.

37. Food Commission, see reference 29.

38. Iceland Frozen Foods, *Attitudes to Children and Food*, 1990/6.

39. B. Livingstone, 'Children's food and snacking, *CHO International Dialogue on Carbohydrates*, 6, 2 issue, 1991.

40. Rugg-Gunn, personal communication, 1991.

41. Dietary Sugars Liaison Group, memorandum to the Advertising Advisory Committee of the Independent Broadcasting Authority, 1990.

42. David Walker, personal communication.

43. *Which?*, 5, 1989, pp. 214-16.

44. Coronary Prevention Group, *The Regulation of Nutrition Claims: Full Report*, CPG, 1991.

45. Independent Television Commission, *Television Advertising Complaints Report,* November 1991.

46. Proprietary Association of Great Britain, *Annual Report* 1990-91, p. 14.

47. *Advertising Standards Authority Report 1992*, 1, 22, p. 8.

48. Advertising Standards Authority, see reference 47.

49. Advertising Standards Authority, *Case Report 191,* March 1991.

Chapter 5

Less Money, Less Choice

Poverty and diet in the UK today
by Suzi Leather

For many consumers in Britain today, healthier eating may not be an option. People living on benefit often cannot afford to switch to a better diet. In this chapter Suzi Leather reports the overwhelming evidence that poverty equals poor nutrition, and argues that government proposals for a healthier nation will be seriously undermined without a new attitude to the cost of nourishing food.

For too long, attitudes in Britain to diet and poverty have been underpinned by the assumption that healthy eating is cheaper than unhealthy eating and that the poor could eat healthily if only they chose more wisely. Instead of focusing on how much healthy eating actually costs, in terms of both price and access, and how much people living on low incomes actually have to spend on food, policy initiatives have concentrated on public information campaigns encouraging people to change their buying patterns. This has reinforced the assumption that income levels are sufficient to permit the choice of healthy food. The evidence contradicts this.

Concern has been expressed in academic, official and public circles that social security benefit rates do not provide an adequate standard of living for poorer people. The reform of the benefit system in 1988, the rise in long-term unemployment and the reduction in the real value of child benefit have generated more anxiety. Evidence has accumulated that – concerning such objectives as providing the means to afford a healthy diet – the income support system is woefully inadequate.

A number of small-scale studies have shown that social security benefit levels are insufficient to allow people to eat a healthy diet, particularly people with special needs (1), and that people on low incomes frequently go without food and eat poorer quality foods (2).

The surprising thing is that, since the inception of the welfare state, the cost of eating, healthily or otherwise, has never been made explicit. This is part of a more general problem: the standard of living that benefits are expected to support are not made explicit. This makes public scrutiny of them difficult. Even the Beveridge report in 1942, on which the welfare state was founded, was based on figures derived from a needs scale constructed in the 1930s (which included essentials like calico and candles). Successive governments have fought shy of quantifying needs in relation to food and other essentials.

But however difficult it is to assess people's needs in relation to a healthy diet or anything else, as Wynn points out, 'it must be done if injustice is to be avoided. For if national scales of need are not devised, then rules of thumb and historical remnants will be used' (3).

5.1 The cost of healthy eating

It is difficult to estimate the cost of eating healthily, but not impossible. The problem is that there are a thousand and one ways of compiling a diet that accords with the latest nutritional guidelines (4). In essence, for the average family, eating healthily means eating more fruit and vegetables (about a pound a day not including potatoes but including about an ounce of pulses, nuts and seeds); eating bread and cereals, especially wholegrain, and potatoes with every meal (but without the spreads or sauces); eating more fish but less fatty meat; and cutting down on full-fat dairy products.

There are ways of making healthy eating seem very cheap, or very expensive, depending on the composition of the 'basket of goods'. Any estimate must stand up to four simple criteria:

- *Is it realistic* – does the 'basket' bear any resemblance to current eating habits; does it depart unrealistically from consumers' existing habits?

- *Would the diet implied by it be acceptable* – and not just for one particular person over one week, but for a wide variety of people and over a period of time?

- *Does it assume perfect conditions* – that consumers have the means to prepare and cook the food and the necessary materials, including staple items like flour and cooking oil, within the budget?

- *Does the consumer really have access* to the goods at the prices costed?

Much work has been done on the cost of healthy eating to see how it compares with a standard diet and in particular whether it is within the reach of people on income support. Some studies have shown both that a healthy diet is more expensive than a standard diet and that this expense is very often well beyond the spending capacity of people on income support (5). Others suggest that even though the cost can be lower than average food spending, it remains beyond the reach of low-income families. However until recently no government has been willing to undertake such an exercise. Within the last two years, however, there have been efforts to cost healthy eating and to relate such costs to income.

(a) The Family Budget Unit's 'modest but adequate' diet

In one study the Family Budget Unit at York University developed a food budget for three family types (6). These trial budgets are based on current patterns of food-purchasing behaviour in the UK, using data from the *National Food Survey* and the *Family Expenditure Survey*, adjusted to bring it into line with other official guidelines on healthy eating. The aim has been to provide, not minimum, but 'modest but adequate' standards that will provide enough food to satisfy the recommended intakes of all nutrients and meet guidelines for healthy eating. The suggested diet is intended to reflect usual purchasing as far as possible and to be reasonably priced. The Family Budget Unit's figure for a 'modest but adequate diet' is £11.34 (at 1990 prices).

(b) MAFF's 'healthy' and 'low cost' diets

In January 1992, in response to a paper by the author to its Consumer Panel (see *Acknowledgements* at the end of the chapter), the Ministry of Agriculture, Fisheries and Food (MAFF) produced some figures on the cost of healthy eating. These estimates are based on the *National Food Survey's* average household diet, adjusted to bring it into line with the nutrient requirements recommended by government, the so-called 'dietary reference values'. MAFF estimates that a healthy diet costs on average £11.71 per person per week (at 1991 prices). This is only slightly above the Family Budget Unit's figure of £11.34 and below the present average household food spending of £12.12 per person per week (see footnote 7).

Out of interest, MAFF constructed another diet which would also meet the dietary reference values but cost only £10 per person per week – its 'low cost healthy' diet. On the basis of these calculations MAFF suggests that a healthy diet can be marginally cheaper than the present British diet – and that 'a healthy diet can cost much less than the present British diet and still retain variety' (8). Table 5.1 shows the detail of this latter diet.

There are problems with some of these figures. Observers have noted shortcomings in the *National Food Survey* on which MAFF based its estimates. It has been found, for example, that all the households in the survey tend to buy more food than usual during the survey week, but that there is a much greater percentage increase in food purchases

Table 5.1: The ingredients of a 'low-cost healthy' diet, costing £10 per person per week in 1991

Type of food	Daily amount in grams (and equivalent helping)
cheese	4 (less than ¼ slice of processed cheese)
carcase meat	20 (less than the edible portion of a chicken wing)
other meat products	17 (less than a rasher of streaky bacon)
fish	13 (less than half the fish in one fish finger)
eggs	5 (less than 1 egg per week)
whole milk	0.29 pint
skimmed milk	0.18 pint
butter/margarine	19 (almost enough for 3 slices of bread thinly spread)
other fats and oils	17 (less than 2 tablespoons)
sugar	29 (7 level teaspoons)
preserves	4 (half a level teaspoon of jam)
potatoes	177 (one medium-sized baked potato in its jacket)
fresh green veg.	46 (less than a small portion of boiled cabbage)
other fresh veg.	66 (1½ medium-sized boiled carrots)
canned beans	49 (1 tablespoon of baked beans)
frozen vegetables	57 (a medium-sized portion of peas)
other processed vegetables	41 (1 heaped tablespoon of sweetcorn)
fresh fruit	85 (1 small apple)
fruit juice	23 (one-tenth of an average glass of fruit juice)
other fruit products	22 (less than one-fifth of an average portion of tinned fruit salad)
cakes, buns and biscuits	9 (1 rich tea biscuit)
breakfast cereals	37 (1 medium-sized average portion of cornflakes)
wholemeal bread	48 (2 slices of a small loaf)
other bread	149 (6 slices of a small white loaf)
other cereal products	71 (an average portion of cooked pasta)
beverages	16 (enough tea, coffee or drinking chocolate to make several cups)

Source: Ministry of Agriculture, Fisheries and Food, 'The cost of alternative diets', Consumer Panel paper, 1992. The equivalent helping sizes are based on H. Crawley, *Food Portion Sizes*, HMSO, 1990.

by the low-income groups during the survey week than by higher-income groups (9). Indeed the probable reasons for this (like embarrassment or shame) may actually deter many households at the bottom of the lowest-income group bracket from participating in the survey at all. Much of the data for the lowest-income groups is missing or misleading. This is partly by design: there are whole population groups that the *National Food Survey* never includes, like families living in bed-and-breakfast accommodation and the single homeless. The low-income groups that are included are accorded no more attention than other groups despite their nutritional vulnerability.

Leaving aside the shortcomings of the *National Food Survey*, the MAFF exercise has been an important contribution to the debate about diet and poverty in Britain. In constructing a diet for £10 a week (a cost which the Department of Social Security is known to be 'happy with'), there is now a degree of transparency about the standard of diet which meets the dietary reference values, and its cost.

However, to conform to such a diet for £10 a week, low-income households would have to cut out meat almost entirely, more than double their consumption of tinned fruit and frozen vegetables (an implicit recognition that they cannot afford enough fresh fruit and vegetables) and of breakfast cereals (in order, presumably, to achieve fibre and fortified vitamins), eat five times more wholemeal bread than at present, and eat more white bread. Of the eight slices of bread to be eaten each day, only three would have even a thin spread of margarine or butter: the rest would have to be eaten dry. Yoghurts and other dairy products are completely excluded. In essence, poor consumers would be expected to adopt a totally different eating culture from the rest of the population. This is discriminatory.

The other issue that needs to be addressed is whether consumers have access to the goods at the prices costed without incurring extra costs. Do they, for instance, have to spend money in order to get to the cheaper food? Do they have the means to prepare and cook food? Since grants for items like cookers and fridges are no longer available and since many low-income consumers have reduced, or even no, access to cooking facilities, this has more than academic significance. One estimate is that the cost of eating a healthy diet is 15 per cent higher using cold food rather than hot.

'If (a) family's cooker were to break down irreversibly and not be replaced for weeks or even months, a cold diet will be more expensive and less varied. Ultimately the nutritional quality will be affected with serious consequences for health.' (10)

The central issue in all this, however, is what the poor have available to spend on food. The MAFF figures are based on a healthy diet constructed on the basis of a notional average which it presents as cheaper than the current average: this is to miss the point. The question is: how does the cost of a realistic healthy diet compare with the resources actually available to low-income consumers? Furthermore, averages, by definition, conceal very significant deviations. These deviations will inevitably take many families' actual costs far above whatever notional average cost is constructed.

As the Family Budget Unit report states:

> 'it is important to note that the costs of the modest but adequate and healthy diets in all three household types are substantially above the average (actual) expenditure in the lowest fifth of the Family Expenditure Survey income distribution. It is unlikely, therefore, that households at the lowest levels of income would be able to purchase a healthy diet which allows a range of food choice commensurate with the notion of "modest but adequate".'

5.2 How much do poor families have, to spend on food?

Often, people are struggling to make ends meet on a weekly income 'that many would not think twice about spending on a meal in a restaurant' (11). While the average UK family spends 12.4 per cent of its income on food eaten at home, for the poorest the spending proportion is far greater (12). As table 5.2 shows, were low-income families to follow the Family Budget Unit's 'modest but adequate diet', the proportion of income spent on food would rise to over fifty per cent.

Even following MAFF's low-cost healthy diet, families living on income support would still be spending about three times more, proportionately, than the average UK family spends on food. For a low-income family with two or more children, the MAFF 'low cost diet' would actually involve a considerable increase in expenditure.

Poor consumers simply do not have this room for manoeuvre. The need to pay for basic essentials like housing, fuel, food and clothes means that people on low incomes have much higher fixed costs proportionately than the better-off. As research has shown, the only room for manoeuvre for many of these people is to go into debt. According to a Policy Studies Institute report in 1992, this is already a problem for 2.6 million households (13).

Table 5.2: The cost per week of the Family Budget Unit's modest but adequate diet and the household's weekly support entitlements in 1991/92

	Cost of modest but adequate diet (A)	Income support* (B)	Column A as percentage of column B
two adults	£34.10	£62.25	55%
single parent, two children (4 & 6)	£35.15	£80.00	44%
single parent, two children (12 & 15)	£45.73	£92.80	49%
two adults, two children (4 & 6)	£54.99	£98.15	56%
two adults, two children (12 & 15)	£65.77	£110.95	59%

* These figures take into account child benefit.

A major difficulty in establishing a basis for discussion about the adequacy of income support is that the value of the food component is not made explicit: it never has been. Before 1988, however, it was at least possible to make an informed guess about the allowance for food via the calculations made for 'special diet additions' - payments made over and above what was considered the 'normal' cost of a diet. The level of these allowances was heavily criticised by academics and dieticians:

> 'The current DHSS allowances for food for normal children and teenagers are inadequate. It is impossible for these age-groups to achieve the recommended daily amounts for energy and protein on the present income-allocation and it is unlikely they will achieve anything like a well-balanced diet ... It is clear that the present normal and special dietary allowances are inappropriate and do not meet fundamental needs. It is suggested that the DHSS should review this system as a matter of some urgency and introduce a realistic arrangement for the monetary needs of all age-groups.' (14)

The Department of Social Security still refuses to identify an amount for food within income support levels, and abolished the special diet additions altogether in 1988, with no compensation for more than half a million people who were dependent on them (15). The current DSS view is that:

'Income support benefit rates ... do not include specific amounts to cover food or any other item of expenditure. They are intended to cover all normal day-to-day living expenses, but claimants, like most people, are free to spend their money in any way they choose.' (16)

In other words, the food element in benefit rates is not costed, and neither is anything else. It is difficult to understand, in the absence of even notional figures for the cost of normal day-to-day living expenses, how the DSS can say that it intends benefit rates to cover them all. It is impossible to assert that claimants are free to spend their money on healthy eating, since their other needs may preclude this. Unless (a) there are notional amounts for different needs, and (b) these are realistic, and (c) they add up to no more than the income provided, the notion of choice is meaningless; people are simply in a position where essential needs compete with one another. This conclusion was reinforced in 1988 by the British Dietetic Association:

'Financial provision for food is insufficient for families in receipt of income support. The healthy diet alternatives to a number of standard food items are generally more expensive. Half the net weekly income of an individual or family on income support could easily be spent on healthy diet – but only at the expense of other essentials such as heat, light, clothes and travel. It is unrealistic, therefore, to expect people to afford a healthy diet without austerity. The deterrent effect of this is likely to contribute to poor health.' (17)

5.3 How poverty inhibits choice

An assumption often made about diet and poverty is that poor people choose less wisely – that they buy the wrong foods. And the *National Food Survey* does indeed show marked differences in the types of foods consumed by low- and high-income groups.

Higher-income groups eat considerably more of the foods generally recommended as part of a healthy diet. Contrast their consumption of skimmed milk, cheese, fish, vegetable oils, fresh vegetables, fresh fruit and wholemeal bread with whole milk, eggs, lard, sugar, preserves and white bread.

At the same time, all income groups have made changes towards a healthier diet. The Health Education Authority found, for instance, that in response to professional healthy eating guidelines, lower-income consumers had changed their methods of food preparation from frying to grilling and/or from lard to oil, and that the main barrier to further change towards a low-fat, high-fibre diet was said to be money (18).

In general, with the exception of vitamin C, poorer people buy more sensibly – in terms of getting nutrients per pence – than the better-off. However, the choices of food by low-income groups, and particularly their high consumption of manufactured convenience foods and foods high in fats and sugars, seems paradoxical. In fact, in order to buy the nutrients they need, their food tends also to be high in fats and sugars – cheap sausages instead of lean meat, for instance. The poor, in effect, incur nutritional costs by satisfying their appetites within their budgets. In terms of dietary energy (calories), sweets and biscuits are much cheaper than fruit.

Table 5.3: The cost of 100 calories of various snack foods

	Amount needed for 100 cals	*Cost*
custard cream biscuits	2 biscuits	3p
sweets	1 small bag	9p
chocolate bar	½ bar	10p
crisps	1 bag	12p
carrots	1 lb	20p
banana	1 medium	20p
apple	3 small	29p
orange	4 small	35p
celery	2½ heads	£1.44p

Source: National Children's Home, *Poverty and Nutrition Survey*, NCH, 1991.

Many bad dietary habits associated with poverty are perfectly reasonable responses to the predicament of the poor. Manufactured foods are a cheap option because they use less energy to prepare, saving on gas and electricity bills. For someone who has been disconnected or has no access to cooking facilities – like some people living in bed-and-breakfast accommodation – they are often the only option. Manufactured convenience foods are predictable and there is less wastage. If you are poor you cannot afford mistakes. If a child does not like what is on offer and there is no back-up in the store cupboard, the child will go hungry. Knowing this, it is rational for parents to avoid variety and innovation, and to provide predictable, familiar food.

You stick with the well known, guaranteed to fill up - this means a diet high in fat and sugar. (And this kind of diet is reinforced by television commercials targeted at children - see chapter 4.)

There are other important restraints on choice. It is as true for food as for other commodities that access and availability are essential components of choice; and both are clearly related to income levels. Access to food depends on where you live, car ownership, the availability and cost of public transport. Fridge/freezer ownership and storage space also combine to affect the economics of healthy eating.

The new structure of the food retail industry and its effects on consumer choice are reviewed in detail in chapter 6 by Spencer Henson. Here we pinpoint just one of the effects.

In the 1980s the multiple food retailers invested in very large superstores located away from high street centres, often near major road networks. With their enormous choice and competitive prices, these stores are attractive to car owners and consumers with adequate credit and storage facilities who can drive to the shops and bulk buy. However, their outside-town locations deny access to many other consumers, often the poorest.

A pilot study of Londoners' access to food argued that these developments in food retailing were responding to and reinforcing the segregation of different income groups. Spencer Henson confirms (in chapter 6) that there is now a market polarisation between consumers who can shop in the large retail outlets offering the greatest choice at lower prices and those who cannot - the poor (often single parents), disabled people, the frail, the non-car-owning sector, elderly people. These groups are highly dependent on small local shops and discount food shops. Discount shops offer low prices but at the expense of choice, often selling a range of only some 750 items (including non-foods) and not stocking fresh fruit and vegetables at all (19). Poor consumers trying to eat healthily have to choose between price and choice: this is no choice.

If you can drive to a big supermarket, stock up on basics and, even better, buy fresh fruit and vegetables from a street market, you can minimise your food bill. If you are poor and don't happen to live near a superstore and street market but on a housing estate on the outskirts of a city, you will be dependent on the expensive local shops which often stock little in the way of healthy food. Shopping elsewhere involves extra costs on public transport or taxis, or walking. This is not feasible with a load of shopping, particularly for women with small children. Once home, you lack storage space and a freezer, maybe a fridge. Cooking with raw materials requires a store cupboard of basics and if you are poor you may not have one. Many people have so little to spend that running out of basics such as flour or margarine destabilises their entire food budget.

In 1989, the Health Education Authority found that for practical reasons single parents with young children were more likely to use local shops;

> 'in order to minimise the frustrations of shopping on a low budget. Respondents characteristically developed a "tunnel vision" approach to buying food, shopping quickly and only looking for familiar items. Consequently choices tended to be habitual, and experimentation was rare. When choosing food, the paramount concerns of most mothers were price, ease and speed of preparation, and family acceptability. "Healthiness" was often pushed down the list of priorities by these more immediate concerns.' (20)

In 1990 a Welsh Consumer Council survey highlighted the disadvantages to consumers of living in rural areas in terms of access to food, and noted that healthy foods generally cost more and were less widely available than their standard equivalent (21). Chapter 6 reports on surveys of prices in all types of food shops in Reading and Oxford in 1991, confirming the lower overall prices of the multiple retailers. In an Edinburgh survey about young people's eating patterns, nutritionists designed a diet to meet basic dietary requirements. It was costed in two contrasting areas in a supermarket and in a corner shop. The corner shops were 20 per cent more expensive:

> 'this bears out other studies which have shown (that in) the poorer areas of Edinburgh as well as other towns and cities the cost of a weekly shopping basket is significantly greater than in the more prosperous areas ... It is an irony that the more deprived area should be the more expensive: add the cost of transport and more difficult access to other facilities ... and you compound an already serious problem.' (22)

5.4 The impact of poverty on diet today

Although the Department of Social Security seems convinced that claimants are able to manage on income support ('our monitoring does not suggest that claimants are unable to manage on income support' (23)), the adequacy of the diet afforded by income support levels counters this assumption.

In 1979 Nelson and Naismith found that a group of children from low-income families were not meeting their energy requirements and correlated this with the poor growth seen in these children. In fact, as the proportion of income spent on food rose, the growth of children deteriorated. A low family income, of which a large but often inadequate proportion must be spent on food, apparently predisposes to shortness (24). Social class differences in height are established by the age of two-and-a-half. A DHSS report on schoolchildren found that children from families with fathers who were unemployed or receiving benefit were significantly shorter than those from social classes I, II and III (non-manual) or families not receiving benefit (25).

In 1990 the *Dietary and Nutritional Survey of British Adults* was published (26). A paper on the nutrition of women on low incomes, based on data from this survey, found that the average intake of several nutrients fell below the target levels recommended by the Department of Health. Over a quarter of women on low incomes appeared to be falling below 'almost certain deficiency' levels for eight essential nutrients (27).

Independent research carried out on 45 families with children who were in touch with local Family Service Units confirms this (28). Managing on inadequate weekly budgets routinely involved cutting down or going without food:

> 'Women in particular went short of food: most single parents and some couples (usually the woman) said they cut down regularly on food for themselves, eg. living on tea and toast for a couple of days at a time, or eating up what was left over once the children had been fed.'

Another study on the nutrition and budgeting patterns of unemployed people found that one of the many conditions that had to be met in order for people living off state benefits to be able to eat a healthy diet was 'a household which believes in fair shares for all' (29).

In 1990 the Family Welfare Association became increasingly concerned at the very small disposable income that families on income support seemed to have for food, after rent and fuel costs had been covered. They found that 47 per cent of families asking for help during the period of their study did not have enough residual income to feed themselves adequately, however carefully they shopped and cooked. Nearly 60 per cent of these were more than £10 a week short – and their sums didn't include the weekly outgoings on family necessities like soap, toothpaste, washing powder and the cost of the launderette and shoe repairs (30).

In 1991 the National Children's Home (NCH) published one of the largest surveys to have looked at the eating patterns of parents and children living on low incomes and at the comparative costs of providing a healthy and unhealthy family diet (31). Its survey of 354 families who used 52 NCH centres around the country (plus in-depth interviews and a shopping basket survey covering locations ranging from inner-city estates to rural areas) showed how difficult it was to provide a nutritionally healthy diet for children on present benefit levels. Twenty per cent of parents and ten per cent of children in the sample had gone without food in the last month because of lack of money. It also found that no parent or child in the survey was eating a healthy diet, and that many parents and children were eating very poor diets. More particularly, it found a direct relationship between those with the lowest income and those with the poorest diet. There was no evidence to suggest that parents were ignorant about what constitutes a healthy diet, evidence supported by the answers given to the question: 'If you had an extra £10 to spend on food for your child, what foods would you like to buy?' Sixty per cent said more fruit, 54 per cent more lean fresh meats, and 38 per cent more vegetables. Less than 10 per cent said items such as cakes, biscuits, ice cream and snack foods.

The impact of homelessness on diet is dramatic. Research has shown that among homeless families nearly one-quarter of women were going without food for themselves because they could not afford it, and ten per cent of children occasionally went hungry. All the health professionals contacted in this survey were concerned about the diets of families living in bed and breakfast accommodation:

> 'On the whole, families in hotels fully understand what food they should be eating, but it falls apart when you have to live in a hotel room. Even if there are cooking facilities in the hotel, invariably there are too many families sharing, and people have to prepare food in rooms. Imagine what it's like with a toddler wanting to eat – you end up giving it crisps and things like that to keep it quiet. It's the same for mothers, they are stressed and cannot prepare a decent meal for themselves, so they live on buns and cups of coffee because those kinds of things can be prepared in a room.' (32)

By the end of 1991 in England alone, there were 12,120 households living in bed-and-breakfast accommodation. This represents more than 34,000 people (33).

The diets of particularly vulnerable groups, 16 and 17-year-olds for instance who are not entitled to income support, give rise to even more concern. A study published in 1991, which focused on homeless young people under the age of 25, found that their actual daily intake as a proportion of that recommended was around one-third for energy, thiamin, riboflavin and iron and under a half for protein and calcium (34). Even if some 16 and 17-year-olds can get discretionary payments, it is at a lower rate than for 18 to 24-year-olds (which is in turn lower than for someone of 25+), even though their dietary requirements are likely to be far higher.

In 1988 the British Dietetic Association (BDA), the professional body of dieticians and nutritionists, found that its members 'have become increasingly worried about the eating patterns of people on low incomes'. The BDA published a report in which it said:

'We have found that when advising people regarding modifying their diet for health, not only are certain groups unable to afford the dietary modifications but in some circumstances they simply do not have enough money for food ... this problem is growing ... Financial provision for food for many people on Supplementary Benefit is inadequate. This is particularly so for children, the elderly, pregnant women, mentally handicapped, physically handicapped, the mentally ill and for some ethnic minority groups.' (35)

Evidence indicates that a healthy diet for a normal person can cost half the weekly income of someone on income support. Therapeutic diets often cost considerably more. In April 1988 all dietary allowances were abolished.

The Maternity Alliance has calculated the cost of a diet considered adequate for pregnant women, based on diet sheets used in maternity hospitals. As a percentage of the income support rate, the cost is 51 per cent of the rate for a single woman aged 18-24, 68 per cent of the rate for a single woman aged 16-17 and 26 per cent of the rate for a couple aged 18 or over. It concluded that women on benefits or on low wages urgently need help if they are to be properly nourished and if their own health and that of their babies is to be protected (36).

Other changes in government policy in the 1980s hit poor children particularly hard. All of them will have been affected by the fall in the real value of child benefit. In addition the Education Act 1980 abolished national nutritional standards for school meals. Throughout the 1980s education authorities came under increasing economic pressure and, as with the household budgets of low-income groups, provision for food was squeezed, standards dropped, and portion sizes were reduced, even for those still entitled to school meals. Under the Social Security Act 1986, families on family income supplement (now family credit) lost their right to free school meals. Similarly, free milk and vitamins are not available to families on family credit. Following the introduction of this legislation in 1988, the British Dietetic Association said 'financial provision for food is insufficient for families in receipt of Income Support' (37).

5.5 Poverty and debt equals reduced choice

In December 1984, the European Commission defined the poor as 'persons whose resources (material, cultural and social) are so limited as to exclude them from the minimum acceptable way of life in the member states in which they live' (38). While recognising that insufficient income is only one aspect of poverty, the European Commission considers it a common denominator of all poverty. The Commission defines the poverty threshold as 50 per cent of the average disposable income per head in the country in question. By this definition one in five people in Britain are poor and nearly one quarter of all the poor households in the European Community are British (39). This inequality has been shown to have significant consequences for health.

> 'Health differences between developed countries reflect, not differences in wealth, but differences in income distribution, in the degree of income inequality within each society. Among the developed countries this seems to be the single most important determinant of why health in one country is better than in another.' (40)

In the UK some 2.6 million households are in debt, mostly as a result of budgeting on a low income, according to the Policy Studies Institute. It found little evidence that 'consumerism' was primarily responsible for debt. 'The evidence in this report will encourage those who have argued that social security rates are too low, and that claimants are in poverty; and it should persuade those who have argued that benefits are already adequate to think again.' (41)

Debt occurs for a variety of reasons, with the following being particularly important for poor consumers:

- many people have had budgeting or crisis loans from the social fund for essential items like a cooker or fridge. The repayment of these loans is deducted at source at a discretionary rate of 5, 10 or 15 per cent of the loan per week. These used to be available as one-off payments;

- if people get into arrears with gas, electricity, water, community charge or mortgage, to prevent disconnection, the bailiff or repossession, these arrears can be deducted at source;

- liability orders from magistrates courts for payment of community charge are an alternative to removal of the household possessions. Many people are now handing over £10 per week out of their income support for this reason;

- income support for mortgage-holders only covers interest payments. Such householders have to find the capital repayment part out of their benefit;

- private debt to shops, loan companies and hire purchase is an increasing problem for people living at or below the poverty line. The most prudent family managing their money very carefully can be totally thrown by such contingencies as all three children growing out of their shoes at once.

It is the difficulty of living month in, month out, year after year, on inadequate benefit that leads to debt. Any margin for error is squeezed. Freedom from debt and social fund repayments have been identified as conditions that must be met if people living on state benefits are to be able to eat a healthy diet (42). Food is a flexible item in a household budget and tends to be cut back when budgets are tight (43). For many of the reasons outlined earlier, people living on income support have their already inadequate disposable income further lowered (and see footnote 44 at the end of the chapter). In addition, there are sections of the population who have been removed from the benefit system altogether.

Most 16 and 17-year-olds, for example, are not eligible for benefit, even if they are unable to find a place on a youth training scheme. They can apply for a severe hardship payment but these are discretionary one-off payments and not a guaranteed safety net (45). The majority of young people living independently who fall into this category live in hostels or emergency accommodation or are homeless. They live on nil or extremely low incomes. Research has shown that their dietary situation is extremely poor.

These youngsters have frequent long spells without food (one to three days is normal). They survive on the good will of slightly older people who are entitled to some support, on hostel-workers and on begging (46). There is one particularly acute problem. Pregnant 16 and 17-year-olds are not entitled to benefit until eleven weeks before their due date of confinement. Unable to find places on training projects by virtue of their pregnancy, they and their unborn babies are in a dire situation. Workers in this field have noted a high rate of miscarriages (47).

Students are also exempt from income support, debarred from housing and unemployment benefit, and have had the vacation hardship allowance removed. During the long summer vacation, a student unable to find work or to rely on parents is entitled, at best, to £9.29 to cover *all* outgoings. This applies even when a student cannot work because of illness. This amount is only one-third of the national income support for 18 to 24-year-olds for whom housing benefit would also be available (48). As a response to these problems, some student unions set up soup kitchens to help their members to eat and continue their studies.

It is clear, by comparing the amount people receive in income support with the calculations we have described of the costs of a healthy diet, that poor people will find it extremely difficult to fund a healthy diet within the present cultural pattern of eating: the absolute level of benefits is inadequate. As we have seen, many thousands of people live below income support levels. While some families may only be able to eat healthily because of their willingness to increase their debts, those who are anxious to avoid or minimise debt suffer nutritional consequences.

> 'Those who were anxious to avoid debt were usually unable to do so ... trying to avoid or minimise debt usually involved going without basic items ... sometimes the whole family would live on soup and sandwiches or dahl and roti (lentils and chapati) for a couple of weeks so as to pay a bill on time.' (49)

5.6 The effects on health

We know that poor health is both a cause and a consequence of poverty. Wilkinson states that,

> 'the vast majority of diseases are more common down the social scale ... Even with a disease such as heart disease which has been much more thoroughly researched than most, the known risk factors explain a good deal less than half the class differences in death rates.' (50)

Socio-economic factors are clearly implicated in many diseases. Plainly, diet is a connecting factor. Cardiovascular diseases and some cancers, for instance, are closely related to diet.

'From a public health point of view, however, there is little room for doubt. Almost without exception, epidemiologic studies have found fruit and vegetables to be protective against cancer as well as a range of other diseases ... It is likely that substantial public health benefits and disease reduction could be achieved if consumption of fruits and vegetables were greatly increased over the low levels seen in the United States and other industrialised nations.' (51)

This chapter has already pointed to the evidence linking socio-economic factors with dietary choice.

One thing that most clearly distinguishes the diets of poor consumers from the better-off is consumption of fresh fruit and vegetables – Table 5.4 gives some examples. The *National Food Survey* also shows marked differences between social groups. The richest fifth consumes 20 per cent more fresh green vegetables, 70 per cent more fresh fruit, and over 400 per cent more fruit juice than the poorest fifth (52).

Table 5.4: Examples of the differences in vegetable, fruit and bread consumption, Britain 1990

	Families with 3 children in income group A	Families with 3 children in income groups D and E2
	(ounces per person per week)	
fresh green vegetables	7.81	4.35
other fresh vegetables	15.46	7.03
processed vegetables	14.99	18.90
potatoes	23.21	43.38
fresh fruit	24.41	6.21
other fruit and fruit products	15.22	2.23

Source: *Household Food Consumption and Expenditure 1990*, HMSO, 1991.

Wilkinson found that,

'controlling for the consumption of fruit and fresh green vegetables revealed significant partial correlations not only with all causes of death for men and women, but also between fat consumption and ischemic heart disease, cerebrovascular disease, hypertensive disease and stomach cancer.' (53)

89

We now understand more fully the links between consumption of fruit and vegetables with diseases such as stomach cancer. The evidence is complicated, not least because consumers who do not eat very much fresh fruit and fresh green vegetables will eat other (less healthy) foods instead and will eat less fibre. But there is ample evidence from dietary surveys that there is an inverse correlation between the consumption of leafy green-yellow vegetables and cardiovascular disease and cancers (54). More is now known about the valuable protective properties of anti-oxidants, such as vitamin C, and other micro-nutrients in preventing these diseases. Fruit and vegetables are the principal dietary sources of anti-oxidant micro-nutrients. It seems that the more we know about micro-nutrients and disease prevention, the more we become aware that poor consumers are also being forced to run significantly higher health risks.

Studying the differences in consumption by different income groups in 1974, Wilkinson concluded:

> 'On the basis of the statistical relationship between the foostuffs and the "all causes" death rate we would expect something like a 20 per cent difference in death rates between these income groups as a result of differences in diets alone.'

Since 1974, the differences in consumption patterns with respect to healthy foods between high- and low-income groups have become more marked (55).

5.7 A healthy nation?

In 1991 the government published a discussion document *The Health of the Nation* with proposals for a health strategy for England (56). It emphasises the need for people to change their behaviour, including diet. The emphasis in the document is on information and choice. One of the objectives is 'to reduce the amount of premature death and ill health related wholly or in part to eating and drinking habits'. Specific government targets for the year 2005 are:

- the proportion of the population who derive less than fifteen per cent of their food energy from saturated fatty acids should be at least sixty per cent;

- the proportion of the population who derive less than thirty-five per cent of their food energy intake from total fat should be at least fifty per cent;

● the proportion of obese adults should be seven per cent or less.

The government will fail to reach these targets unless priorities are sustained in other areas of policy. For instance, under the common agricultural policy, fruit and vegetables have been destroyed in order to keep prices up (see footnote 57). Chapter 4 details how the practice of advertising and promoting highly processed and largely 'unhealthy' food products, often aimed specifically at children, is defended.

Income is also ignored in policy on food consumption. However, for poor consumers it is precisely the inadequacy of their income that is at issue. Ability to pay plays a crucial role in structuring people's food-purchasing decisions and patterns of food consumption. Despite confident official assertions to the contrary, all the detailed evidence shows that for many people a healthy diet is beyond their means. For this reason they run a much higher risk of illness such as heart disease and some cancers.

The explanation for many of the unhealthy dietary choices made by poor people lies in problems intrinsic to poverty - lack of money and indebtedness, higher prices, a lack of access and facilities. What this amounts to is a lack of choice. Nowhere in *The Health of the Nation* is there any recognition of the need to ensure that people have the resources to permit freedom of choice. It is time that pious hopes and good intentions gave way to a recognition of the continual struggle that some have to eat properly. The first target for health is that income support be set at a level which truly covers all the normal day-to-day living expenses, including the real cost of a healthy diet. Unless and until this happens, better health will remain the prerogative of those who can afford a good diet.

This chapter is based on By Bread Alone: Poverty and Diet in Britain Today, *a paper discussed by the Ministry of Agriculture, Fisheries and Food's Consumer Panel in January 1992. The author would like to thank Isobel Cole-Hamilton, Spencer Henson, Ann Hobbis, Mike Nelson and Richard Wilkinson for their help in its preparation.*

References and footnotes to chapter 5

1. F.A. Hanes and A. Macdonald, 'Can I afford the diet?', *Journal of Human Nutrition and Dietetics*, 1988.

2. T. Lang and others, *Jam Tomorrow*, Manchester Polytechnic, 1984.

3. Cited in S. Stitt, *Of Little Benefit*, Campaign Against Poverty, 1991.

4. Department of Health, *Dietary Reference Values for Food Energy and Nutrients for the United Kingdom*, HMSO, 1991.

5. Welsh Consumer Council, *Shopping for Food: a study of food prices and availability in Wales*, WCC, 1990; National Children's Home, *Poverty and Nutrition Survey*, NCH, 1991; I. Cole-Hamilton, and T. Lang, *Tightening Belts – a report on the impact of poverty on food*, London Food Commission, 1986; C. Burrows and others, *Shopping Basket Survey (1991)*, Sheffield City Council, Health Education Authority and Sheffield Health Authority.

6. Family Budget Unit, *Establishing a Food Budget for Three Family Types*, York University, 1991.

7. Both the FBU and MAFF figures exclude food eaten away from home, soft drinks and confectionery.

8. Ministry of Agriculture, Fisheries and Food, 'The cost of alternative diets', Consumer Panel paper, 1992.

9. M. Nelson, 'A dietary survey method for measuring family food purchases and individual nutrient intakes concurrently, and its use in dietary surveillance', PhD thesis, University of London, 1983.

10. F.A. Hanes and A. Macdonald, see reference 1.

11. R. Berthoud and E. Kempson, *Credit and Debt*, Policy Studies Institute, 1992.

12. Ministry of Agriculture, Fisheries and Food, *Household Food Consumption and Expenditure 1990*, Annual Report of the National Food Survey Committee, HMSO, 1990.

13. Berthoud and Kempson, see reference 11.

14. A. Macdonald and W.I. Forsyth, 'The cost of nutrition and diet therapy for low-income families', *Human Nutrition: Applied Nutrition*, 1986.

15. Letter to the author from Department of Social Security, 16 April 1992.

16. Letter to the author from Department of Social Security, 1 November 1991.

17. Policy statement from the British Dietetic Association, November 1988.

18. Health Education Authority, *Diet, Nutrition and 'Healthy Eating' in Low Income Groups*, 1989.

19. London Food Commission, *Food Retailing in London*, 1985.

20. Health Education Authority, see reference 18.

21. Welsh Consumer Council, see reference 5.

22. *Fat, Fizz and Fasting*, Bridges Project/Edinburgh District Council (undated).

23. Department of Social Security, see reference 16.

24. M. Nelson and D. Naismith, 'The nutritional status of poor children in London', *Journal of Human Nutrition*, 1979.

25. Committee on Medical Aspects of Food Policy, *The Diets of British Schoolchildren*, Department of Health report no. 36, HMSO, 1989.

26. J. Gregory and others, *The Dietary and Nutritional Survey of British Adults*, Office of Population Censuses and Surveys, HMSO, 1990.

27. Food Commission, *The Nutrition of Women on Low Incomes*, 1991.

28. R. Cohen, *Just about Surviving: Debt and the Social Fund*, Family Service Units, 1991.

29. A. Hobbiss, *Wanting for Nothing*, Horton Publishing, 1991.

30. Letter from Family Welfare Association to the *Independent*, 14 August 1991.

31. National Children's Home, see reference 5.

32. J. Conway (editor), *Prescription for Poor Health*, London Food Commission, Maternity Alliance, SHAC, Shelter, 1988.

33. Department of the Environment figures quoted by Shelter to the author.

34. *It Makes You Sick*, Nottingham Hostels Liaison Group, undated.

35. British Dietetic Association, *Can't Afford the Diet*, 1986.

36. *Maternity Services*, vol. 1, Health Committee (second report), HMSO, 1992.

37. British Dietetic Association, see reference 17.

38. The European Commission, *The European Poverty Programme, Background Report*, August 1991.

39. The European Commission, *Final Report on the Second European Poverty Programme 1985-89*, COM(91) 29 final, 13 February 1991.

40. A. Quick and R. G. Wilkinson, *Income and Health*, Socialist Health Association, 1991.

41. R. Berthoud and E. Kempson, see reference 11.

42. A. Hobbis, see reference 29.

43. T. Lang, see reference 2.

44. In future single mothers who refuse to name the father of their child will have a financial penalty deducted from their income support.

45. Numbers applying for severe hardship payments in September 1991: 5,408 of which 4,301 were successful.

46. *Excluding Youth*, Bridges Project and Edinburgh Centre for Social Welfare Research, 1991; and Nottingham Hostels Liaison Group, see reference 34.

47.   Telephone evidence, Rita Brophy, Nottingham Hostels Liaison Group.

48.   National Association of Citizens Advice Bureaux, *Diminishing Options*, NACAB, 1991.

49.   R. Cohen, see reference 28.

50.   A. Quick and R.G. Wilkinson, see reference 40.

51.   G. Block, 'Dietary guidelines and the results of food consumption surveys', *The American Journal of Clinical Nutrition*: supplement to vol. 53, no. 1, January 1991.

52.   *National Food Survey Annual Report*, see reference 12.

53.   R.G. Wilkinson, 'Socio-economic differentials in mortality – the importance of diet', *Getting the Most out of Food*, Van den Berges and Jurgens Ltd., 1977.

54.   A.T. Diplock, 'Antioxidant nutrients and disease prevention: an overview', *The American Journal of Clinical Nutrition*: supplement to vol. 53, no. 1 January 1991.

55.   Ministry of Agriculture, Fisheries and Food, see reference 12.

56.   Department of Health, *The Health of the Nation*, HMSO, 1991.

57.   In 1988/89 277,292 tonnes of fruit and vegetables were destroyed in the European Community under CAP rules.

Chapter 6

From High Street to Hypermarket

Food retailing in the 1990s
by Spencer Henson

Food shops – and the way they are owned and run – have changed out of all recognition in recent years. A few businesses now own a vast slice of the UK food retail market. One-stop, once-a-week shopping for food has become the norm for many of us. Superstore prices are lower, and the quality often better, than in the local corner shops. But the power of a handful of companies over the price, quality and range of the food we buy and their effect on the economics of small, neighbourhood shops are hotly debated. This chapter reviews these trends and the effects they have had on consumer choice.

The food retailing business has undergone a sea-change in recent years. This chapter reviews these changes – focusing on the UK market for food, the new structure of the industry, and the effects of concentrated ownership on margins, efficiency and competition. We then look at what this means for their customers – at the price, quality and choice of food, and the problems of access to the new food shops for many consumers.

6.1 The market for food

A major factor behind the changing structure and performance of the UK industry has been the very particular economic conditions in which it operates.

While the 1980s saw an unprecedented surge in consumer spending generally, consumer expenditure on food in shops hardly grew at all – just 5.9 per cent in real terms between 1985 and 1990 (1). One reason for this relatively static demand is the UK's low population growth – averaging only 0.35 per cent over 1985-90 – which inevitably limits the growth in the total number of food consumers. The second is that when household incomes rise, there is no corresponding rise in spending on food, particularly food for consumption at home. There has been a persistent decline in the proportion of consumer expenditure on food. So food retailers have not been able to rely on increases in sales through natural market growth but have had to fight their competitors for a bigger slice of the same-sized cake.

At the same time, demand for food is more stable than most other retail markets. It is virtually recession-proof, and sometimes actually picks up during an economic downturn. Demand is also fairly constant over the year as a whole, although sales of individual food items of course vary dramatically between seasons.

But despite the low growth in total consumer spending, there have been large shifts in demand for individual products. Consumers have shown increasingly different requirements – some, for example, still buying on the basis of price, others now shopping as much on the basis of quality, convenience, product range and other non-price considerations. This segmentation of the market has been a major factor in the changing competitive structure of the food industry.

6.2 The concentrating ownership

(a) Who runs food retailing?

Food retailing has moved a long way from the variety of small, family-run shops along every high street. The industry is now a complex mix of different business organisations.

The multiples: a small number of large organisations now dominate food retailing. Six major multiples – Sainsbury, Tesco, Gateway, Asda, Kwik Save and Safeway – held around three-quarters of the market in 1990, according to one estimate (2). The multiples include some 'discounters' – like Kwik Save and Aldi – which stock a limited range of products and compete entirely on price. There is also a number of smaller, but still important, regional multiples (like William Low and Budgens).

Independent retailers: these are the small owner-retailers with just one shop or a small chain. They have been the major casualties of recent years. Between 1980 and 1987 the number of single retailers fell by 16,794 and the independents' market share fell from 24.9 per cent to 15.5 per cent (3). Small retailers now often trade as members of a wider 'symbol group' under a common name (like Mace or Londis) and together accounted for 2.7 per cent of retail food sales in 1991.

Co-operative stores: these were traditionally operated by local co-operative societies, buying their supplies from the Co-operative Wholesale Society (CWS) and their marketing services from the Co-operative Retail Society (CRS). The co-operative sector is still important, with over 11 per cent of market share in 1990 (4). Recently the CWS and CRS have expanded into direct retailing and now operate a number of their own stores as well as continuing to provide their traditional services to local co-ops.

Non-food retailers: the mixed retailing sector includes Marks and Spencer which, although not classified as a food retailer, commands a significant share of the UK food market. In 1987 non-food retailers accounted for 16.4 per cent of all food sales (5).

This chapter only looks at retailers whose chief business is food. In practice, most of these also sell a variety of other household goods – non-food products can represent up to 40 per cent of a food retailer's total sales.

(b) The growing polarisation

While there has been a large drop in the numbers of independent food businesses, the total number of multiples – large and small – has also been cut, through takeovers and mergers. So the overwhelming trend has been towards concentration of ownership by a few large companies.

This has gone along with a concentration in retail capacity. According to Business Statistics Office figures, over the period 1976-87 the total number of food shops fell by 44,531 (or 31.2 per cent), 28,311 of them independents. The one area where the independent sector has managed to stave off the multiples has been in specialist food outlets – greengrocers, delicatessens and dairies, for example – which have actually increased.

While there are fewer food stores, their average size has gradually increased, along with total sales per store. This largely came about as the major multiples moved out of inner-city high streets and into out-of-town, green-field sites. By 1988 just two per cent of food stores accounted for 52 per cent of all retail food sales and the top twenty per cent of stores accounted for 90 per cent of sales (6).

According to the Institute of Grocery Distribution, the major multiples held 73.7 per cent of the market share in 1987, a growth of 21 per cent in seven years (7). Other estimates put the share even higher, at 79.9 per cent in 1990 (8). (Both estimates include non-food sales.)

The aspect of the new retailing pattern that has attracted most critical attention has been its concentration – the handful of businesses commanding such a large share of the market. Although there is no universally agreed way of calculating market share, the slice held by the largest two multiples (Sainsbury and Tesco) are significant by any standard – nearly 12 per cent each in 1989 according to one estimate (9), and between 16 and 19 per cent in 1990 according to another (10).

In fact, though, there are real differences in the competitive scene in different parts of the country. For instance, for the UK as a whole in 1988 the total market share held by the independents was 15.5 per cent; in Scotland, though, it was more than 30 per cent while in the east Midlands it was 5 per cent (11). There are equally sharp regional contrasts for the multiples themselves: in 1989 Sainsbury's market share was 21.5 per cent in the south east, only 6 per cent in the north of England and nothing at all in Scotland where the company did not operate (although now it does).

The restructuring at the top end of the business has reverberated through the rest of food retailing. One response to the threat to independent food stores has been the growth of symbol groups like Spar, Londis and Mace, which provide their small-shop members with marketing and merchandising support. Symbol groups accounted for an estimated 30.7 per cent of the independents' market share in 1990.

Co-operatives are a significant force in UK food retailing, with a bigger total market share than some of the large multiples. The co-operatives, too, have had to rationalise. During the ten years up to 1989, a mass amalgamation of small, local co-operative societies led to a 61 per cent fall in their total number. By 1989 the ten largest held 65 per cent of the co-operative market share (12).

The multiples have recently faced a new threat – the arrival of retailers like Aldi and Netto from outside the UK. These have entered at the discounting end of the retail chain, in direct competition to the existing discount operators although, given the success of these outsiders in their parent countries, all the UK multiples see their arrival as a serious threat.

Further back up the food chain, the manufacturing industry has also undergone a structural shift, again towards concentration. The top five manufacturers of organic oils and fats, for example, command 79 per cent of their market and the top five grain millers 69 per cent (13). So the multiple retailers are often dealing with suppliers who themselves hold comparable, or even greater, levels of market power. It is possible that initially the shift towards concentration in food retailing was in part a reaction to the power of the major food manufacturers.

So recent years have seen a polarisation. At one extreme are a few vast multiples, operating through a limited number of large outlets. At the other are many small multiples and independents, operating through a large number of small shops. Although in theory the whole range compete with each other, in practice each end of the market is a distinct sub-group and serves different groups of consumers. A few multiples, like Argyll, have tried to cover both ends of the market but this is the exception rather than the rule.

6.3 How competitive are the multiples?

Although no one food multiple owns a 25 per cent share of the total market (the classical definition of a monopoly), the largest of them are certainly well placed to take advantage of size, and there has been heated debate about their conduct and performance.

The food retail sector as a whole has greatly increased its returns. 'Gross margins' (meaning, roughly, the difference between turnover and purchase costs *less* the value of stocks) rose 9.5 per cent between 1980 and 1987, although this was a smaller increase than for the retail trade as a whole. The smaller food retailers made the greatest gains in gross margins, the large multiples the smallest (14).

However, gross margins are not the best indicator of a company's performance. 'Net margins', on the other hand, incorporate both gross margins and operating costs – in other words, it also takes account of a company's efficiency. The major multiples have achieved significant increases in net margins in recent years. Net margins of 6 to 8 per cent are commonplace. Sainsbury's, for example, rose 38 per cent, to 7.2 per cent, from 1985 to 1990. The larger co-operatives and smaller multiples generally earned net margins of around three to four per cent (15).

Major concern has focused on this rise in the multiples' net margins. How has it been achieved?

Part of the explanation has been the sharply rising lag, since 1985, between rises in food manufacturers' prices (what retailers pay their suppliers) and retail prices (what retailers charge their customers). As this margin widened, the multiples' margins rose proportionately, suggesting that the benefits of lower manufacturer supply prices (for example through discounts) have not been entirely passed on to consumers.

Another factor is the multiples' increased efficiency. One measure of efficiency in retailing are the gross margins earned per employee. These rose significantly for food retailers of all sizes between 1980 and 1988 (16) and rose the most for the large food retailers. (Compared to the rest of the retail trade, all food retailers remained relatively inefficient by this measure, although differences in handling disparate products make comparisons between retail sectors uncertain.)

Another measure of efficiency – the rate of turnover per employee – shows the large food multiples as markedly more efficient than either smaller food retailers or larger retailers in the UK retail sector as a whole.

Higher efficiency has certainly been achieved, through major improvements in food product management and merchandising and better distribution systems. Scanning systems, for instance, which streamline merchandising and help maintain the ideal stock ratio, were used in around seventy per cent of grocery sales in 1990, compared with just two per cent in 1984 (17). Scanners also feed in to direct product profitability – a system of stock planning based on unit profitability of shelf space, now widely used by the larger retailers.

The multiples see 'superstores' – meaning shops of 25,000 square feet or more – as important in increasing operating efficiency. In 1978 there were 176 superstores. In 1989 there were 578, a rise of 328 per cent.

The multiples often defend their own high net margins by pointing to the even higher levels earned by the UK food manufacturers who supply them. In 1988/89 the manufacturer Hazlewood Foods achieved an operating margin of 16.3 per cent (18). In fact, though, the returns in food retailing and manufacturing are probably comparable – in 1988/89 the average operating margin for the top 120 manufacturers was 7 per cent and for the top eight retailers 6.6 per cent. Another way of comparing retailers and manufacturers is by rate of return on capital employed. Here, manufacturers have managed significant growths, in contrast to the static levels of the major food retailers.

A comparison is also often made with the net margins earned by food retailers in other countries. The six to eight per cent net margins earned by major retailers here compare with two to four per cent earned by comparable retailers in the United States and Europe. A number of reasons have been put forward to explain higher net margins in the UK – including differences in store development costs and in levels of market saturation. However, another important factor is the greater regulation of discriminatory pricing in these other countries, which prohibits discounts that are not attributable to lower supply costs. (This is discussed again in the next section.)

So the multiple food retailers have undoubtedly improved their operating efficiency at shop and distribution levels, and consumers will have benefited from the lower food prices these have brought. However, there is some evidence, too, that the multiples could be reaping benefits from their size beyond those that follow simple economies of scale. This leads us on to a key issue in debates about the concentration in food retailing.

6.4 How far do the major multiples compete on price?

(a) Our price surveys

Price competition was ferocious in the late 1970s and early 1980s. Today, although the major retailers remain sensitive about the level of their prices compared to their main competitors, competition on non-price factors – like product quality and range and the comfort and quality of the shop itself – is increasingly important.

A low level of price competition does not mean, however, that we would expect identical prices across the major multiples. In any market, identical prices for all products across all the major operators can only happen if:

- it is a perfectly competitive market in which all products are totally undifferentiated in the eyes of consumers;

  or

- there is collusion between the major operators to fix the prices or to follow one operator's lead on price.

As background for this chapter, we conducted a survey of prices across a range of food shops in the Reading (Berkshire) and Oxford areas. Although the findings only strictly apply in these two regions, the major multiples price their products on a national basis and our findings can therefore be used to indicate the level of price competition in the UK as a whole.

We collected prices from large and small multiples and from independents for two types of product: 11 generic – or unbranded – items (like sugar and eggs) and 28 manufacturer-branded items (like Nescafe and Typhoo tea bags). We also priced 26 own-brand products in the major multiples. And we looked at some total shopping basket bills, again in all types of shop.

101

Generic (or unbranded) products: as table 6.1 shows, in 1991 there was very little price variation on some of these products in multiple stores. The prices of granulated sugar and a pint of milk, for instance, are identical in all the major multiples except one. There is much more price variation between the independent retailers. Other generic products on sale in multiples, like cottage cheese and canned peaches, varied more (although there may also have been marked differences in their quality).

Manufacturer-branded products: for these, there was a wider spread of prices across the shops as a whole (see table 6.2), especially compared to the prices of the 11 generic items. The variations are usually smaller in the large multiple stores, where 36 per cent of manufacturer-branded food had identical price tags. But when we include the smaller multiples, especially the discounters, there are bigger price differences.

Table 6.1: Generic food: examples of price variations, June 1991 (prices are in pence)

	Asda	Safe-way	Gate-way	Wait-rose	Bud-gen	Lo-Cost	Kwik-Save	Coop	Sains-bury	Sava-centre	Tesco	Indep.
granulated sugar: 1000g	66	66	66	66	66	66	64	66	66	66	66	67
white rice: 500g	57	56	52	56	65	68		55	56	56	56	69
white spaghetti: 500g	55	49	52	51	52	49	41		54	51	52	63
canned peach slices in syrup: 400g	31	34	38	34	36	36	27	37	31	31	31	48
canned whole carrots: 300g	26	26	26	26	28	27		25	22	22	25	31
fruit yoghurt: 150g	27	27	28	27	27	28	26	27	27	27	27	30
eggs size 4: 6	49	49	49	51	52		49		47	44	46	51
ordinary milk: 1 pint	30	30	30	30	30	29	27	30	30	30	30	33
lard: 500g	31	31	31	36	31	31	27	31	31	29	31	32
cottage cheese: 8oz	74	74	75	78	78	88	69	65	66	66	73	72
canned tomatoes: 14oz	21	21	24	25	24	27	21	30	21	21	25	31

Table 6.2: Manufacturer-branded food: examples of price variations, June 1991 (prices are in pence)

	Sains-bury	Sava-centre	Tesco	Asda	Safe-way	Gate-way	Wait-rose	Bud-gen	Lo-Cost	Kwik-Save	Coop	Indep.
Flora oil: 1 litre	109	109	109	109	109	109	109	109		105	109	128
Nescafe: 100g	139	134	139	137	139	139	139	139	139	135	139	177
Typhoo tea bags: 80g	159	159	159	157	159	159	159	159	149	155	159	170
Green Giant sweetcorn: 340g	45	45	45	53	53	53	53	45			53	63
Heinz tomato soup: 435g	37	37	37	37	37	37	37	37	37	36	37	45
Heinz baked beans: 450g	29	28	29	29	29	29	29	29	29	28	29	34
Stork soft margarine: 250g	39	39	39	39	39	37		39	37	35	38	38
Birds Eye fish fingers: 10	117	112	117	117	117	117	117		117		117	160
Sunpat peanut butter: 12oz	109	109		109	109		109	111	111		109	126
Ambrosia creamed rice: 439g	42	39	42	41	42	42	42	43	42	39	42	53
Carnation milk: 410g	49	46	45	49	49	49	49	49	51	46	49	59

So on the basis of these findings, the degree of price competition varies according to the product. Some vary widely, others are more or less standard across all the major multiples. It was evident at the stores we surveyed that what price competition there is takes the form of large, well advertised price cuts on a few products, no doubt the products on which consumers show most price sensitivity. However, this does not explain the similarity in the prices of most other items. The major multiples are known to monitor their competitors' prices and, once these are established, probably have little incentive to undercut. There may therefore be a natural degree of price leadership.

Own-brand products: these are increasingly important in the trade. Although still often promoted on the basis of a lower price, the quality of own-brand goods has also improved over recent years. Table 6.3 shows that the prices of own-brand food in major multiple stores vary more than the prices of generic or manufacturer-branded products, but not always.

Table 6.3. Own-brand food from major multiples: examples of price variations, June 1991 (prices are in pence)

	Sains-bury	Sava centre	Asda	Tesco	Safeway	Gateway	Waitrose
butter: 250g	54	54	54	54	54	54	54
instant coffee granules: 100g	109	109	109	109	109	109	119
tea bags: 80g	92	89	89	92	92	99	97
canned sweetcorn: 340g	38	39	39	42	39	42	42
canned tomato soup: 435g	34	34	34	34	34	34	31
baked beans: 450g	27	27	27	27	27	27	27
soft margarine: 250g	34	34	34	34	34	37	
frozen fish fingers:10	109	110	110		109		
peanut butter: 12oz	103	193	103	103	103	105	95
canned creamed rice: 439g	39	39	39	39	39		
evaporated milk: 410g	45	45	45	45	45	45	45

We also compared the prices of own-label and manufacturer-branded products (although there were some differences in package size or quality). Own brands were mostly cheaper although, as table 6.4 shows, there were marked differences in the size of the price discount – from 37 per cent at one extreme to nil at the other. Very often, the own-label products with the standard prices are the exact equivalents of manufacturer brands which have limited price differences.

Table 6.4: Own-brand and manufacturer-brand food: average differences in price, June 1991

	Difference in price
sunflower oil	32-37%
butter	3.6%
baked beans	6.9%
bottled pasta sauce	15.7%
frozen fish fingers	6-11%
sunflower margarine	23-25%
evaporated milk	0-8%
creamed rice	7.1%
peanut butter	5.5%

Shopping basket prices: when it comes to the total bill for a whole shopping basket of goods, many surveys have shown the lower overall price of the multiple retailers. A study for the Welsh Consumer Council in 1988, for example, costed a basket of 30 grocery items and found an average difference of 9.7 per cent between multiple and independent shops (19). There were some differences among the multiples (from £16.69 to £18.20), but their trolleyfuls were consistently cheaper than in independent outlets (from £18.27 to £21.94).

In 1991 we also chose 30 food items for our shopping basket survey. We found, though, that only the large multiples stocked all 30 items, so a second basket of 21 items was also costed in all types of shop.

The bills for the multiples' shopping basket are in table 6.5. They show far less variation than the Welsh Consumer Council's basket in 1988. The cheapest multiple – Savacentre – charged only 2 to 4 per cent less than the others, suggesting a very limited level of price competition.

Table 6.5: The cost of a 30-item shopping basket in seven multiple retailers

	Cost
Savacentre	£19.58
Sainsbury	£20.05
Tesco	£20.09
Safeway	£20.15
Gateway	£20.37
Waitrose	£20.23
Asda	£20.14

For the smaller 21-item basket, costed in multiple (large and small), co-operative and independent stores, there were wider variations (see table 6.6). The discount store Kwik Save cost 5 per cent less than the cheapest of the major multiples, while the average for independent shops was 24.5 per cent higher than the cheapest multiple. So in our 1991 survey, the discounters were the best buy on price, with the major multiples a close second.

Table 6.6: The cost of a 21-item shopping basket in different food shops

	Cost
Savacentre	£13.43
Sainsbury	£13.77
Tesco	£13.86
Safeway	£13.82
Waitrose	£13.88
Gateway	£14.14
Asda	£13.83
Kwik-Save	£13.07
Lo Cost	£13.99
Budgen	£14.27
co-operatives (average)	£13.98
independents (average)	£16.27

Table 6.7: Manufacturer list prices compared with shop prices, May-June 1991 (prices are in pence)

	Manufacturer list price	Average multiple selling price	Average independent selling price
Heinz tomato ketchup: 570g	71	64-69	90
Carnation milk: 410g	57	45-51	59
Nescafe: 100g	149	134-139	177
Birdseye cod fillet fish fingers: 10	132	117	160
Saxa table salt: 750g	37	35	45
Bisto: 8oz	60	58	67

Sources: The Grocer *1991 and the author's surveys in Reading and Oxford, 1991.*

(b) Competition or market power?

How can the large retailers afford to undercut prices to the extent they do?

The major factor is undoubtedly the discounts they can obtain from manufacturers. Table 6.7 shows the manufacturers' list price and the average price actually charged in multiple and in small shops. For all these branded products, the multiples actually charge customers less than the manufacturer list prices – a major competitive advantage.

Two questions arise in connection with what is termed 'discriminatory pricing' by the food manufacturers:

● are the discounts passed on to customers in the multiple supermarkets?

and

● what are the implications for the small independent shops unable to get the manufacturer discounts?

We have already touched on the mixed evidence in answer to the first question. Given the lower prices offered by the major multiples, consumers have clearly benefited from discriminatory pricing. But it is also clear that the multiples have retained some of the benefits and converted them into higher net margins.

The second question has concerned representatives of independent grocers for many years. They allege unfair competition – that the discounts to the major groups are based on market clout rather than cost economies. Certainly from the consumer point of view, the competitive strength of the major multiples has been a key factor in the closure of countless local shops and the trend in many of the survivors towards a so-called convenience format.

While there is little doubt that prices in a multiple supermarket are a good deal cheaper than in a corner grocer, among the multiples as a whole prices are remarkably similar, sometimes identical. Competition seems to be confined to price cuts on a few items. It is also clear that the major multiples gain significant advantages from their market power through lower supply prices which are not totally passed on in full to lower consumer prices. This inevitably raises the question: would their prices be even lower were it not for their commanding place in the market? Any increase in price competition would have to be balanced by a reduction in non-price competition – including food

107

quality, range of products and the quality of the stores. Consumers would have to choose according to the value they place on price versus non-price factors.

6.5 Non-price competition: choice, quality and in-store extras

Among the multiples in recent years, the trend has been away from competition on price and towards competition on other factors like own-brand quality and the convenience and comfort of the stores themselves. This is reflected in the level of their advertising.

Traditionally food retailers were not great advertisers. This has changed. Sainsbury, for instance, increased its spending on advertising from £9.2 million in 1986 to an estimated £22.2 million in 1990 (20), a rise reflected in the advertising budgets of all the big multiples. Advertising expenditure by the smaller and regional stores is largely restricted to local and in-store promotions.

How do the multiples compete on services other than price?

Own-brand products are an increasingly important competitive tool. Between 1978 and 1988, the share of package grocery turnover for own-brand labels rose from 23.1 to 29.6 per cent. But there are variations among the multiples. Sainsbury's own brands accounted for 51.1 per cent of its turnover in 1989, Gateway's for only 20 per cent. For Asda, own-brand sales increased from 7.6 per cent of turnover in 1985 to 30 per cent in 1988, a massive 395 per cent rise. At the other extreme, the discounting chains rely solely on manufacturer brands – and lower prices – as their competitive tool.

Increasingly, own brands give the retailer both competitive edge and better returns on sales. The multiples have gradually gone for improved quality products that both benefit from, and support, their own trade names. This helps to cut spending on corporate promotion and advertising, giving margins on the actual sales of own brands of up to 25 per cent. Own-brand products also give greater flexibility in responding to changing patterns of consumer demand. Today the retailers themselves often prompt new product development for their own labels, rather than automatically accepting the products offered by manufacturers.

From the consumer point of view, own-brand food products seem at first glance to be entirely sensible. They tend to be cheaper, as we saw in section 6.4, and to offer more choice. However, as shops give more shelf space to their own-label food, they may well reduce the total range of brands, especially manufacturer brands, on offer to consumers – in effect, a cut in consumer choice.

The quality of the shop itself, and the services it offers, have progressively become a focus for competition among the big retailers, and they now devote a good deal of effort to identifying – and marketing – the factors that will attract customers.

According to Sainsbury surveys (1984 to 1990), store cleanliness, value for money and high quality products are the three most important factors for their customers, although other features, like ease of getting to the store and convenient car parking, have played an increasing role in distinguishing one store from another.

A 1990 Consumers' Association survey (see table 6.8) indicates the importance to consumers of factors other than special offers or discounts.

Different groups of consumers will rate factors differently, and choose their shops accordingly. A high-income shopper may choose a large superstore (for its wide range of products), a less well-off shopper a discount chain (for its lower prices), and a pensioner the independent round the corner (for its convenient location). (The next section looks in detail at the question of access.)

More products: the major multiples stock a wider range of food products than other types of retailers – a point confirmed during our price surveys. We checked the availability in all the shops we visited of 81 manufacturer brands or own-label equivalents. The major multiples stocked virtually all of them, the rest a significantly lower proportion (for the discount chains, this is deliberate trading policy).

Larger stores: the range of non-food products and in-store extras like bakeries, fish counters and restaurants is increasingly important to some consumers, and an increasingly important part of the multiples' marketing strategy. This is reflected in the expanding floor space of their stores: in 1980 more than 30 per cent of multiple stores were smaller than 2,000 square feet, in 1989 only 9.6 per cent were (21).

Car parking is an increasingly important feature for stores and for customers. Between 80 and 90 per cent of new multiple stores incorporate car parks, reflecting the trend towards out-of-town sites,

Table 6.8: Key factors for consumers in their choice of food store, from a Consumers' Association survey, 1990

	Proportion considering as important %
clean floors and shelves	86
well-stocked shelves	79
wide selection of produce	73
a lot of staffed check-outs	70
helpful knowledgeable staff	69
access for disabled people	68
wide shopping aisles	59
ample car parking	57
cash/basket/express tills	54
free shopping bags	52
environmentally friendly goods	50
toilets	49
near to home	45
wide check-outs	45
special offers and discounts	39
late opening	36
fresh bread baked there	33
separate delicatessen	32
packing service	32
nappy changing room	26
seats	24
fresh fish counter	24
own-branded products	23
organic produce	20
early opening	16
payment by credit card	10

From: Which? February 1990, published by Consumers' Association, London.

increased bulk shopping and the new importance of time spent shopping.

Check-outs: consumers commonly complain about too few check-out counters and the length of queues in large food shops, and indeed the number of check-outs per unit of sales area remained more or less constant over 1980 to 1988. At the same time, the stores have tried to increase turnover through each check-out, for instance by installing scanning systems.

Opening hours: supermarkets have responded to some extent to customer demand for longer weekday and Sunday opening. By 1988,

30 per cent of new multiple stores were open after 7pm on two evenings a week and 33 per cent on six evenings. Small independents, however, have traditionally opened later, with opening hours of 8am to 10pm becoming usual.

So in multiple stores consumers are increasingly offered a wider range and better quality of food products and extra services and standards in the shops themselves. This is in part a reaction to consumer demand, in part fuelled by the retailers' own attempts to outwit competitors. Whether these non-price benefits compensate for higher food bills, however, will be a matter for individual consumer judgement.

6.6 Access to food shops

The trends in food retailing we have discussed so far undoubtedly benefit some consumers. But a superstore offering lower prices overall, wider choice, better quality and extra in-store services is of no benefit to someone unable to use it.

(a) Distant shops

The growth in the average size of shops has taken the largest of them out of the high street and the purpose-built shopping centre and into out-of-town sites.

In 1988 around 65 per cent of new superstores were opened on the edge of towns, just over 10 per cent in shopping centres or high streets (22).

Even out of towns, the multiples select their sites with care, targeting areas with higher-income car owners and reducing investment in lower-income areas. A 1989 survey studied the households within easy reach of the stores operated by the major food retailers (23). There were differences between the different retailers, but even the most accessible to low-income families – Kwik Save – had only 20 per cent of its shop area within their easy reach. By contrast, the most accessible retailer to high-income groups – Waitrose – had 68 per cent of its sales area within their easy reach. In a 1984 London-based study, 60 per cent of all superstores and 80 per cent of new store planning applications were in the higher-income outer London boroughs. In two of the poorest inner London boroughs, Hackney and Southwark, there were no superstores and no applications to build any (24).

The growth in out-of-town superstores has had a depressing effect on the total numbers of food shops. A study in Reading, for example, showed a 10 to 20 per cent drop in the number of food outlets in suburban shopping areas between 1974 and 1984 (25), following the relocation of major food stores outside the town. In high streets, too, supermarkets have replaced smaller stores, leaving mostly the more peripheral or specialist food retailers like department stores, mixed retailers and delicatessens.

Some food discount chains – offering low prices but on a limited range of stock – have taken the place of multiples in inner-city sites. Many independent grocers, in a bid to stay in business, have moved to stocking a smaller range of basic food and non-food goods, with longer (often seven-days-a-week) opening and – inevitably – higher prices.

(b) Out of town – out of reach

These changes in the location of a large proportion of the UK's food retail capacity have left consumers with little choice. They have had to adapt their shopping habits. There have been four particularly marked trends:

- using just one store to buy all or most food;
- shopping less often for food;
- travelling further to the food shop; and
- using the car more to get there and back.

A once-a-week food shop is now the norm for 61.7 per cent of consumers, with 13.5 per cent shopping even less often than that. The majority – 70.2 per cent – go there and back by car. But as table 6.9 shows, there are striking differences between households.

Elderly, low-income and unemployed people generally shop more often and only 38.5 per cent of those in socio-economic group E use the car, compared to nearly 87 per cent in the AB groups. More people on lower incomes get to the food shop by bus or on foot.

As the major food shops move out of town, consumers pay the price in time, physical effort and transport. These costs can be prohibitively high, especially for people without the use of a car – often those who are less well-off or physically disabled. Low-income consumers, who in any case spend a higher proportion of their income on food, are often unable to reach the food shops with some of the lowest prices in the UK. This is partly offset by the discount food shops which have moved into some high streets and local shopping centres and which offer the lowest food prices in the UK. However, we have also seen the limited range and quality of the discounters, local independents and small multiples.

Table 6.9: How often people shop for food, 1990

	every day %	2/3 days a week %	once a week %	once a month %	less frequently %
all consumers	3.7	16.3	61.7	6.3	0.4
aged 15−24 years	3.2	9.0	66.9	6.1	0.5
aged 23−34	4.0	10.0	64.5	7.6	0.3
aged 35−44	4.0	15.3	62.3	7.5	0.3
aged 45−54	3.5	14.8	64.4	6.6	0.3
aged 55−64	3.7	19.6	59.9	4.7	0.3
aged 65+	3.5	23.1	57.1	5.1	0.5
socio-economic group					
AB	1.2	15.6	60.7	8.6	0.7
C1	2.6	14.6	61.6	7.9	0.4
C2	4.1	15.6	64.5	6.1	0.2
D	5.5	15.3	64.5	4.1	0.2
E	5.5	22.0	55.5	3.6	0.4
working full time	2.1	10.8	66.3	8.6	0.4
working part time	4.1	14.6	62.8	7.1	0.2
not working	4.2	19.0	59.6	5.1	0.4

Source: Mintel, 1991.

A typical multiple superstore will stock 20,000 different products. The quality, especially of fresh food, is generally superior to that of other shops.

The importance of access is underlined by the 1986 survey of consumers in Reading referred to earlier. Asked to rank the factors that influence where they shop for food, low-income consumers rated 'near to home' as the most important, even ranking it above low prices. High earners, on the other hand, put 'near to home' as the sixth most important factor, along with the size of the store and its suitability for bulk buying. Both high- and low-income shoppers thought that hypermarkets and superstores offered low prices, wide choice and good quality and that market stalls and local grocers were accessible but more expensive and gave less choice.

In chapter 5, Suzi Leather discusses in detail the effects of poverty –
including the price of healthy foods and the costs of access – on
consumer choice.

(c) The future

The policies of the powerful food retail outlets in recent years have
both reflected and reinforced social and income disparities among UK
consumers. They have brought shoppers a number of benefits in terms
of price, choice and quality. But both directly (by siting shops outside
town centres and in high-income areas) and indirectly (by undermining
the economics of small local outlets), the major multiples have also
imposed costs on consumers – and there is little evidence that the costs
are borne by the consumers who get most of the benefits. Some
multiples have started to offer free bus services to out-of-town stores,
teleshopping and home deliveries. But for many people these are no
substitute for local neighbourhood shops.

However, the 1990s may see some changes. It is open to the authorities
responsible for regulating new retail developments to develop policies
to encourage the revival of local food retailing. And the multiples
themselves may provide some of the answers. As the retail market for
food approaches saturation point and UK income levels polarise, low-
income consumers may come to be seen as a potential source of growth.

References to chapter 6.

1. Mintel, 'Food retailing', *Retail Intelligence*, 1, 1990.

2. Letter to the author from AGB Market Information, 1991.

3. Institute of Grocery Distribution, *Food Retailing 1989*, IGD, 1990.

4. AGB Market Information, see reference 2.

5. Business Statistics Office, *Business Monitor SDA 25: Retailing 1986*,
   HMSO, 1989.

6. *The Retail Pocket Book*, Nielson, 1991.

7. Institute of Grocery Distribution, see reference 3.

8. AGB Market Information, see reference 2.

9. Mintel, 'Specialist food retailers', *Retail Intelligence*, 4, 1990.

10. AGB Market Information, see reference 2.

11. Henderson Crothswaite, *Food Retailing into the Nineties*, 1989.

12. Economist Intelligence Unit, 'Co-operative societies', *Retail Business
    Quarterly Trade Review*, 16, 1990.

13. S. Henson, 'The food retailer-manufacturer interface within Europe', paper presented to IAMA conference, 1992.

14. Business Statistics Office figures, 1980-90.

15. Mintel, 'Food retailing', *Retail Intelligence*, 1, 1991.

16. Business Statistics Office, *Business Monitor SDA25: Retailing 1988*, HMSO, 1991.

17. Institute of Grocery Distribution, see reference 3.

18. 'How big are the European food retailers?', *The Grocer*, 9 June 1990.

19. Welsh Consumer Council, *Shopping for Food: A Study of Food Prices and Availability in Wales*, WCC, 1990.

20. Economist Intelligence Unit.

21. Institute of Grocery Distribution, see reference 3.

22. Institute of Grocery Distribution, *Food Retailing 1991*.

23. Henderson Crothswaite, see reference 11.

24. J.C. Lewis, *Food Retailing in London: a pilot study of the three largest food retailers and Londoners' access to food*, London Food Commission, 1985.

25. S. Opacic and R.B. Potter, 'Grocery store cognitions of disadvantaged consumers groups: a Reading case study', *Tijdschift voor Econ. en Soc. Geografie*, 77, 1986.

Chapter 7
Food Quality

What does it mean?
by Ann Foster and Sandra Macrae

Down the ages, butchers and bakers, grocers and greengrocers have used the word 'quality' to describe their goods. It is still a popular marketing term today. But what does 'quality' mean to retailers and producers? And does it have the same meaning for their customers, as they try to choose fruit or meat or cheese that meets their own standards for a quality product? This chapter charts the latest initiatives by the industry, the government, the European Commission and, not least, by consumer organisations to find some common ground when it comes to defining quality in food.

'Quality' in food – as in any product or service – means different things to different people. A quality product for one shopper may be a waste of money for another. The word 'quality' on a label may mean that the food has been produced to the highest standards of excellence – or just meets the basic legal minimum.

Recently, however, there have been serious efforts by consumer organisations, the food industry, the government and the European Commission to agree some definitions for quality as it applies to food. In 1990, for example, Consumer Congress, the body that brings together consumer organisations nationwide, called for a research programme on 'quality definitions and consumer information'. Some producers have joined certification schemes, backed by independent inspections, that set and monitor standards for the production of dairy, meat and fish products. In the name of quality, the European Commission is discussing measures to protect the titles of some traditional foods.

Against this background, it is increasingly important to examine quality in food from the point of view of those who actually pay for and eat the product. This chapter starts with the consumer approach. In section 7.2 we examine some legal definitions of quality, at both UK and European levels. Section 7.3 examines recent quality initiatives at the other end of the food chain – among retailers, producers and farmers.

7.1 The ingredients of 'quality': a consumer approach

What distinguishes a 'quality' food? The answer will vary, of course, both from one food to another and one shopper to another. Consumers' perceptions of, say, a quality cut of meat are subjective and depend on their own personal needs and expectations. On this basis it could be argued that a quality food product is one that meets the consumer's requirements in every way.

But what are consumers' requirements in relation to food production and processing?

(a) From safety to ethics

The Consumer Congress resolution in 1990 suggested that consumers' interpretations of quality can cover a very wide range of attributes, from taste, look, texture and smell, through storing and cooking qualities, to the environmental or animal welfare policies of the food producer.

In 1992, the National Food Alliance of voluntary and consumer organisations considered six distinct headings as an analytical framework for setting legal and regulatory standards for quality food products. These are:

- *sensual*: the food appeals to the senses (look, taste, smell);

- *'real'*: it is authentically traditional or 'natural' (which can cover both fresh and manufactured foods);

- *functional*: it is useful for the purpose to which it is put;

- *nutritional*: it is a good source of nutrients for promoting health and preventing disease (a standard that shifts as nutritional knowledge develops);

- *biological*: it is a good supporter of useful life (live yoghurt is one example); this also refers to the pharmacological qualities of foods and herbs;

- *environmental*: this covers three related points – ethical (for example, animals reared with kindness), social (foods from factories with good working conditions) and political (produce from democratic countries).

Our own approach to a definition of quality has been to separate the various attributes of food into layers, according to their priority when it comes to consumer choice. The 'wheel' in Figure 7.1 shows those banded layers. The inner circle – food that is safe – is the first and most basic priority. Each succeeding circle represents an increasingly sophisticated set of consumer requirements. These may sometimes – importantly – incur a higher price; the heavy black rules on our wheel show where an extra quality layer usually has a price premium.

Figure 7.1: Food quality: the consumer priorities

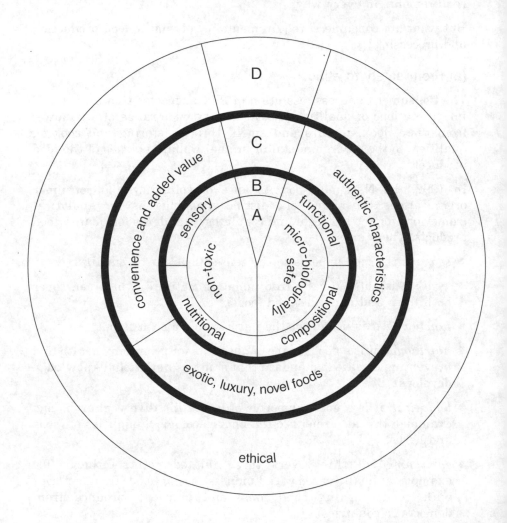

Note: ■■■■■■■ the heavy black lines show where extra quality usually means extra price.

The two inner circles arguably represent the minimum consumer criteria for all food – not just so-called quality food. And satisfying these basic criteria should impose no extra price.

118

Circle A

Safety: Consumers must be confident that the production, processing, packaging, labelling, distribution and storage of food are within acceptable safety limits.

Circle B

This band covers four related characteristics of food.

Nutrition: with increasing concern about diet-related health risks, consumers' perceptions of nutritional quality have shifted towards lower fat, sugar and salt concentrations in food, more fibre-rich carbohydrates and the optimum conservation of vitamins in, for instance, fruit.

Composition: regulations that set specific compositional standards (like the minimum amount of meat in sausages or fruit in jam) are gradually being replaced by labelling regulations, largely as a result of European Commission policies (please see chapter 9 for a fuller explanation). Many consumer organisations fear this trend will lower food quality standards overall.

Function: food should be fit for its purpose. So potatoes sold for roasting or baking or boiling and cream sold as whipping cream should do what they promise. 'Quality' here may include informative labelling, to tell consumers how to prepare and use the food.

Sensory: many consumers decide to buy, or not, on the basis of taste, smell, texture and look. For them, a quality tomato feels firm, a quality avocado feels soft, fish smells fresh. People often complain today that flavour and taste are being sacrificed for uniform size and colour. (On the other hand, many retailers assert that customers spurn unshapely or unwashed vegetables in favour of perfectly shaped, clean ones.)

The four attributes we have banded together in circle B are closely linked but not always compatible, as recent attempts to develop a virtually fat-free food have shown. The US company NutraSweet has developed a fat alternative called Simplesse, made from milk whey and egg white proteins by a process called micro-particulation. It may be of superior nutritional quality since it can be used in a whole range of low-fat products, but it has restricted functional qualities since it cannot be deep-fried or baked. According to some opinions, the sensory qualities of fat-free products may also be somewhat lacking: some of

119

those on the market in the US have been described as having 'all the texture and taste of a plastic eraser' and leaving 'a nasty chemical aftertaste' (*Scotland on Sunday*, 9 February 1992).

Circle C

This is a category of optional consumer requirements – and the first that could add to the price of a food.

Authenticity: this means that a food has been produced by a particular time-honoured method (curing, smoking or fermenting, for instance) or in a particular place (Stilton cheese or Scottish salmon) or with particular ingredients (cream in ice-cream).

Consumers may well be sceptical about some claims to authenticity and traditional methods. Parma ham can be made from pigs reared mainly in Denmark but slaughtered and cured in Parma. The Farm Assured Scotch Livestock scheme only requires that the animal was born and has spent its final twelve weeks in Scotland and slaughtered in a Scottish abattoir to qualify for the Farm Assured Scotch Beef quality label. (The European Commission's attempt to protect geographical origin and other characteristics are discussed more fully below.)

Convenience: many consumers will happily pay more for products which have 'added value', such as the recipe-dish meal or vegetables already washed and chopped, sliced or grated. This has been one of the fastest growing sectors in the UK food market.

Exotic, novel and luxury: for a select group of consumers, 'quality' means the exotic or the unusual, for which they must pay more. Vintage champagne, truffles and exotic, imported fruit could come into this category, although examples become harder to find as supermarkets bring the exclusive within the reach of all. Exclusivity alone, however, is no guarantee of quality.

Circle D

The outer circle of our wheel represents a set of ethical values which consumers can express in their buying decisions and so exert influence over the way food is produced. Increasing concern has been shown about the use of pesticides in crop production, intensive rearing techniques in animal production, animal pharmaceuticals, some feeding practices and methods of slaughtering. (Chapter 10 describes the growing role of biotechnology and science in today's food products.)

Concern about animal welfare and the impact of modern farming practices on the environment has provoked a growing number of consumers to include ethical considerations in their interpretation of food quality.

The important point is that where premium prices are being asked, the exact nature of the superiority of the food product should be explained to the consumer.

(b) Consumer perceptions of quality schemes

In 1991, on behalf of the National Farmers' Union of Scotland, a market research company, System Three Scotland, investigated consumer attitudes to quality and quality schemes, as part of background research for the introduction of the Scottish Farm Assured Scheme (we look at this scheme again in section 7.3).

The research showed that consumers assess the quality of fresh foods on the basis of:

- freshness;

- appearance;

- colour (especially for meat); and

- the reputation of the retailer.

The respondents thought the planned food quality scheme was a good idea on the basis that a properly run scheme would control farm practices, improve standards and result in a better quality product.

Respondents were shown a checklist and asked which items on the list they would expect to see incorporated in a quality scheme for meat. (See table 7.1.) The answers reveal a perception of quality that places heavy emphasis on food safety, animal welfare and more natural methods of food production. Although respondents wanted fewer chemical inputs, they stopped short of equating quality with fully organic methods of production. What appears to matter most to consumers is that food quality should reflect a more humane, natural and environmentally sensitive approach.

Respondents were also asked to identify the implications of a food quality scheme (see table 7.2). In other words, if they saw an identifying label that the produce was 'quality assured', what should this mean in practice? The answers confirmed the importance of food safety, product superiority and animal welfare.

121

Table 7.1: How respondents ranked the components of a new meat quality scheme (rank 1 is the most important for respondents, rank 13 the least important)

Ranking

1.   Uses no recycled animal matter in animal feed.
2.   Uses lowest possible level of chemicals in animal feed.
3.   Uses no growth hormones on any animal.
4.   Uses safe and humane technology.
5.   Uses lowest possible levels of fertiliser to ensure healthy growth without adverse side-effects.
6.   Uses lowest possible levels of pesticides to ensure plant protection without compromising quality.
7.   Is subject to a disciplined and monitored food production system.
8.   All animals are given a balanced diet.
9.   Provides at least the internationally recognised space allowance per animal.
10.   Guarantees that their produce is entirely wholesome.
11.   Farmers are trained to professional standards in the use of science and technology.
12.   Protects the environment by planting hedgerows and trees.
13.   Uses controlled technology.

Source: System Three Scotland for National Farmers' Union of Scotland.

Table 7.2: What should the scheme mean about a product's standards (rank 1 is the most important to respondents, rank 8 the least important)

Ranking

1.   Is guaranteed completely safe for human consumption.
2.   Is a superior quality product.
3.   Ensures high quality of life for livestock.
4.   Surpasses all European guidelines.
5.   Is a high quality product.
6.   Contributes to the high regard in which Scottish produce is held.
7.   Marries the best of the old with the best of the new.
8.   Sets the standard to which other countries aspire.

This research supports the view that consumers' perceptions of quality now go far beyond the more superficial aspects of freshness, appearance and colour. The results have encouraged the National Farmers' Union of Scotland to undertake further research into consumers' views on food safety, its wholesomeness and environment issues, in the belief that any industry-wide quality assurance scheme should be designed only after consumers' preferences and priorities have been clearly identified and understood. The marketing director of the National Farmers' Union of Scotland, Alastair Alexander, said: 'we need a scheme based on a knowledge of consumer concerns and wants, rather than farmers' own opinions of an assurance label'.

(c) What do quality symbols mean to consumers?

Are the symbols, slogans, claims and labels that use the word 'quality' really symbols of quality or simply marketing gimmicks? The Consumers' Association put quality marks to the test and the results were published in *Which?* April 1991.

Consumers' Association (CA) sent shoppers to nine major supermarkets, to buy any foods they found with symbols on the packs, and then selected 23 different symbols for group discussions. Twelve of these symbols are shown in Figure 7.2. The group discussions revealed some interesting examples of the level of understanding - and misunderstanding - of quality marks.

Symbol 1 is the official mark of the food quality scheme operated by Food From Britain (FFB), supported by the Ministry of Agriculture, Fisheries and Food. Companies which use the symbol must meet the standards devised by FFB and must comply with the scheme (described fully in section 7.3). No one in the Consumers' Association discussion groups was aware of the official status of the symbol and very few said that it would influence them to buy a product.

Symbols 1 to 6 are backed by independent inspection schemes. Not surprisingly, though, people found it difficult to distinguish between symbols denoting official schemes and symbols that were merely marketing claims. Equally, there was confusion about those backed by an independent inspection scheme and those which are not.

The discussion groups liked symbol 11 'ideal for vegetarians' and symbol 12 'organically grown' because they used words which made the meaning quite clear. But in fact symbol 12 has no official status and on its own does not guarantee that the product meets any recognised organic standards, such as those of the Soil Association (indicated by symbol 5). Symbol 6, 'conservation grade', is also an indication of how the food was produced. It is part of a scheme run by the Guild of Conservation Food Producers, which aims to produce food by less intensive, but not organic, methods. This was judged by the discussion groups to be confusing since the term 'conservation grade' meant nothing unless accompanied by an explanation.

Figure 7.2: Twelve 'quality symbols' from food labels, tested on consumers

From: Which? April 1991, published by Consumers' Association, London. The symbols were originally reproduced in colour.

Consumers' Association verdict was as follows:

'Despite the problems, our research with food-shoppers shows that symbols can be useful as a shorthand for people looking for particular types of products. It also shows that it is not always clear to consumers when symbols are just a design feature or a claim, and when they guarantee something about the product. Where there is any room for doubt, symbols should have words which clearly explain the characteristics guaranteed by the symbol. It is not enough to expect that the people the symbol is intended for will recognise it. Others may be misled if they think it has a different meaning.

'... Symbols should be as self-explanatory as possible. There should also be an easy way to find out more details if you want to. The agreed standards and details of monitoring or policing should be available to anyone who wants to know about them. Accurate explanatory leaflets or posters in shops could help.'

We agree: any symbols used on retail packs relating to quality standards should be accompanied by a simple explanation of what is guaranteed.

7.2 Quality: laws and regulations

Food production and sale is subject to a raft of laws and regulations made at national and, increasingly, at European levels. Chapter 9 covers the legal ground very fully. Here we focus on how the law views one specific aspect of the food on sale in shops – its quality.

(a) United Kingdom law

The Food Safety Act 1990 section 14 (reproducing the Food Act 1984, section 2) makes it an offence for any person to sell – to the purchaser's prejudice – any food which is not of 'the nature, substance or quality' demanded by the purchaser. There is some overlap between the three terms and the prosecutor can choose whichever is most appropriate.

The court may be able to measure quality against a legally prescribed standard – one that lays down, for example, the ingredients or composition of the product. Here the decision to prosecute is straightforward; the food is either within the standard and so meets the required quality, or it is not and an offence has been committed.

Where there is no specific legal standard, there is an implication that the purchaser wants food of a reasonable quality, measured by general trade practice. The test for the court is to decide on the evidence what it considers to be the proper minimum standard. Since 1915 a series of cases has evolved this principle. There may be an accepted view among traders and analysts that, to be of reasonable quality, certain substances should be present in fixed proportions – for example, the amount of fish there ought to be in a 'mock salmon cutlet'.

The courts will always say that the food fails the quality test if there is a foreign body in it that is a source of danger – a sliver of glass in a bottle of milk, for example. Despite one case which decided that a bottle cap in a bottle of milk did not necessarily mean there was an offence, normally the mere presence of a foreign body will tend to show a lack of quality, even if it has caused no actual harm.

In a recent case, the court decided that a drink described as 'containing less than 1 kilocalorie per serving' and which actually contained 29 times that amount failed to meet the quality demanded by a prospective purchaser. So the court may also treat a 'description' as equivalent to 'quality'.

(b) The European Community and quality

Chapter 9 describes the problems that beset early EC efforts to agree detailed standards for the composition and production of some foods (taking a legendary fourteen years to agree a definition for jam) and the shift towards more general directive frameworks that set down broad principles on consumer information and public health. No EC country is allowed to ban the entry of food that is *legally* produced in another member state, unless there is reason to believe it could injure health. Consumer organisations generally welcome such moves towards freer trade and greater choice for consumers.

However, the European Commission has proposed two measures that touch on the issue of food quality but which both trade and consumer groups in the UK consider to be protectionist and restrictive.

Geographical origin

This proposed regulation would protect products from a specific area – Arran cheese, say, or Loch Fyne kippers. Its chief purpose would be to help the Community's rural economy by protecting regional agricultural and food products – extending the wine industry's *appellation controlée* principle.

126

Specific characteristics

This second proposal similarly aims to promote the Community's rural areas. It proposes schemes to register, certificate and protect the name of a product possessing 'specific characteristics' (like an ingredient or production method) which distinguish it from other similar food products.

It is generally agreed in the UK that such proposals would restrict consumer choice, inhibit marketing opportunities for producers and limit future technological developments. A sounder quality yardstick for consumers would be informative labelling. When one cheese is clearly labelled 'Somerset Brie' made in the UK and the other 'Brie' made in France, the consumer is free to choose between them. Furthermore, guaranteeing the origin or even the ingredient of a product can hardly guarantee its quality – beyond the fact that it is 'authentic'.

The proposals were still under discussion as this chapter was being written (mid-1992). They find favour with southern European member states which may benefit from protection for local culinary traditions and employment.

Of perhaps more importance in the context of food quality and Europe is the setting up of the European Organisation for Testing and Certification. This will manage certification schemes and mutual recognition arrangements between national bodies. In this country, for example, Food From Britain is recognised by the UK government as the national body with the power to award quality certificates to food producers (this scheme is discussed again in section 7.3). It remains to be seen whether mutual recognition of national schemes or a single Europe-wide quality scheme will find more favour. From the consumer's point of view, the single quality label idea would certainly be the best solution.

7.3 What does 'quality' mean to the industry?

(a) Management systems

'Quality' has been a well-worn marketing slogan for the food industry down the centuries. In recent years, though, in the wake of new management and marketing trends, new UK and EC legislation, retail mergers, food safety alarms and consumer pressure, new meanings have been attached to the word. A variety of management systems are now used to set and maintain quantified standards. 'Quality' often features in the name or description of these systems. But how far do they control quality as consumers understand the word?

Quality control is a basic, long established system for inspecting and testing foods during their production and distribution. The tests tend to be *after* the event and sometimes, as with microbiological tests, there is a long time lag before the results are known. So this is a policing rather than a preventive system.

Quality assurance is rather more integrated into the production process. It aims to monitor all operations, from supply of the raw material to the finished product, for consistency and safety. It was evident in our discussions with a sample of multiples, for example, that the emphasis on 'quality assurance' is here to stay. Most have large and sophisticated food technology departments, product development specialists and quality assurance schemes. According to a newspaper article (*Scotland on Sunday*, 26 May 1991), the Argyll Group spends around £4 million a year – two per cent of its 1991 profit – on product inspection, random testing and visiting factories and growers.

British Standard 5750, developed initially for the engineering sector, is now being applied in a wide variety of UK businesses, including food. (Its principles are internationally recognised, via ISO9000 in the US and EN29000 in Europe.) To get a BS5750 certificate, a company has to examine all its management and document systems and define its quality controls for each stage. The procedures are independently inspected, and a company can lose its certificate if it fails to reach the standards it has set itself. Critics say that a scheme that allows companies to define their own standards is flawed in that a certificated business might follow all its procedures to the letter and still produce a poor end-product.

Hazard Analysis Critical Control Points, or HACCP, is another internationally recognised procedure for assessing and controlling standards, principally safety standards. It assesses the hazards associated with every stage of manufacture, from raw material to finished product, and identifies the critical points at which the risks need to be controlled. The philosophy is to get it right first time – to build quality in, not inspect faults out. HACCP is set up and run by individual companies and is not independently monitored.

Total quality management is another regime for improving performance that has now been adopted by some food companies. Quality in this context is, at its simplest, what the customer needs and expects. Companies aim to ensure that the activities of all employees are directed towards satisfying the customer at minimum cost. Total quality is based on problem solving and 'getting it right first time, every time'.

Whichever management scheme is adopted by a manufacturer or supplier, however, it is likely to be subject to the individual demands of the major retailers. Most multiple retailers place some kind of requirement on their suppliers, of both own-label and manufacturer-branded products, in terms of specifications and the production environment. They may insist on regular inspections, unannounced visits, manuals which detail the specification, or compliance with recognised standards such as BS5750.

The multiple retailers in general have displayed a reluctance to accept any inspection systems other than their own. And one supplier told us that the presence of retail customers on the factory floor had had a greater influence on product quality assurance than any other single factor.

However, the retailers' definition of quality does not always coincide with their customers. Criticism is voiced over the way in which the multiples – while proclaiming that 'the consumer is king' – in effect control the quality criteria of products.

The uniformity and tastelessness of much meat and many fruit and vegetables in today's shops, for example, often come in for criticism. For the retailer, 'quality' does not necessarily embrace taste. A major supermarket was reported as asserting that strawberries had to be of a certain size and colour and delivered at a specific temperature; customers, it argued, tended to buy on quality and price, taste was of lesser importance. So this type of quality assurance scheme is aimed at guaranteeing size and colour – only *part* of a consumer's view of quality.

It is interesting that concessions are now being made to taste, with the reintroduction into some supermarkets of traditional varieties of British apple, although at a premium price. Perhaps the perception of quality in some products will go full circle, with taste once more triumphing over appearance.

Recent legislation has also strongly reinforced the industry's approach to food safety and therefore to basic quality. A food trader charged under the Food Safety Act 1990 can defend himself by demonstrating that 'he took all reasonable precautions and exercised all due diligence' – the so-called due diligence defence. For the defence to be successful, a trader would have to show that positive systems of control were in place, covering:

- hygiene of both staff and premises;
- raw materials, including packaging;
- production;
- recipe, specification or compositional standards;
- packing and storage;
- labelling and advertising;
- staff training;
- monitoring of complaints.

(b) Quality schemes for food

Since the early 1980s there has been increasing interest in various parts of the food sector in product quality certification schemes. The best known is the scheme set up by Food From Britain, an organisation funded by government and the food industry to promote British food at home and abroad.

The scheme is run by a Quality Council whose members are appointed by Food From Britain, and its stated aim is:

'to provide, through approved quality certification schemes, a means by which a range of quality assured food and drink products can be supplied to retailers, wholesalers and caterers and through them to consumers in a way that is demonstrated by a certificate of registration, and where practicable by means of a certification mark, that they have been produced only by producers who can operate to standards, procedures and practices defined and approved by the certifying authority.'

The FFB Quality Council is made up of members with a wide range of interests in food and drink products, including retailing, catering, science, enforcement, the Ministry of Agriculture, Fisheries and Food, consumer organisations and those involved with the individual commodity schemes. The chairman is independent and the wide range of interests represented on it underlines FFB's commitment to independent monitoring.

The Council is the recognised UK authority for the certification of quality foods. It is the government's aim that it will become the controlling authority under any European Community measures on food product quality certification (mentioned in section 7.2 above).

The commodities covered by an FFB certificate in mid-1992 were:

- Charter Bacon;
- Scotch Beef and Lamb;
- Welsh Lamb;
- Quality British Turkey;
- Scottish Farmed Salmon;
- Smoked Scottish Salmon;
- eggs;
- sugar;
- hand-made cheese;
- Shetland Salmon.

So with the exception of hand-made cheese and sugar, the scheme so far covers primary rather than processed products.

Each scheme has a 'quality manual' which sets out:

- the standards that identify the distinctive features and characteristics of the product (the product should be distinct from others of the same kind; this can cover origin or special conditions of production or manufacture) and which define the level of quality;
- standards for the production environment, production stages and distribution;
- defined operational procedures and practices for the production and distribution processes, including how non-conforming products will be dealt with.

A certificate is awarded to a producer complying with the scheme, renewable annually, and the Food From Britain mark can appear on his products.

Inspections are carried out by bodies independent of any commercial interest in the activities being monitored. The inspectors report to Food From Britain. Any breaches are discussed with the operator and a timetable for putting them right is agreed. The most common 'minor breaches' are things like failure to provide nail brushes at washbasins, not wearing hairnets, and so on.

The certificate will be withdrawn for:

● a major breach in complying with the scheme's requirements;

● failure to correct smaller deficiencies identified during several surveillance visits;

● misuse of the certification mark;

● refusal to allow the inspectors to carry out surveillance visits or hindering them;

● any action that may have an adverse effect on the integrity or reputation of the scheme.

According to the FFB quality controller, the standards are high and are stringently inspected by the third party inspectors. In theory, with capital investment and some changes in work practices, most of the food industry should be able to reach the required standards. In practice this has not happened. Food From Britain says the scheme is designed to assist companies to improve their competitive performance. It uses 'quality' in relation to standards, which can apply equally to basic products with mass market appeal and to luxury, up-market products. The Charter Bacon and Scotch Beef and Lamb schemes have, by setting realistic standards, encouraged a high percentage of the industry to join.

The quality standard levels have been criticised, however, as being too low. Food From Britain representatives argue that this is not so and indeed some of the schemes seem to have floundered because of unwillingness to comply with the required standards or the inspection procedures – apples, pears and cheese, for example. The FFB says that in some food sector industries, where there is little by way of legislation, it is necessary to go back to basics and document exactly what is required. The schemes are not meant to be static, but to be responsive to consumer demands. They will gradually raise standards by introducing more stringent requirements as time goes on and the schemes mature.

Many multiple retailers have been unwilling to use the Food From Britain quality mark on their stock, particularly fresh produce. It is clear that it is difficult to persuade these large retailers that the quality marked products can bring any advantages; indeed the last thing they may want is to be identified as having the same standards as their retail competitors.

Food From Britain argues that the absence of quality marked products on the shelves does not necessarily mean non-participation since many major retailers will use the schemes to identify their preferred suppliers. This may be true but, during our discussions with three multiples, it was clear that the FFB schemes did not carry much weight. All the supermarkets we spoke to indicated that they would still carry out their own inspections and produce their own specifications, regardless of whether the producer had been approved by FFB.

The lack of co-operation by retailers has been a factor behind the demise of some of the schemes, particularly those for fresh salad products, vegetables and chicken. Conversely, some, particularly those for meat, are now increasingly used. After various health scares, consumers are seeking added reassurance. However, even here there has been a tendency for the labels to be customised to encompass both the supermarket name and the quality scheme, thus giving an impression that the product is unique to that particular chain. As we have seen (section 7.1), the Food From Britain symbol – a red, white and blue triangle and the words British Quality Food – is not readily understood by shoppers.

So while the trade may be aware that Food From Britain is the official body for recognising quality schemes in the UK, it has obviously been difficult to fund any kind of promotion campaign to alert the consumer to this. The scheme standards are laid down independently and assessed by independent inspectors. This obviously confers greater credibility. For the reasons we have outlined, however, it does not seem to have been successful in raising standards within several sectors. Furthermore, for whatever reasons – including trade and public ignorance – FFB does not seem to command great respect either from the food industry or from consumers. It has been very difficult to get industry funding for the organisation which remains largely dependent on government financing.

(c) Quality schemes for Scottish food

Scotland, according to recent consumer research, has the image of a green and pleasant land producing fresh food in natural conditions. In the face of tough commercial competition, however, a pleasant image is not enough. For success in the market place, the industry has to back up a good image with a range of agricultural products which meet agreed quality standards.

With this in mind, the National Farmers' Union of Scotland, Scottish Enterprise, and Highlands and Islands Enterprise are jointly developing a Scottish Farm Assured Scheme which will address consumer concerns about the quality, wholesomeness, safety, and animal welfare and environmental responsibilities of modern agricultural practice. The initiative is being guided by a strategy group which includes consumer representatives.

There are already various quality assurance schemes in Scotland including Farm Assured Scotch Livestock, covering beef and lamb, and the Scottish Pig Industry Initiative. The new Scottish Farm Assured Scheme will provide the umbrella for these and hopes to bring in new commodity groups, such as soft fruit, cereals, salmon and trout.

At the heart of the scheme will be a major consumer research project. Five hundred householders will be asked for their attitudes towards food safety, food quality, animal welfare, environmental issues and quality assurance schemes.

The organisers will then draw up codes of good farming practice, reflecting consumer priorities. The objectives of the codes will be:

- to satisfy consumer and trade concerns about the wholesomeness and safety of food;

- to develop the link between farm assurance and quality control wherever possible;

- to surpass statutory guidelines on primary food production;

- to follow environmentally sound farming practices.

The National Farmers' Union of Scotland is under no illusion about the challenges that lie ahead. Good initiatives have foundered before. In our view, quality schemes like these should be encouraged within the food industry, so long as they meet consumer requirements and reflect standards of production and processing which are higher than the legal minimum. The Scottish Consumer Council has welcomed the steps taken by the National Farmers' Union of Scotland to undertake research into consumers' views, to ensure that the scheme genuinely takes account of their interests as well as those of the producers. To succeed, it will need commitment - and investment - from the industry and, most important of all, it will need to win and retain consumer confidence.

Chapter 8
Freedom of Choice

Principles and practice
by Roger Straughan

Freedom of choice is a key consumer principle, everyone agrees. But what exactly do they mean? Should consumers be free to choose food that might harm them? If not, where should the line be drawn between 'definitely toxic' and 'slightly suspect'? Should some food processes be banned on ethical grounds? If so, how are these ethical decisions to be made? Can there ever be too much choice? If information is an essential ingredient of real choice, how much information do consumers need about food? In this chapter Dr Straughan takes us back to intellectual basics, to sketch the philosophical background to the principle of consumer choice and the practical issues it raises.

Freedom of choice is widely acknowledged as a fundamental economic and moral principle. In terms of consumer principles, choice has been described as 'the most precious of all consumers' rights' (1) and, by a former director of the National Consumer Council, as 'the engine of consumer power' (2). The principle of free choice can be justified economically in terms of market efficiency and morally in terms of respect for persons as responsible decision-makers.

But one of the problems with principles is that they are expressed in such generalised and abstract terms that their precise meaning and application are often unclear. As soon as one asks exactly what these principles mean and how they should be applied in particular cases, major disagreements result. Further confusion is caused by the fact that terms like 'freedom' and 'equality' imply *commendation*. This emotive feature of language is evident in many discussions of consumer principles.

To propose freedom of choice as a consumer principle, therefore, leaves many questions unanswered. What exactly is meant by freedom of choice here? What constitutes a free choice? How is freedom of choice related to breadth of choice? Are there necessary limits to any choice? If so, how are these limits set out and at what point do they remove freedom of choice? Do consumers actually do much conscious choosing, or are most purchases made in an unthinking, reactive way? More questions will then arise about the *desirability* of 'free' consumer choice in particular cases and whether consumers *ought* to have the freedom to buy any product they choose (even if it might harm them).

This chapter focuses on the abstract principle of freedom of choice and applies it to the practical concerns of consumers, particularly the consumers of food and drink. Section 8.1 looks at some constraints on the broad ideas of 'freedom' and 'choice'. Section 8.2 examines some factors – psychological, safety and risk, and ethical – that are particularly relevant when applying the principle to food. Section 8.3 draws the main threads together by returning to a key theme – the importance of information for consumers. So the scope is a broad one, and this short chapter offers just a sketch map of the whole area, not a detailed guide book. Its central reference point is freedom of choice.

8.1 What is freedom of choice?

(a) How free?

In any context, 'freedom' must always be relative. Total freedom is unattainable and indeed unimaginable. Physically I am not free to run a two-minute mile, to go shopping on Jupiter or even to go shopping around every supermarket in England on a Friday afternoon for the best buy. Economic constraints too mean that consumers' freedom is limited by their income and the money in their pockets; if I can only afford a packet of fish fingers, I am not, in practice, free to choose a side of smoked salmon.

Availability is another obvious limiting factor. Consumers are only free to choose what is in fact on offer, a point well illustrated by news pictures of empty shelves in Moscow shops.

Market forces also limit the range of products from which consumers are free to choose. Consumers cannot expect the freedom to choose between a thousand different varieties of condensed milk, because it would not be profitable to offer so many virtually identical alternatives. Choice will again be restricted or removed where there is a monopoly, although there are few clear examples of this in UK food and drink products – except perhaps water.

So free choice for consumers cannot be unlimited. The key question is not whether consumers have or ought to have absolute freedom of choice, but rather what *degree* of freedom they have or ought to have, and what constraints are justifiable and acceptable.

(b) How much choosing?

'Choice' is also a more complex concept than might at first appear, and a closer analysis reveals some interesting implications for the consumer.

Choosing has been defined as 'making up one's mind with regard to a particular object, action or state of affairs, in a context of alternatives (where) the particular choice is made in the light of best fulfilling some aim or requirement the agent has in mind' (3). The process of choice, according to another account, 'involves listing valued goods, weighing them in comparison with each other and calculating what choice will best maximise their attainment' (4).

So two different kinds of judgement seem to be required. Consumers do not simply 'choose a product'; they choose what they believe will attain some objective better than another product. I may, for example, choose a packet of 'organic' cornflakes in preference to a packet of 'ordinary' cornflakes if my objective is to eat the healthiest possible cornflake and if I believe that the organic variety meets that condition. Or, I may choose the cheapest tin of baked-beans on the shelf if my aim is to satisfy my baked bean-addicted family as cheaply as possible.

This might seem to suggest that choosing is always a highly rational, deliberate and thoughtful activity. But it does not follow that, in practice, we always consciously go through these separate mental processes when choosing something. Our objectives (such as, to fill the shopping basket as cheaply as possible) may be so engrained in our minds that they have become second nature, and require no conscious decision or judgement when we are choosing individual items of food. Similarly, no great deliberation is involved in choosing a packet of 24 tea bags in preference to one of 200 if you live alone and drink tea only occasionally. Analysing the logical components of choice tends to make choosing sound a much more complicated activity than it often is in practice. However, many consumers today are probably making conscious judgements more often about what to choose. For instance, do I choose an allegedly 'environmentally friendly' kitchen roll in preference to the one I usually buy which is cheaper and a more pleasing colour?

(c) Whose values?

Even if there is little or no deliberation, values and value judgements are a necessary component of choosing. These fall into various categories – such as moral, aesthetic, economic, political, religious – depending on why the goal or objective is thought to be desirable.

Some of these categories may sound too grandiose to apply to the average consumer choosing a tin of tuna in the supermarket, and certainly many consumer choices will be based on down-to-earth, commonsense economic values – trying to get the best value for money.

But even the choice or rejection of a tin of tuna could reflect other categories of value, which might take account of such things as the country of origin, aesthetic appeal or the methods used to catch the fish.

We have to bear in mind this evaluative basis of choosing when it comes to possible restrictions on consumer choice, discussed in some detail in section 8.2. Deliberately to restrict consumers' freedom of choice by not allowing certain products to reach the market place is, in effect, to make value judgements paternalistically on behalf of those consumers. But the validity of a value judgement cannot be tested or established in the same way as a factual statement; the amount of salt in a tin of tuna, for example, can be measured and this factual information conveyed to consumers, but the judgement that tuna *ought not* to be offered to the consumer because certain methods of tuna fishing are *morally wrong* is not factual and cannot be proved or disproved by experts or authorities.

So although consumers should be able to rely on those with knowledge and expertise to establish facts about food products, there can be no similar experts or authorities in the area of value judgements. What expert, for example, could judge on behalf of others that vegetarianism is 'right' or 'wrong'?

This is not to say that deliberate restrictions of consumer choice may never be justified, but that any proposed restrictions must be scrutinised carefully and that the onus of justification rests upon those wishing to impose the restriction and thereby to make a judgement about what is right for other individuals.

(d) How much information?

Choosing must be distinguished from merely picking or guessing on a random basis. I cannot properly be said to be choosing if I point to a dish on an Italian menu without any idea of what it or the alternatives are. I am not choosing an organic product if I do not understand what 'organic' means. I have not chosen a pot of marmalade if I take the first one off the shelf that happens to catch my eye. What is missing in these examples is *knowledge* about the product and its alternatives. To exercise a choice, one must necessarily know something about what one is choosing and what one is choosing it from. As such knowledge is far from being universal, probably a lot of consumer behaviour concerned with the buying of products cannot be accurately described in terms of making choices.

What sort of information should be provided about food and drink products, and how should it be given? What kind of language should be used, and what level of understanding should be assumed? Which information is most relevant to the making of consumer choices? When does information become misleading or confusing? Can all necessary information be conveyed on labels? These questions raise a host of issues, explored further in sections 8.2 and 8.3.

8.2 Possible restrictions on consumer choice

Two important points emerge from the last section:

- that consumer choice is already inevitably limited by a variety of physical and economic constraints; and

- that the onus of justification for any more restrictions will rest upon those wanting to impose them.

The discussion of further restrictions in this section will inevitably highlight a clash of principles. In the debate about the sale of unpasteurised milk, for example, attention has been drawn to 'a clear conflict between the principle that goods should be safe from foreseeable risks and the principle that consumers should be free to make choices on their own behalf' (5). The principles at stake will vary in different cases - protection from risk will not always be a factor. But the conflict will always be between what might be called paternalism on the one hand and autonomy on the other - a conflict between the desirability of making judgements about what is in the best interests of others and of allowing individuals to make their *own* judgements.

In practice, few people would probably want to rule out all possible restrictions (in addition to the unavoidable physical and economic ones). In the unlikely event of a product being discovered to possess so lethal an ingredient that anyone eating it would not survive long enough to choose (or reject) it a second time, it would be perverse to claim the freedom to choose that product in the first place or to object to an immediate ban on its sale.

Unfortunately, almost no case is as clear cut as this. In reality, it is much less obvious what the range of freedom of choice should be and when it might be justifiable to override it. To tackle this problem, we need to investigate some factors which might be put forward as justifications for restricting free choice.

139

(a) Psychological factors

Free choice is by no means always an unmixed blessing. It can incur a variety of costs.

Some of these arise in the gathering and processing of information which the individual needs in order to make his or her own free choice. Consumer publications like *Which?*, that gather and process information about consumer products and services, illustrate how these activities require specialist knowledge and techniques and incur high costs in terms of time, money and effort. It is clearly unrealistic to expect individual consumers to undertake such research themselves.

Apart from economic costs like these, the freedom to choose may bring with it even more daunting psychological costs for the individual consumer. Simply trying to remember and manipulate the relevant data may lead to 'information overload' (6). Even more fundamental is the sense of responsibility which the act of choosing can impose, often bringing worry and anxiety that one may make or have made a 'wrong' or 'bad' choice. These concerns are likely to be most acute when major decisions about career, family or medical treatment have to be made, but they may also be felt in more trivial decisions about consumer products. In an interesting discussion of whether more choice is always better than less, Dworkin describes how car manufacturer Henry Ford offered his customers a choice of colours – black!

> 'This undoubtedly restricted the range a customer had to choose from, but it also eliminated the need to answer questions such as: Which colour is the safest in terms of visibility? Which colour is likely to show the least dirt? Which colour is my spouse likely to prefer? Which colour will "last" in terms of fashion, etc?' (7)

To have a wide range of alternatives can be disturbing and disorientating, as we realise when driving into an empty car park with a huge number of alternative spaces. Our desire for security may even lead to what has been called a 'fear of freedom' (8). As another writer puts it:

> 'The individual's sense of security may be undermined by the widening of the area of his discretion. He may be unable to tolerate the uncertainty involved in having to make so many choices himself and may welcome with relief some more womb-like type of existence in which things are decided for him.' (9)

It is probably far-fetched to suppose that many consumers will long to return to the womb as a result of having to choose between tins of cat food (though one might imagine some people, haunted by indecision in the supermarket, who wish their range of choice to be reduced). However, these psychological factors do raise some important general issues.

Breadth of choice

Although freedom of choice can be defended on various grounds, it does not follow that more choice is always necessary or desirable. Freedom of choice is not to be equated with breadth of choice. Consumers do not, for instance, need their choice of tinned peaches to be extended to cover a range of two hundred alternatives; the most they could require would be a choice of different sizes of tin, of different pieces of fruit (slices, halves, etc.) and of different liquids (syrup, fruit juice, etc.), offered in a reasonable selection of qualities and prices. There seems little value in multiplying alternatives for its own sake, if the alternatives do not possess significantly different, desired characteristics.

Good enough or best possible?

Some economists and philosophers have argued the merits of a policy of 'satisficing' rather than of 'optimising'. In other words, it may often be more sensible to settle for what is 'good enough' rather than pursue the best possible option:

> 'The moderate individual ... is someone content with [what he considers] a reasonable amount of satisfaction; he wants to be satisfied and, up to a certain point, he wants more enjoyments rather than fewer, to be better off rather than worse off; but there is a point beyond which he has no desire, and even refuses, to go.' (10)

It is not difficult to see how this approach could be applied to questions about the consumer's range of choices and how a 'satisficing' consumer might operate:

> 'The satisficer need not consider and compare as many possibilities as the optimizer - indeed, quite typically, the satisficer will pursue the first option he notices; if it seems reasonably satisfactory, he will not bother even to consider other possibilities' (11).

Whether the majority of consumers are in fact satisficers or optimisers is a separate question. But the possibility of rationally pursuing a policy of 'satisficing' at least suggests that maximising the range of consumers' choice may not be universally accepted as a top priority.

141

Imposing freedom of choice

Consumers who, for some of the reasons above, might wish their range of choice to be reduced or even removed, pose a difficult and paradoxical problem. If freedom of choice is something to be valued and respected, what is to be done about those who choose to relinquish all or some of that freedom? To impose freedom of choice in such circumstances could be seen as denying freedom of choice.

This is a puzzle that arises in various political and social contexts and has no simple answer. As far as consumer choice is concerned, a partial solution may lie in offering not only a wide choice of products to those who want that, but also a wide choice of outlets and markets. The out-of-town hypermarket, for example, will not suit the shopping habits or psychology of all consumers, and many may prefer the much more limited range and the more personal atmosphere of the small corner shop.

So various kinds of psychological factor offer a possible justification for limiting consumers' freedom of choice, or at least their range of choice, in certain circumstances.

There is one area where psychological factors appear to offer a particularly powerful justification. Do consumers want or need the freedom to choose products that are unsafe or harmful? There may be some psychological costs for some people in merely trying to choose between ten varieties of rice pudding, but if some rice puddings were believed to have highly toxic qualities and no restrictions were placed upon their production and sale, choosing a rice pudding would become a form of Russian roulette – and a highly stressful exercise for everybody. However, even if consumers were not worried by the possibility of choosing a lethal rice pudding, the basic question of whether we should have the *right* to choose unsafe products would remain.

(b) Safety factors

Can restrictions on the consumer's free choice be justified in terms of safety and protection? Let us approach this complex problem by formulating two extreme, diametrically opposed viewpoints:

- that *all* potentially harmful or risky products should be banned and thus excluded from the consumer's range of choice; and

- that *no* products whatever should be banned, but that consumers should be given all the available information.

Should everything risky be banned? The main weakness of this first view is its inadequate and naive concept of risk. As Lawlor puts it:

> 'In reality, the market does not present the consumer with two categories of products, the one dangerous and the other risk-free. It is rather a question of varying degrees of risk: everything that can be bought, from a proprietary medicine to a ladder or a pencil, is potentially dangerous in certain situations.' (12)

In other words it is impossible to prove a universal negative. No one can guarantee, on the basis of present evidence, that a particular event will never happen in the future; we can only talk in terms of apparent probabilities. A conclusive answer can never be given to the question 'Is this product safe?' because all products, processes and activities carry with them some degree of potential risk. A recent document from the International Organisation of Consumers Unions makes the point effectively:

> '... the word "safety" implies zero risk, a situation and degree of certainty that cannot be achieved. Yet scientists and politicians have been known to state without qualification that a substance or process is "safe". In fact science is about probabilities, not certainties, and the history of toxicology and safety assessment is a story of constant revision in the light of new evidence and newly identified risks to humans, animals and the environment. In reality, decisions have to be made about acceptable and unacceptable risks.' (13)

Should nothing risky be banned? This second viewpoint is almost as hard to maintain. While it might perhaps be defended in the case of some products involving certain levels of risk (considered later), few consumers would welcome 'total freedom' of this kind, for the reasons noted in the last section. If a food additive, for example, is shown to be toxic with no compensating benefit, it is unjustifiable to expose consumers to the risk of eating it, even though a ban will, strictly speaking, restrict their choice. To quote Lawlor again, 'unacceptable product risks must be eliminated, so that the consumer may approach the market without excessive fear' (14). Not surprisingly, there is evidence that an overwhelming majority of consumers are in favour of government safety regulations (15).

While it is relatively easy to demolish these two extreme positions, it is much more difficult to decide where the line should be drawn in the space between them. If restrictions are justifiable and indeed necessary in certain circumstances, at which point do they become unjustifiable and unnecessary? What criteria should be used to identify the kind of risks which will justify restrictions? When does a product risk in fact become 'unacceptable'?

Food safety and risk assessment are specialist, technical subjects and it is not this book's job to make recommendations about specific products that should be banned or regulated. Instead, we shall attempt to clear the ground a little by categorising a few factors which may increase or decrease the justifiability of restrictions. Rather than trying to prescribe exactly where the dividing line should be drawn, we shall discuss which considerations are most relevant to decisions about moving that line in the direction of more or less restriction.

Level and extent of risk

How much risk is involved in a particular product will obviously be one major factor. Again, though, this is not a simple matter. 'Zero risk' is impossible, as we have seen. Further complications are created by another logical point. A product carries risk if it may cause harm or damage of some kind, but it is never strictly possible to prove conclusively that x *causes* y, only that y *seems to be associated* with x; some unknown factor - z - may be a contributory, interacting cause or even the 'real' cause. If I suffer indigestion after eating apples treated with a certain chemical, I cannot conclude that it is the chemical which is the cause. It may be the time of day when I eat apples, or that apples are the one food I always eat too quickly. This point is expanded in a helpful discussion of food health by Payne and Thomson:

> 'A complete demonstration of cause and effect between phenomena is an impossibility. Rather, we will have a range of degrees of confidence in the prediction that phenomenon B follows phenomenon A, starting at a low level with evidence simply of association, and increasing to higher degrees of confidence through the description of more and more interlinked processes starting with A and ending with B.' (16)

A further complication is that consumers will vary in their reactions to food and drink products. To quote Payne and Thomson again:

> 'Individuals differ, not only in respect of their habits of diet, but in the degree to which they are susceptible to harm. This may be in part because of metabolic or physiological behaviour eg. some take more exercise than others, some smoke, some lead more stressful lives than others.' (17)

Finally, the relationship between intake and risk may not be straightforward. The risk may be very low when the intake of a food or drink is moderate, but rise sharply when the intake increases. Individual differences again come into play here; it may be that only a tiny percentage of consumers eat or drink large quantities of the product and are likely to suffer harm as a consequence. The result is that:

> 'In practice, we are not in a position to describe the form of the intake-risk function for any food component which is at present suspected of having significant effects on health: neither are we in a position to describe with any accuracy the frequency distribution of habitual intakes in the population, or to characterise the people who depart markedly from the mode.' (18).

So there are enormous complexities in determining the level and extent of risk. All that can be concluded in general terms is that the case for restricting consumers' choice in any particular instance will become stronger in proportion to the strength of the cause/effect link, the number of people judged to be at risk and the level of intake at which the risk appears to become significant. The seriousness of the possible harm is another more obvious criterion; possible death is clearly a more potent justificatory factor than possible indigestion.

Sources of risk

Important distinctions need to be drawn between risks arising from different sources, but which may be associated with the same product or class of product.

A product may be *intrinsically* risky, or it may be particularly risky *in certain forms*, or it may be risky because of defects, pollution or poor quality. Wine, for example, might be seen as intrinsically risky because of the general dangers of alcohol; red wine might be judged to be more risky than white wine if it contains more substances associated with serious illness; and wine sweetened with anti-freeze solution will present risks of a much more direct and tangible kind. The same sort of distinctions could be drawn between full-cream milk, 'green-top' untreated milk, and milk polluted during production.

Few consumers will want the freedom to choose toxic wine or polluted milk, so the strongest case for restrictions of choice here clearly applies to the third category. The other two categories present more difficult problems.

145

Category (i): Intrinsically risky products: Wine, full-cream milk and many other products may be judged to present certain intrinsic risks, but could this kind of risk ever justify restricting consumers' freedom to choose them? Intrinsic risk is not generally thought to be a sufficient reason for a ban – cigarettes, fireworks and chainsaws can easily be purchased despite their potentially lethal properties. These examples have some significant common features, which can also be applied to food and drink products.

Firstly, we should again distinguish between an intrinsically risky product and a defective version of it (which would fall into our third category). Chainsaws are *potentially* dangerous if not used properly, but a defective chainsaw could be *actually* lethal and should therefore be removed from the range of consumer choice, together with toxic wine and polluted milk. Secondly, potentially dangerous products are allowed on the shelves on the assumption that any purchaser will be aware of the risks involved, and this is underlined by the fact that children are prohibited from buying many such products because they may not be aware of those risks.

What level of 'commonsense' knowledge can be assumed to be possessed by all or most adult consumers, however, is a delicate matter of judgement. Warnings are printed on fireworks and packets of cigarettes, for example, but not on bottles of wine or milk, although it might be thought that the risks associated with fireworks and cigarettes were more obvious and more widely understood. Perhaps the *comparative* level of estimated risk explains the discrepancies (cigarette smokers are judged to be running far greater risks than milk drinkers).

Another issue involving intrinsically risky products bears even more closely on the principle of freedom. If certain patterns of eating and/or drinking are thought likely to contribute in the long term to serious health problems, how free should consumers be to buy products which encourage these 'unhealthy' patterns? The practical and ethical objections to imposing restrictions of this more comprehensive kind are formidable. How would one set about 'regulating' the traditional, high-fat, English breakfast of bacon, eggs, sausages and fried bread? Apart from the practical obstacles, it would be difficult to justify measures to remove the consumer's right to eat an 'unhealthy' diet if he or she wanted to.

So restrictions on the consumer's freedom to choose intrinsically risky food products do not appear on the whole to be easily justified.

Category (ii): Risky versions of products: Particular problems can arise when some versions of a food or drink are believed to present significantly higher risks than the 'standard' form. Unpasteurised green-top milk is a case in point. In England and Wales between 1980 and 1989, 5,791 people were infected and twelve died from drinking untreated milk, compared with 1,192 cases of infection and one death from pasteurised milk, despite the fact that less than one per cent of all milk consumed is untreated. As a result, proposals were made to ban sales of untreated milk in England and Wales, as it already is in Scotland.

How do such products differ from those in category (i)? One difference is the possibility of *comparative* evidence of a significantly higher risk associated with the more unusual form of the product. This suggests at the very least that clear identification of the riskier version is essential along with full information about why it is riskier. Without this, there is a danger of confusion and ignorance, particularly if the 'safe' version of the product is presented as having a 'healthy', 'natural' image. This apart, however, there do not seem to be any significant differences between categories (i) and (ii) and, given identification and information, additional restrictions are difficult to justify.

Category (ii) products such as untreated milk do, nevertheless, highlight a further important aspect of risk-taking which impinges directly upon the question of free choice – the balancing of risks.

The balance of risk

Consumers who choose to drink untreated milk do so not because they wish to expose themselves to more risk, but because of the *benefits* which they believe the product offers:

> 'the vast majority of those people who drink raw milk do so from choice because they consider it healthier, more nutritious and better tasting then its pasteurised counterpart.' (19)

As no product can ever be guaranteed one-hundred-per-cent safe, all consumer choices represent a balancing of risks against benefits, though a conscious, deliberate weighing up is most likely in problematic cases like whether or not to buy untreated milk:

> 'the decision to buy involves assessing the risk, measuring it and other disadvantages against the benefits offered and, in that light, considering whether to pay the price demanded' (20).

So, consumers will decide to buy a riskier product such as untreated milk if they feel the risk to be *acceptable*, and this judgement will of course be influenced by all manner of individual factors. What is acceptable to one consumer will be unacceptable to another.

Two related implications follow from this:

(i)   information has to be made available to consumers to make them aware of the comparative risks involved and to enable a genuinely informed choice to be made;

(ii)   provided that such information is adequately publicised, the general presumption should be in favour of extending freedom of choice for consumers rather than restricting it; restrictions cannot help but deprive some consumers of perceived benefits which they value and judge to outweigh the risks for them.

(c) Ethical and social factors

A final set of factors which might be put forward as a possible justification for limiting consumers' freedom of choice may be loosely labelled 'ethical and social'. This could cover a wide range of arguments. We discuss two examples here.

Animal welfare arguments

These claim that if the production of certain foods involves animal suffering, those products should not be allowed on the market. Some products are already banned in the UK on these grounds, although imported varieties are often available. Veal produced from calves reared in crates, for example, is now subject to a ban, and one supermarket chain at least is labelling its UK and Dutch veal to enable customers to distinguish between the different methods of rearing.

From the viewpoint of consumer choice, we are again faced here with conflicting moral principles. However, we do not need to become embroiled in the whole emotive question of animal rights in order to identify a few points relevant to the question of restricting consumer choice.

(i)   Freedom of choice cannot be the only moral principle. Few people, for example, would want to argue for the consumer's freedom to choose soap produced from human victims of mass extermination. Respect for persons (despite the difficulties of interpretation in particular cases) is probably accepted by many as a fundamental moral principle, while respect for animals appears to be more dependent upon culture; some foreign methods of producing and preparing food, for instance, are considered barbaric by westerners, though animal welfare campaigners would claim that western methods of 'factory farming' are equally immoral.

The only general conclusion we can draw, then, is that animal welfare issues raise important moral questions which must be publicised, debated and judged *on their own terms* and not as a 'consumer issue'. If that debate suggests that legislation and regulation are required on moral grounds, any restriction of consumer choice should not be allowed to override that moral judgement.

(ii) The provision of full information to enable consumers to draw distinctions in terms of animal welfare, as happens to some extent with veal and with 'free-range' eggs, is again to be welcomed. Some products may disappear if enough consumers refuse to buy them. 'Welfare labelling' is likely to become increasingly common.

(iii) A further justification for limiting consumers' freedom of choice on grounds of animal welfare might be that animals are unable to argue for their own welfare and that measures to increase *their* freedom sometimes need to be taken on their behalf.

Arguments of 'need'

Safety, quality and efficacy are widely accepted as basic guidelines for assessing products of various kinds – though the interpretation of each of them raises many problems, as the discussion on safety factors has shown. Recently, however, there has been some debate about the possibility of a fourth criterion or 'fourth hurdle', relating to socio-economic need. It is hard to find a clear statement of what precisely this fourth hurdle might refer to, and the arguments remain nebulous. Critics claim with some justification that the 'fourth hurdle has defied definition, either by its supporters, or independent experts' (21).

An example of how the fourth hurdle argument might be applied is the case of BST milk. Bovine somatotropin (BST) is a genetically-engineered growth hormone which, when administered to cows, can increase milk production by almost a quarter. Objections have been levelled against the process on grounds of safety and of animal welfare, and some people are opposed to all forms of genetic manipulation on religious grounds (22). But even if all of these objections were met, there could still be a fourth hurdle argument to the effect that BST milk is not *needed* on socio-economic grounds. Is there any need for such technological developments which can put dairy farmers out of business, when there is already a surplus of milk in many countries?

The example shows how the concept of 'need' can be used to advocate restrictions on certain products and processes. The danger of statements or claims about needs, however, is that although they sound factual, descriptive and objective, they cannot, in practice, avoid being evaluative, prescriptive and subjective.

Needs cannot be measured and analysed as the ingredients of a food product can. Different judgements about what is 'needed' will be made by different individuals and groups, depending on their beliefs, values and perspective. Moreover, it might be agreed that a product, process or new development is not 'needed' here and now, but who can predict what 'future needs' will be at another time and place? It is always conceivable that restricting developments today may result in future catastrophes.

(d) Conclusion

This section has shown that there are few obvious points of demarcation where restriction on consumers' freedom of choice becomes justified. Fine distinctions will often need to be drawn. Each set of factors we have examined – psychological, safety and ethical/social – suggests that a complete absence of limitations, restrictions and regulations is neither practicable nor desirable. But the overall thrust has been that there is in principle an overall presumption in favour of extending, rather than reducing, consumer choice, and that the onus must be on those wishing to impose restrictions to justify them. In the last section we draw some of the threads together by returning to a recurrent theme of this chapter – the importance of knowledge and information.

8.3 Free choice, knowledge and information

We have seen that choice involves knowledge. To exercise choice, one must necessarily know about what one is choosing and what one is choosing from. The emphasis laid by consumer organisations upon '*informed* choice' underlines this essential ingredient. However, there are various questions about what precisely this means in practice.

(a) How much information is necessary?

Clearly there is a practical limit to the amount of information that can be provided about any product. No consumer wants to wade through pages of technical reports before every trip to the shops, and the psychological factors (examined in section 8.2) suggest that for some consumers in some circumstances, too much information may be as unwelcome as too little. Most consumers are not equipped to make detailed scientific assessments of risk levels, for instance:

'... how confident do we feel that we understand the risks associated with various levels of the substance? Is five parts per million of benzene hexachloride a lot or a little? If the bacteria count in a frozen egg is one million per gram, should we be alarmed? ... consumers do not ordinarily have anything approaching perfect information for judging the safety of most consumer products themselves.' (23)

Even a full description of a product's ingredients can be daunting:

'Too often the cumulative effect of measures taken in the consumer's name is confusion: how meaningful to the consumer is the list of 'E-numbers' on a packet of sweets? How many of us realise that the large 'E' on the packet, implying Community approval, refers to the weight and nothing else? In principle, the more complete the information on the packet, the better – proper information on the nutritional value of the contents is clearly desirable, for instance. Comprehensiveness will be of no avail, however, without clarity.' (24)

So the *quality* of the information provided is probably more important than its quantity, a point succinctly made in a report from the Consumers in the European Community Group:

'Meaningful information must be given, and it must be the truth. It must not be misleading; it must not be made false by reason of what is omitted; it must allow easy comparison between products.' (25)

Inevitably, though, judgements will have to be made about the level of knowledge and understanding to be assumed in the 'average' consumer, and that level will never be wholly appropriate for all consumers. One course may be to provide a basic amount of direct information on the label which will be helpful to the majority and also to offer easy access (perhaps by leaflets or consumer telephone services) to more detailed or technical information for those who want it.

There are strong arguments (as we saw in section 8.2) for extending this information to methods and processes of production, as well as ingredients. In the case of BST milk, for example, consumers who might object to the process involved (using a genetically-engineered growth hormone) have been unable to choose not to buy and consume the product, as the milk has been assimilated into the common pool, making it impossible to label and distinguish it. This procedure has been defended on the grounds that the product is in fact indistinguishable from 'ordinary' milk (though there has been some controversy over this). Yet even if this is true, the distinctive *process* involved and the possible ethical issues which it may raise seem to require that consumers should be given the necessary information in order to be able to choose whether or not to buy the product.

Although the provision of information is often discussed in a somewhat negative or defensive context – in terms of *warnings* – there could also be a more positive dimension, as Lawlor points out:

> 'Consumer information is not simply a matter of warning about possible risks: it should also be possible for a customer to read on the label about the product's positive qualities – and believe what it says. The Commission has become interested in the possibilities for certifying these positive qualities: such certification, if properly carried out, could overcome the scepticism of consumers and encourage suppliers to add to the value of their product by offering higher quality.' (26)

Some implications of this are discussed under section (c) below.

(b) How should information be conveyed?

We have said that the amount of information that can or should be given on labels is limited and there is increasing use of leaflets at the point of sale and of consumer telephone services.

But as the National Consumer Council has long argued, 'consumer education' is not just a matter of giving information. Education involves equipping learners with the knowledge, skills and understanding to form their own judgements and make their own decisions; it is therefore highly relevant to the exercise of *choice*. But education is a long process – many would say a life-long process – and while consumers certainly need *information* about products, consumer *education* is a much more lengthy enterprise. Consumer decision-making is a perfect example of an interdisciplinary educational activity, drawing upon virtually the whole range of subjects on the school curriculum and providing opportunities for gathering, analysing and interpreting many kinds of data and for making balanced value judgements, often about controversial issues. Some work of this type is being done in schools, but not enough.

One area where a more limited programme of adult education might be attempted is 'risk education'. The impossibility of 'zero risk' is not widely understood, though the argument is not particularly difficult to demonstrate or to grasp. A more general appreciation of the need to make judgements about the balance of risks and benefits would be a great step forward, an objective not helped by media debate and official pronouncements about whether or not a particular product is 'safe'.

(c) How should information be regulated?

Consumers cannot make informed choices on the basis of faulty information. Their freedom of choice will thus be restricted if inadequate, inaccurate or misleading information is provided. An important means of safeguarding freedom of choice, then, is to monitor closely the quality of information (paradoxically, strict regulation is justified here, to protect and extend freedom). (See also chapter 9 for a further discussion of enforcement procedures.)

The use and misuse of language is one obvious area on which such regulation should focus. Advertising standards, among other things, require that extravagant claims are not made for a product, but 'information' can mislead without being empirically inaccurate. Many products, for instance, claim to be 'natural'; yet 'naturalness' is an extremely difficult attribute to define and even if a definition can be agreed, 'natural' products or processes are not necessarily more desirable or beneficial than 'non-natural' ones. Many natural substances are of course lethal. The dangers of confusion here have led to the formulation of guidelines for the use of the word 'natural' in this context. Similar problems arise with such words as 'organic' and 'pure'. (Chapter 4 discusses the influence of advertising and labelling on consumer choice and purchasing behaviour.)

Product description and labelling raise many complex questions which take us beyond the range of this chapter. An excellent review can be found in a report, *Food Labelling and Standards: A New Beginning*, which suggests the following principles:

> 'Choice will only be possible if the information which consumers are given about a product is prominent, clear, legible and easily visible when the product is on display; so that they are informed of the true nature of the food and can distinguish it from other, similar products ...

'Food names should never mislead. The law should be based on the principle that labelling should be judged from the point of view of the customer and what the customer is likely to think or assume about the product.' (27)

But two specific points on descriptive labelling deserve a brief mention here, as they bear directly upon consumer choice:

(i)   Many of the detailed regulations on descriptive labelling embody distinctions which are far from obvious to the average consumer. Even food experts find them confusing. 'Bacon crisps' or 'bacon-flavoured crisps', for example, must derive their flavour entirely or primarily from bacon, while anything labelled 'bacon flavour' need contain no bacon at all (28). When such arcane knowledge is required in order to know precisely what one is buying, consumers have little chance of exercising an informed choice.

(ii)   Debate about EC regulations has highlighted 'those cases in which the free choice of the consumer is restricted on the basis of purely notional conceptions alone' (29). This raises the vexed issue of so-called 'recipe standards':

'The recipe standards provide for rules on the composition of the products. These products may then be marketed under a certain designation (reserved designation) or, in a stronger version, must be sold under that designation (mandatory designation). The result of a recipe standard in combination with a reserved designation is a relative sales prohibition. Products which are not in conformity with these composition rules may be sold but not under the name in question. The French provisions reserving the names "lait en poudre" or "lait concentré" for products which are exclusively derived from milk are an example of this type of measure.' (30)

The main justification for such restrictions has been to protect the consumer against confusion and to maintain 'quality'. Against this, it has been argued that standards 'are being used as a justification for banning the marketing of certain products' (31).

This is another controversy which cannot be explored in any depth here. However, the general thrust of this chapter suggests that informative and comprehensible labelling is more preferable than rigid rules about composition, though the maintenance of 'quality' (another concept in need of clarification, and discussed in chapter 7) is a legitimate concern of legislators and consumers alike.

Conclusion

This chapter has demonstrated how freedom of choice cannot be examined in isolation as a consumer principle. Indeeed, four of the National Consumer Council's 'essential consumer principles' – safety, quality, choice and information – have been shown to be closely inter-related; one cannot be adequately analysed and discussed without reference to the others.

However, the aim has been to sketch out a map rather than to write a detailed guide-book, and that map has taken freedom of choice as its central point of reference. Freedom of choice has accordingly been scrutinised as a consumer principle, its implications probed and its limitations explored, in the hope that this will enable specific recommendations and decisions to be made on a firmer basis.

References to chapter 8

1. E. Lawlor, *Individual Choice and Higher Growth*, Office for Official Publications of the European Communities, Luxembourg, 1989, p. 26.

2. Maurice Healy, *Consumers and the Free Market*, National Consumer Council, 1990.

3. T.F. Daveney, 'Choosing', *Mind*, LXXIII, 1964, p. 524.

4. S. Kelman, 'Regulation and paternalism' in *Rights and Regulation: Ethical, Political and Economic Issues*, edited by T.R. Machan and M.B. Johnson, Ballinger, Cambridge, Massachusetts, 1983, p. 245.

5. T. Hincks and M. Healy, *Untreated ('Green Top') Milk*, National Consumer Council consultation paper, 1989.

6. See S. Kelman, reference 4, p. 228.

7. G. Dworkin, 'Is more choice better than less?', *Midwest Studies in Philosophy*, 7, 1982, p. 60.

8. See E. Fromm, *The Fear of Freedom*, Routledge, 1942.

9. R.S. Peters, *Ethics and Education*, Allen and Unwin, 1966, p. 190.

10. M. Slote, 'On seeking less than the best', in *Philosophical Issues in Moral Education and Development*, edited by B. Spiecker and R. Straughan, Open University Press, 1988, p. 67.

11. M. Slote, see reference 10, p. 71.

12. E. Lawlor, see reference 1, p. 25.

13. International Organisation of Consumers Unions, *Consumers, International Food Standards and the General Agreement on Tariffs and Trade*, IOCU, The Hague, 1990, 5.5.2.

14. E. Lawlor, see reference 1, p. 25.

15. See S. Kelman, reference 4, pp. 236-7.

16. P. Payne and A. Thomson, 'Food health: individual choice and collective responsibility,' *Royal Society of Health Journal*, 99,5, 1979, p. 185.

17. P. Payne and A. Thomson, see reference 16.

18. P. Payne and A. Thomson, see reference 16, p. 186.

19. T. Hincks and M. Healy, see reference 5.

20. E. Lawlor, see reference 1, p. 25.

21. National Office of Animal Health Ltd, *Socio-economic Assessment for Animal Medicines – An Analysis*, NOAH, 1990.

22. See R. Straughan, *The Genetic Manipulation of Plants, Animals and Microbes: the Social and Ethical Issues for Consumers*, National Consumer Council, 1989.

23. S. Kelman, see reference 4, p. 226.

24. E. Lawlor, see reference 1, p. 48.

25. Consumers in the European Community Group, *Food Labelling and Standards: A New Beginning*, 1988.

26. E. Lawlor, see reference 1, p. 48.

27. CECG, see reference 25, p. 9.

28. CECG, see reference 25, p. 13.

29. R. Barents, 'The image of the consumer in the case law of the European court', *European Food Law Review*, 1990, p. 8.

30. R. Barents, see reference 29, p. 13.

31. CECG, see reference 25, p. 5.

Chapter 9
Food Law and Regulation
Is the consumer voice heard?
by David Jukes

Like most developed countries, the UK imposes legal controls on the ingredients, processing and labelling of food, in the interests of its citizens' health – and consumer confidence. These legal controls are strongly influenced by our trade agreements with other countries. This chapter outlines how food regulation now develops at UK, European and worldwide levels and highlights some of the questions that follow from these developments. Is the consumer interest fully taken into account when decisions are being made by remote institutions? Does freer trade inevitably mean lower safety standards? Should consumers in the developed world be prepared to relax health and hygiene standards to give consumers in developing countries a better standard of living?

The earliest food law in the United Kingdom dates back many hundreds of years and was designed to protect consumers from poor quality or low-weight bread. Even further back, some religious food practices provided a form of consumer protection. Here, though, we concentrate on modern food laws and how they affect consumer choice today.

(a) Consumer protection today

Legislative controls on food divide broadly into three categories, covering health and safety, standards and labelling.

Health and safety

Minimum standards are laid down to protect people's health. A common phrase in food law is that it is an offence to produce food for sale that is 'injurious to health'. Detailed technical regulations control additives (like colours, preservatives and sweeteners) and contaminants (like lead or arsenic, pesticide residues or harmful components of packaging), based on scientific evidence of their toxicity.

It is also an offence to sell food which is 'unfit for human consumption', usually taken to refer to food that is microbiologically unfit. The manufacturers of the hazelnut purée which led to the UK outbreak of botulism poisoning in yoghurt were found guilty of this.

Food standards

Governments commonly establish minimum standards for foods. Early types of fraud included watering down milk and alcoholic drinks.

157

While these did not affect health or safety, they did lead to the consumer being sold material below the accepted standard. Typical examples of minimum standards are the levels of water in butter or the amount of meat in a beefburger.

Food labelling

Where a standard is laid down, it will go along with a restriction on using the name of the food unless it complies with that standard. In some cases this can extend to banning foods which *look like* the specified food. In the UK, consumers are generally regarded as informed and aware of the need to read food labels and the trend now is to specify that labels should give the necessary information to enable the consumer to make an informed choice before buying. Labelling controls have increased over the past decade. In the early 1980s the new regulation that labels must declare most food additives led to a reaction against additives. More quantitative ingredient declarations are likely in the future. With more information on labels, there has been a decline in the numbers of food standards. The revision of the UK meat product standards in 1984 was typical of the trend. A lengthy list of detailed compositional standards was replaced by a general requirement that meat products carry a statement of the meat content and a much more limited list of minimum standards for basic products like sausages, beefburgers and pies.

(b) How is legislation made?

Most developed countries have a legal system that includes controls on food. The details vary significantly, of course, but the process and certain other features are often identical.

Food legislation is normally introduced at two levels – primary and secondary. In the United Kingdom, these are Acts of parliament and regulations respectively.

The primary powers normally establish a general principle. They provide for the main offences (like those listed above) and give the courts the power to penalise offenders. They lay down the powers of enforcement officers and some of the detailed administrative provisions. These primary controls are normally subject to detailed parliamentary scrutiny and debate. But parliamentary time is limited and, in any year, only a limited number of Acts become law. So it is not possible to follow this procedure for all the detailed technical controls needed in a modern society. The primary power therefore contains provisions for the introduction of more detailed or technical controls by a simplified procedure – secondary legislation.

The quantity of technical controls in a modern society is enormous. In the UK, for food alone, there are up to a hundred different sets of regulations. They give specific details of, for example, quantities, levels or wording on labels. They do not normally need full parliamentary debate but can become law after a specified consultation procedure.

This system of *secondary legislation* has two key advantages. One is that the law can usually be changed rapidly when a new hazard is identified. The other is that it provides industry, and the courts, with a specified standard against which to judge any item. Primary controls are usually worded in a general way. A manufacturer might find it difficult to know what is legal and what is not simply by reading an Act of parliament. Detailed regulations usually make it obvious when a product meets the specified standard.

The two-level system described here is followed in many countries. In some, though, the power to issue the detailed technical controls may be delegated to, for example, a separate national agency. In many developing countries, standards organisations take the lead in the development of legal standards. A national standard can be introduced that is initially voluntary. If appropriate, it can then be made compulsory on all manufacturers.

(c) Do consumers have a say?

The legislative structure is meant to provide consumers with protection. But how far are consumers involved in the development of that legislation? And to what extent are decisions taken without involving them? What are the effects of European and international trade and food agreements on UK consumer protection? Should the protection of consumers in a developed country like the UK override the economic needs of consumers in developing countries?

The rest of this chapter addresses these interlocking questions by looking at food legislation and control via the three levels at which they are decided - national, European Community and international.

9.1 The United Kingdom

(a) The scope of UK food law

In the modern era of food law, since about 1860, controls - especially on contaminants and toxic ingredients - have been progressively extended. For example:

Minimum standards

Controls have often been applied to prevent manufacturers adding ingredients which could reduce the quality of food below a specific minimum. Margarine was an early target. Other major controls were introduced and extended during and after the second world war, including controls on meat products, soft drinks and jams.

Additive controls

Some detailed additive controls have been around since about 1935. Preservatives and colours were regarded as important areas. Controls were greatly extended and strengthened during the late 1950s and 1960s, resulting in almost total control of most categories of additives. Flavourings – the largest category (by numbers of substances) – are still without detailed controls, but since the quantity of any one flavouring is now very much smaller, their priority for control is lower.

Hygiene

If the conditions of production or distribution of food are unsatisfactory, serious food poisoning can follow. Hygiene standards are therefore established through legislation, and enforcement officers spend a lot of time checking on compliance. Some standards apply to all food businesses, others apply to a single sector – like milk or meat.

Contaminants

As with additives, there is a need to ensure that the chemicals in food are safe. But the controls on contaminants are more complex because, by definition, they have usually found their way into food by accident. Although legal controls are harder to establish, where a known hazard exists, limits can be applied. The food industry, sometimes backed by government programmes, then monitors the contaminant levels to make sure they stay within the safety limit.

(b) How UK food laws are made

The first step in the legislative process – the impetus for a decision to introduce or alter a control – is in practice one of the hardest steps to identify. The most obvious example would be the release of new scientific data which indicates that a substance, currently permitted in food, may be a hazard to health. There could also be pressure from enforcement officers that, as a result of a court case for example, the law is no longer clear or effective. Sometimes action is initiated as

160

a result of consumer concern. In the past, this might have been related to the numbers of letters to *The Times* or questions in parliament. Today public anxiety might be measured by television coverage or articles in the popular press (although of course this raises the issue of whether media coverage is a true reflection of the majority view or the result of a campaign by a small group of activists).

By whatever route a minister of state decides that change is needed – the process begins. In most cases, consideration would first be given to new or amended regulations. A new primary Act requires enormous pressure and is unlikely in the UK for many years now that we have the Food Safety Act 1990. Most problems can be dealt with under its regulation-making powers. The Act states how regulations may be issued. With two minor exceptions, 'Ministers shall consult with such organisations as appear to them to be representative of interests likely to be substantially affected by the regulations or order'.

While this implies that the minister (or secretary of state) undertakes the consultation, in practice it is civil servants who consult and bring forward proposals to the minister.

Most ministers find it useful to operate with a series of specialist committees which give them detailed advice, much of it very technical. Within the area of food, there are many such committees, including:

- the Food Advisory Committee

- the Committee on Toxicity

- the Committee on Medical Aspects of Food Policy

- the Advisory Committee on Novel Foods and Processes

- the Steering Group on Food Surveillance

- the Consumer Panel

- the Committee on Microbiological Safety of Foods.

Each committee works within its own special terms of reference. Members are appointed by ministers, usually on the basis of their knowledge and experience. Some committees have specific consumer representation – the Food Advisory Committee, for example. The Consumer Panel is made up of individuals not linked to any major interest group – a real attempt to get a valid consumer view.

Most committees have a specific job, such as evaluating the safety of food additives and related chemicals. In terms of the general development of legal controls on food, the Food Advisory Committee (FAC) is the most important. The publication of FAC recommendations for new controls is always a major stimulus to government to adopt them. Once the report and recommendations are published, comments may be made on it by industry, the enforcement authority, retailers and, of course, by consumers. The minister or department then circulates draft regulations for comment. Only when this stage is complete will the minister finally sign the regulations into law.

One extra stage is possible, in that the Food Safety Act 1990 provides for possible 'annulment in pursuance of a resolution of either House of Parliament'. In theory, a regulation could be annulled if a vote is taken in parliament and a majority vote against. In practice, this never happens since the consultation process is extensive and regulations represent the best compromise between conflicting views. And of course no government tries to implement measures which could lose its majority in parliament.

The procedure outlined above sounds reasonably well constructed. There are, though, occasions when conflicts arise and difficult decisions have to be taken. Often these will greatly extend the total consultation and discussion period and it is not unknown for more than ten years to elapse between initiation and implementation of a new regulation. Significant changes can be made and, sometimes, suggested regulations are quietly dropped.

(c) Food law enforcement

Once a control has been introduced, consumer protection is only achieved if the measure is put into effect. As with any law, respect for it is partly related to the perceived risk of being found out and the penalty in the event of a successful prosecution. The penalty in food offence cases also includes the costs associated with any lost business or unsold goods resulting from the prosecution.

In the United Kingdom, enforcement is mainly the responsibility of environmental health officers and trading standards officers. Precise responsibilities vary around the country.

9.2 The European Community

Today the whole system is actually more complex than described above. The United Kingdom is also a member state of the European

Community and has agreed to comply with the provisions of the Treaty of Rome. This provides for the development of Community legislation in many areas - food being no exception. UK legislation is often merely the final stage in a process started within the Community's structures.

(a) The Treaty of Rome and the Single European Act

The European Economic Community was established in 1957 with the signing of the Treaty of Rome and currently has a membership of twelve countries. Although there have been modifications -principally by the Merger Treaty of 1965, the various treaties of accession when additional countries join the Community, and most recently by the Single European Act - the Treaty of Rome remains the basis of its activities.

The intentions of the Community are clearly stated in the Treaty. Article 2 says that the task of the Community will be:

'by establishing a common market and progressively approximating the economic policies of Member States, to promote throughout the Community a harmonious development of economic activities, a continuous and balanced expansion, an increase in stability, an accelerated raising of the standard of living and closer relations between the States belonging to it.'

Article 3 amplifies this, by specifying that the activities shall include:

'(a) the elimination, as between Member States, of customs duties and quantitative restrictions on the import and export of goods, and of all other measures having equivalent effect ...

'(h) the approximation of the laws of Member States to the extent required for the proper functioning of the common market.'

So the Community is first of all an economic community. Legislative developments are therefore chiefly designed to improve its economic and trading conditions. In the process of developing the legislation to achieve this, account is taken of the need to protect human health. So, while article 30 of the Treaty forbids restrictions to trade, article 36 allows them if they are necessary to protect the health and life of humans, animals or plants. What is 'necessary' has been the subject of much discussion.

In July 1987, major amendments were incorporated into the Treaty of Rome by the Single European Act. A new article 8A in the Treaty of Rome states:

'The Community shall adopt measures with the aim of progressively establishing the internal market over a period expiring on 31 December 1992 ... The internal market shall comprise an area in which the free movement of goods, persons, services and capital is ensured in accordance with the provisions of this Treaty.'

Again it is worth noting the economic character of this amendment.

(b) The administrative structure

The European Community is structured around four 'institutions'.

The Council

The European Council of Ministers consists of one representative minister from each member state. The actual minister varies depending on the subject under discussion. When it is agriculture or food, the Council will be the agricultural or food ministers of each member state. The Council has been described as the 'decision maker' and the 'legislature' of the European Community.

As decision maker, the Council takes major decisions about the future of the Community – the amendment to the Rome Treaty is an example. As the legislature, the Council agrees to measures which, in most cases, have been presented to it by the Commission. The Treaty allows for voting within the Council. Some measures may be adopted on majority vote; others on a qualified majority vote (which protects the interests of the smaller countries); others require a unanimous vote.

The Commission

The European Commission is a permanent body of seventeen commissioners, responsible for the functioning and development of the Community. Its responsibilities can be summarised as supervision, decision making and making delegated legislation.

In its supervision role, the Commission ensures that the Treaty obligations are being undertaken by the member states.

While the Council has powers of decision making, the Commission equally has extensive powers to influence the direction of the Community. Since the Council usually acts on a proposal from the Commission, the Commission has power to decide in advance the form a proposal will take. Some measures agreed by the Council may provide for the Commission to agree points of lesser importance. Thus the Commission may issue directives of a technical nature once the Council has agreed the main framework of the legislation.

The parliament

There are 518 delegates, or Euro-MPs, allocated to countries in proportion to their population and also providing smaller countries with sufficient delegates to represent their interests. Members were originally appointed. There are now direct elections, with members serving for a five-year term.

The general function of the European parliament is in article 137 of the Treaty of Rome, which says that it shall exercise 'the advisory and supervisory powers conferred on it by the Treaty'. Separate sections of the Treaty provide for actions by the parliament. Specifically, article 149, amended by the Single European Act, provides for certain consultation and co-operation procedures.

The court

The European court has thirteen judges appointed from member states, assisted by six advocates-general. The court ensures that the Commission, Council, member states and others observe the requirements of the treaties. This task is complicated by the fact that much Community law is economic in nature, is evolving and is in constant need of revision. Thus, when called upon to state what the treaty obligations are in a given field, the court interprets existing rules and formulates new ones by reference to the objectives of the Community. It often uses the expression 'at the present stage in the development of the Community'. This means that the court does not observe a strict rule of precedence. Every case is considered on its own merits and different decisions might be reached at different times, if conditions have changed within the Community.

Several Community committees also help in the development of legislation.

The Economic and Social Committee

This consists of representatives of the various categories of economic and social activity, in particular representatives of producers, farmers, carriers, workers, dealers, craftsmen, professional occupations and representatives of the general public. Although this committee was established by the Treaty of Rome and is thus an important part of the process of formulating legislation, it has only an advisory role.

The Standing Committee for Foodstuffs

This was established in 1969 as part of an agreed programme of work. It is composed of representatives of the member states.

The Advisory Committee for Food

This was established in 1975, following advice in 1972 from the economic and social committee. It has thirty members divided into five groups to represent industry, consumers, agriculture, commerce and workers. Members are nominated by the various European associations established by the groups concerned to represent their interests. This committee may be consulted by the Commission on any problems concerning the harmonisation of legislation relating to foodstuffs.

The Scientific Committee for Food

This is an expert committee established to give the Commission advice on technical and scientific matters. Its structure is now under review since the amount of work given to it is too great and new arrangements are being considered.

(c) How EC legislation is adopted

Food legislation within the Community is usually either in the form of a regulation or a directive. The major difference between these two is that the regulation is 'directly applicable' as law in each member state, while the directive is only 'binding as to the result to be achieved' and requires member states to incorporate its provisions into their own national legislation.

Under the original Treaty of Rome, new legislation required the unanimous agreement of the Council. It also says that the European parliament and the Economic and Social Committee shall be consulted. To help ensure that more measures were adopted, the Single European Act provided for the possibility of qualified majority voting and for 'co-operation with the European Parliament' as distinct from the original 'consultation'.

A first reading in the European parliament is now to be followed by the adoption of a 'common position' (by qualified majority vote) in the Council. The parliament then has an opportunity to study the common position. Depending on the view of parliament at this stage, the Council can act either by qualified majority or by unanimous agreement. Following the adoption of a common position, fixed time limits have to be observed by the various institutions. The maximum is likely to be six months. However, long delays can still arise in the discussions prior to the adoption of the common position.

For the food products covered by the common agricultural policy – including dairy products, margarine and milling products – an additional procedure is available. For these, article 43(2) applies, which states: 'The Council shall, on a proposal from the Commission and after consulting the Assembly, acting ... by a qualified majority, make regulations, issue directives or take decisions without prejudice to any recommendations it may also make'.

(d) Completing the internal market

When discussion started on completing the internal market, it was apparent that the foodstuffs sector was one area in which improvements were required if the objectives were to be met by 1992. In the Commission's white paper of June 1985, *Completing the Internal Market*, the foodstuffs sector was named as one in which any transfer of powers from the Council to the Commission on technical matters was likely to require particular emphasis. The Commission said that it would submit separate specific proposals to the Council on foodstuffs. This it did in November 1985.

By analysing the directives adopted by member states, the Commission found that they had been more willing to adopt measures of a 'horizontal' nature, containing general food legislative principles. Matters relating to the composition of individual foodstuffs (the 'vertical' measures) had faced difficulty in reconciling differences of opinion. It was therefore proposed that a distinction would be made between those matters which by their nature must be the subject of legislation, and those whose characteristics are such that they do not need to be regulated. The Commission indicated that future Community legislation should be limited to provisions justified by the need to:

- protect public health;
- provide consumers with information and protection in matters other than health;
- ensure fair trading;
- provide for the necessary public controls.

A timetable was agreed for preparing and adopting the measures which the Commission felt were justified on this basis. Of major importance were additives, food labelling, packaging materials, special nutritional foods and enforcement powers.

(e) Mutual recognition of each other's standards

So legislation tackled measures deemed essential for common standards, in particular health-related matters. There are, however, many other areas in which individual countries have imposed their own legislative standards. These are often compositional controls, designed to prevent consumers being presented with many similar foods but of varying compositions. It was this type of legislation – the 'vertical standards' that often constitute significant barriers to trade – which proved very difficult to remove by agreement between member states.

Given that all member states have this type of legislation and given that it was almost impossible to harmonise, it was recognised that a new approach was needed – 'mutual recognition'. Does it matter if the compositional standards are different from one country to another so long as the consumer knows the origins of the food? Travellers are exposed to such foods. The concept in an internal market is that there should be no need to travel to buy them, they should be available in local shops.

Mutual recognition therefore implies that imports from other countries may comply with different standards but so long as they are manufactured in accordance with the legislation of the manufacturing country and meet any agreed EC controls, they should be allowed in to any other member state.

In the United Kingdom, new compositional legislation is starting to allow for the sale of foods manufactured in another member state provided they comply with the legislation in force in that country. It is still early days and we do not yet know how, in practice, the system will operate. Enforcement officers in the UK, for instance, do not know the legislation of all the other member states. How will they be able to decide whether food is legally on sale in this country?

Mutual recognition also implies recognition of others' control systems and laboratory techniques. The removal of checks at frontiers means greater reliance on the enforcement officers and official controls operating inside other countries. Common standards are needed against which any official information can be judged. At this point it becomes important to consider the quality standards applied within factories, within official laboratories and by enforcement officers. There is therefore a need to develop a system of certification or accreditation whereby the results submitted by one country to another country are accepted as being true statements.

(f) The internal market and food choice

The intention of the internal market programme is to remove any barriers to trade that are the result of national borders. The Community is to be regarded as a single entity and industry should be able to sell its goods from Birmingham to Barcelona to Berlin to Bologna, with no major restrictions arising from the fact that they are all in different countries.

For the UK consumer, this may initially cause concern. Are the standards in other European countries as high as ours? Will it allow in food that is sub-standard or a health hazard? But these questions can be viewed from another angle. Many UK citizens look forward to their annual trips to the Mediterranean and other resort areas. They enjoy soaking up the sun and eating the local food. Should the pleasure of eating Greek, French or Portuguese food be restricted to those who can afford to fly there? Why should we in the UK be prevented from buying that food in our local supermarkets? If we are happy to buy it from a local shop on holiday, why not from our own shops at home?

The internal market aims to achieve just this freedom. But this is not to say that health issues can be ignored. Indeed, it is in this area that the Commission is concentrating its programme of food legislation. It is vital, if the internal market is to work effectively, that confidence in health and safety controls is maintained.

Confidence only comes when the consumer believes that the products on sale have been manufactured to minimum standards - that they are safe to eat. If the controls introduced by the European Community are effective, then the foods will be safe. If the controls fail to maintain safety, problems will surface and consumer confidence will be lost. It is for this reason that major manufacturers are determined to establish a reputation for quality based on valid controls of their own products (chapter 7 discusses quality in the food industry in detail). Should there be a breakdown in confidence, consumers will automatically purchase those products which they regard as safe - or those with a 'quality' image.

All these developments should lead to a greater choice of products for the consumer, supported by agreed Community minimum standards. But there is a negative side. The minimum standards are developed by the Community's institutions. Public access to these institutions is significantly harder than access to a national ministry. The power to influence the decision-making process is therefore more restricted. It could be that influence comes only from the larger organisations, which will inevitably include such groupings as agriculture and industry. Will consumers have sufficient access to the process? This has still to be addressed adequately.

9.3 Decisions at international level

(a) The background

What is true for groups of countries - like the European Community - is also true of the world as a whole. International harmonisation of standards has been an objective for many years. However, just as the Community has faced difficulties in establishing common standards and so lifting barriers to trade, so has the world as a whole.

If it is widely believed that the world economy benefits from a freeing of trade, then the objective should be to remove any national provisions which prevent or limit this. The European Community has used two main approaches to the removal of barriers - harmonisation and the newer approach, mutual recognition. As we have seen, harmonisation - agreeing common standards - proved difficult. Mutual recognition of each other's standards is now the preferred route. The basic standards in member states are similar (if not identical) and it has been accepted that consumer protection can be maintained even if goods from other member states are allowed in under different standards.

Extending this to the international situation poses problems. If harmonisation between twelve European countries was difficult, it is likely to be impossible between some 150 countries, from the poorest of developing countries to the richest of the developed. The mutual recognition approach can only be adopted if there is confidence in the food controls of other exporting countries - including basic food law and its administration and enforcement. Different international organisations are involved in attempting to solve this. They are described below. Before that, it is worth considering the issue of food choice, this time on an international scale.

The question of choice only arises once the total quantity of food available is greater than that needed by consumers. The consumer is then able to decide what food to buy. However the price of that food will also be crucial. Choice is only available when the consumer has the necessary money to purchase different foods.

On an international scale, this raises the question: *which consumers should have a choice*? Are there aspects of the international food system which favour one group of consumers over another? The choice in a hypermarket in the United Kingdom is immense – the choice in a village in the heart of Africa is usually non-existent. The shoppers involved are all consumers, but it is almost impossible to reconcile their different situations.

Two main organisations have a key role in the development of international controls on food trade – the Codex Alimentarius Commission and GATT.

(b) The Codex Alimentarius Commission

This was established in 1962, following recommendations from the Food and Agriculture Organisation (FAO), the World Health Organisation (WHO) and a joint FAO/WHO conference on food standards. Membership is open to all countries which are members of either the FAO or the WHO – nearly every country in the world. Membership has increased steadily and is now about 140 countries. The consumer interest has also now been recognised and the International Organisation of Consumers Unions has observer status at general (non-expert) Codex committees.

The objectives of the Commission include:

● protecting the health of consumers and ensuring fair practices in the food trade;

● promoting co-ordination of all food standards work by international governmental and non-governmental organisations;

● determining priorities and initiating and guiding the preparation of draft standards with the aid of appropriate organisations;

● finalising these standards and publishing them as a *Codex Alimentarius*; and

● subsequently amending the standards.

To accomplish this, the Codex Commission has established an extensive network of committees. Control is exercised by full Commission meetings, held every two years. The majority of the technical work is done by subsidiary committees, some of which meet every year. There are two main groups – 'subject' and 'commodity' committees.

The subject committees have responsibility for developing standards and codes on, for example, labelling, additives, contaminants and sampling. These can then be applied to all food and are called 'horizontal standards'.

171

The commodity committees develop standards for individual items of food, such as oils and fats, sugars, tropical fresh fruits and vegetables. These 'vertical standards' cover details like the composition, additives, contaminants and labelling for the specific food. About two hundred commodity standards are agreed at present.

The development of any Codex standard usually follows an eight-step progression that allows for extensive consultation and discussion. All member countries are allowed to attend all subject and commodity committee meetings and if unable to attend, can submit written comments which are carefully considered during the meetings.

This lengthy process is designed to ensure that any Codex standard has been thoroughly discussed. The final version should thus represent a consensus and provide the world with a standard that protects health and promotes trade. Has this actually been achieved?

The Codex Commission is a voluntary organisation. Once a Codex standard is published, member countries are required to consider how to adopt it into national legislation. But there is no compulsion to accept it and, unfortunately, Codex standards have not met with overwhelming success. Far from it. The vast majority have only been accepted by a small proportion of countries - often between ten and thirty - and most of these have only limited trade.

(c) GATT – the general agreement on tariffs and trade

The general agreement on tariffs and trade was agreed in 1948. It provides a set of rules for the conduct of international trade and is the forum where negotiations on trade take place. GATT's aim is to ensure that there is a fair and equal trading arrangement between countries, by which trade is subject to defined, recognised and mutually accepted rules. Over a hundred countries are now members. It is an organisation of governments. No non-governmental organisations have formal observer or consultative status.

The keystone of GATT's trade rules is the principle of non-discrimination, known as the 'most favoured nation' or MFN clause. This requires that any trade advantage granted by a member country to another should be extended to all of them. Similarly, any import restrictions should apply equally to all imports of that product from all sources. So every GATT member, regardless of size or power, should have the same trade opportunities and face the same barriers as its competitors.

GATT also provides a framework for settling trade disputes between members. The first stage is for the GATT secretariat to organise consultations between the countries concerned. If this fails, the dispute is referred to a GATT panel of experts, usually officials from the national delegations to GATT, who mediate between the two countries and apply GATT rules to the dispute. Their recommendations go to the GATT Council which normally adopts the report by consensus. If the offending country fails to comply with the recommendations, retaliation can be sanctioned.

Food standards and GATT

Food standards are covered by article 20 of the general agreement on tariffs and trade. This says, among other things, that nothing in the agreement shall prevent the adoption or enforcement by any member country of measures necessary to protect human, animal or plant life or health, provided this is not used as a means of arbitrary or unjustifiable discrimination between countries or as a disguised restriction on international trade.

During the Tokyo round of GATT negotiations between 1973 and 1979, a new agreement on technical barriers to trade - usually known as the 'standards code' - was agreed. This acknowledges the right of a country to take measures to protect human, animal or plant life or health in its own way, so long as this is non-discriminatory and does not erect unnecessary trade barriers. The code then lays down the procedures countries should adopt when considering new standards.

The standards code encourages the use of international standards and certification and stresses that there should be no unnecessary duplication in work under the code and in the Codex - meaning that GATT should not get into the business of setting international standards.

Food standards also feature in the Uruguay round of negotiations which started in 1986 and which, at the time of writing (mid-1992), had failed to reach a conclusion. If and when the Uruguay round is completed, a revised version of the 1979 standards code will be incorporated into the general agreement and there will be a new agreement on sanitary and phytosanitary measures - the SPS agreement. This covers any measure applied to protect human, animal or plant life or health from risks arising from the spread of pests and diseases and from additives, contaminants and toxins in food.

The agreement says that, where they exist, international standards should be used as the basis for national standards. It refers specifically to the international standards developed by the Codex Alimentarius Commission. It also says that nothing in the agreement should prevent countries from introducing higher standards than existing international standards, provided there are justifiable grounds for doing so.

So the GATT Uruguay round, like the Tokyo round before it, will enhance the role of international standards and the organisations that develop them. For food standards, this means the Codex Commission.

(d) A new status for Codex standards?

This was the state of affairs in the GATT round when the Food and Agriculture Organisation and the World Health Organisation convened a conference in March 1991 in Rome. International food standards were high on the agenda.

The need for this had been apparent for a few years. The failure of most countries to adopt Codex standards into law was the starting point – the realisation that, throughout many different countries, food law had moved away from legislation on standardised foods (the 'vertical' approach) to legislation on health, safety and consumer information (the 'horizontal' approach). The view had been developing that Codex should also move this way.

The view prevailed that a new approach was needed. Given the possible new status of Codex standards in the event of a GATT agreement, they must all be critically assessed to see that they do include essential health and safety and consumer protection measures. They should not include other non-essentials. In addition, the major effort on international food standards would be concentrated in the subject committees, to develop standards and codes applicable to all foods. Work has now started on a detailed re-examination of Codex standards.

With the emphasis now on health, safety and consumer information, the harmonisation of national laws by the adoption of internationally established standards is likely to be speeded up. For the low-income countries of the world this must be good news. A greater degree of harmonisation must reduce, if not remove, technical barriers to trade, making exports easier.

The progress will not be rapid or easy. Developed countries have established legislative systems which take many years to change. The mere existence of the GATT sanitary and phytosanitary agreement will not, on its own, remove barriers. Aggrieved countries will have to resort to GATT's dispute settlement procedure and await the outcome.

There is another important point. With the greater influence of Codex standards, developed countries will inevitably seek to ensure that those standards do now adopt a high level of protection for their citizens - not least by participating in all important Codex meetings. Developing countries, however, often find it difficult to finance attendance at meetings.

The Rome conference also discussed a series of recommendations from the International Organisation for Consumers Unions (IOCU) which aimed to increase and improve consumer participation in setting international food standards. Although unable to support many of IOCU's proposals, the meeting was able to recommend that national governments should consult their national consumer organisations before developing their position. This was endorsed by the Codex regional meeting later the same year.

9.4 The implications for consumer choice

So legal controls at every level - national, European and international - accept that consumers are justified in seeking protection from unsafe and fraudulently marketed food, and have procedures designed to provide that protection.

However, the institutional structures that decide those controls have other objectives too. The most obvious, at European and world levels, are the pressures to improve trade between countries. While this should lead to wider choice for consumers, it is arguable that increased trade can in practice reduce consumer protection. Does more choice lead to less protection? In this last section, we examine some of the potential problem areas.

(a) A remote system

As a system becomes more international, it becomes more remote from the people it serves. There are already concerns within the European Community about access by consumers to the decision-making process. Extend this to the international scale, with the developments taking place with the Codex, and the problem becomes even greater.

175

Membership of the Codex Commission is open only to national representatives, chosen by governments. It is therefore up to the individual governments to establish links with consumers in their own countries, to ensure that the views expressed in the Commission take their interests into account. This is an important issue. Unless they have confidence in the process, consumers will press their own governments to set national standards above the Codex standards, undermining all the Codex Commission's efforts. Codex must be seen to stand up for consumer protection and to involve consumers in decision making. The influence and active involvement of the International Organisation of Consumers Unions will ensure that these issues are kept high on the agenda.

(b) Access to information

Consumer confidence in food safety often rests upon the ability of governments to act on the basis of independent advice following scientific research. This is best guaranteed if the research and the advice are open to public scrutiny. In the United Kingdom, there have been concerns about the availability of information about food, although in recent years the government has been acting to promote a more open system.

While the UK system is certainly not the most open, it is also not the most secretive. When negotiations are at international level, there is likely to be concern that decisions may not be wholly based on sound science. Only when a system is fully open, when reports are published rapidly and when everybody has equal access to the relevant documents will it be possible to assess the validity of decisions about food standards.

(c) Equality of enforcement

The ability of the United Kingdom enforcement authorities - trading standards and environmental health officers - to maintain consumer protection has been questioned, given that it is a local government function and that different local authorities have different priorities. The development of codes of practice has certainly helped. Any doubts about UK enforcement, though, are dwarfed by concerns about the enforcement of minimum standards in other countries.

Each country within the European Community has its own system of protection. Each is different and any one system may, in parts, be weaker than another. However, it is generally held that the internal market system can be made to operate without major risks to health and safety.

On an international scale, with the much greater diversity of standards, questions will remain. In this context, the removal of all frontier checks seems a long way away.

Conclusion

Legislation does restrict food choice. However, it ensures that consumers' choices are restricted to those foods which are safe and which enable the consumer to buy with confidence. Manufacturers are permitted to produce foods with a range of other quality characteristics and to offer them at a range of prices. The consumer should be able to choose, confident that all of them are safe – in so far as safety can be defined.

Chapter 10
Science at the Supermarket
What's on the menu tomorrow?
by Lucy Harris

Artificial sweeteners ... fat substitutes ... food irradiation ... genetically-modified fruit, vegetables, cheese and meat ... these are just a few of the products of the rapidly growing partnership between science and the food industry. Biotechnology and other scientific techniques are bringing major advances in agriculture and food production. They also raise concerns about long-term safety and about the economics and ethics of food production, as well as the traditional consumer issues of information and choice. This chapter is both a layperson's guide to the new foods and processes and a review of their implications for consumers.

New, highly technical ways of producing and processing food are transforming the choice available to consumers. Many 'novel foods' are now on sale. (In the context of food, novel has taken on a special meaning – explained below.) They include exotic fruits and vegetables not previously available in the UK, meat substitutes, new sweetening agents and, most recently, fat replacers. New processing methods are also increasingly being used – genetic modification for instance, and licences may now be granted for the use of food irradiation. Rapid growth in the use of new biotechnologies for food production looks set to continue.

The first part of this chapter – sections 10.1 and 10.2 – explains what is meant by 'novel' foods and processes and looks at some of the most important developments.

Sections 10.3 to 10.7 focus on one of those processes – biotechnology – and its increasing impact on food production, particularly through the genetic modification of plants, animals and micro-organisms. It has been hailed as one of the most significant developments in scientific knowledge this century, with important contributions to make in the fields of medicine, food production and environmental management. It also raises broad-ranging questions about the use of scientific research, the role of regulations and information, and a host of social, economic and ethical issues.

The last section – 10.8 – looks at the consumer concerns raised by these developments and their impact on consumer food choice. It assesses the extent to which these developments are likely to extend, or to endanger, consumer choice.

Section one: Novel foods and processes

10.1 What are 'novel foods'?

In the UK, novel foods have been broadly defined as:

> 'foods or food ingredients which have not hitherto been used for human consumption to a significant extent in the United Kingdom and/or which have been produced by extensively modified or entirely new food production processes.' (1)

So the use of a new raw material, a new processing or preparation technique or the novelty of a food's role in the diet, may all contribute to a food being classified as novel.

Before a novel food or process is introduced, thorough safety evaluations, including toxicological and nutritional studies, must be carried out to ensure there is no health risk. These studies are then assessed by the government's Advisory Committee on Novel Foods and Processes (ACNFP) which advises the agriculture and health ministers responsible for giving final clearance.

Several products have been cleared for use in recent years, including a genetically-modified baker's yeast; three genetically-modified enzymes for use in cheese production; a new fructose syrup to be used as a sweetener in diabetic and diet foods; and the process of food irradiation. In addition, a number of other new products have had an important impact on the food market and consumer choice in recent years.

(a) Artificial sweeteners

These are not officially classified as novel foods and are covered, at the UK and European Community level, by specific legislation on additives. However, their increasing use over the last twenty years is an important development, raising questions about safety, consumer choice and information, and it seems appropriate to include them in this discussion.

The 1980s saw dramatic growth in the market for 'diet' foods. The success of products like low-calorie soft drinks, desserts, and table-top sweeteners shows that consumers welcome this widening choice. Sweeteners like aspartame and saccharin are mostly taken by people trying to reduce their sugar intake, and lose weight. They also have an important role in diabetic and other dietetic products. However, a number of concerns have been raised about them.

179

A European Commission directive on sweeteners was being negotiated at the time of writing (mid-1992) (2). The current draft lists twelve permitted sweeteners, and sets limits for the range of foods to which they may be added and the maximum amounts to be used. Consumer organisations are concerned that the draft directive includes *all* the sweeteners currently permitted throughout the EC, and at higher levels. For most countries, this would mean increasing the permitted range. In the UK, for example, Cyclamate and NHDC (neohesperidine dihydrochalcone), which are not approved at present, would be allowed under the directive. Questions are still being raised about the safety of these products and the need for them (additive legislation includes the requirement that a 'need' for a new product must be established before it can be approved).

Also, it appears that sweeteners have not contributed to reducing the overall consumption of sugar (3). Although less 'visible' sugar is consumed than ten years ago, many people are eating more processed foods which are often high in 'invisible' sugar. In addition, the substitution of intense sweeteners for sugar does not necessarily help in the reduction of weight or the prevention of obesity, as Peter Rogers and David Mela describe in chapter 2 on biology and the senses. Sweeteners are unlikely to help people to lose weight without other changes in their food intake or lifestyle.

This raises questions about consumer information and, in particular, whether claims for 'diet' products can be justified or whether they are misleading.

Currently, the labels of all products which claim to be low or reduced calorie, have to state that they can help slimming or weight control only as part of a calorie-controlled diet. They also have to give nutritional information on energy, fat, protein and carbohydrate. However, the whole area of what constitutes a health claim needs review and clarification.

(b) Fat replacers

The message from health advisers and nutritionists for some time now has been to cut down on fatty foods which contribute to obesity and coronary heart disease. Most people find this difficult because fat gives foods like butter and ice-cream their rich, creamy texture. Without fat, or with less of it, many foods taste bland and unappetising.

Food technologists have now developed ways of imitating the texture and feel of fat with products much lower in energy and without the risks associated with fat consumption. Most fall into one of two general categories.

Calorie-reduced fat substitutes: these are made of carbohydrates and proteins which can be digested and absorbed, providing between one and seven calories per gram compared to nine calories per gram for fat. One such product, Simplesse, was launched in the UK in early 1992. It is made from egg and milk proteins and uses a process called 'micro-particulation' which, through heating and blending, produces minute particles that imitate the texture of fat. Another is Prime-O-Lean, an animal fat replacement made from vegetable oil, proteins and sugars being developed for use in sausages and hamburgers in the USA. The manufacturers claim that its use can reduce saturated fat levels by fifty per cent.

Calorie-free fat substitutes: these are being developed from plant compounds combined in new ways so that they cannot be digested or absorbed. One of them, Olestra, is made from sugar and fatty acids and has been the subject of much publicity. It has not yet (mid-1992) been approved either in the USA or Europe.

Like artificial sweeteners, fat replacers could play a part in increasing consumer choice and helping people to change their diets. But again, there is doubt about whether they will necessarily help people reduce total fat consumption or lose weight (4). Although fat replacers widen the choice of lower-calorie foods available, they are unlikely to encourage people to lose a taste for fatty food. Unless people make a deliberate effort to lower their overall calorie intake, they may compensate for the 'missing' calories by eating other fatty foods. Another potential concern is that a diet of very low-fat foods is not suitable for children under five who need some energy from fat for adequate growth.

Simplesse is currently sold as an ingredient of a so-called bioyoghurt, a low-fat spread and a low-fat ice-cream. It will probably be the first of many fat replacement products on the UK market. Their success will depend on the extent to which they meet consumer expectations in terms of taste, quality, usefulness and value for money. (Chapter 7 examines consumer perceptions of quality in food.)

(c) Health foods, probiotics and functional foods

Over the last few years, there has been rapid growth in the 'health food' sector. Products once considered to be of interest to a small minority are now readily available in most major supermarkets.

Many products now use a 'healthy' image as a marketing tool. Medical claims (that is, claims that foods prevent, treat or cure disease) are not

181

permitted. However, increasing numbers of foods make general claims such as 'low fat', 'high fibre', or 'no artificial sweeteners', implying that they are healthy in comparison with other, 'unhealthy' versions.

Another trend is to promote a food product as having health-enhancing properties. The new 'bioyoghurts', for instance, contain an added strain of a bacterium called bifidus (in addition to the lactobacillus or streptococcus traditionally used to make yoghurt). Bifidus is normally found in the human gut, and is thought to play a role in the digestive process. These bacteria may be able to survive passage through the gut in an active form and thus help digestion and guard against the growth of harmful organisms. So, it has been claimed, bioyoghurts containing active bifidus may be able to promote good health if eaten regularly, although this has not been proved. Foods like this are sometimes classed as 'probiotic'.

In Japan, the last few years have seen a trend towards the development of a group of foods called 'functional foods' (5). These are alleged to have certain health-related benefits – such as the reinforcement of the body's natural defence systems; protection against high blood pressure, diabetes, cancer and coronary heart disease; control of appetite and nutrient absorption; and treatment of the symptoms of ageing. Whether any of these claims can be substantiated remains doubtful.

Specially formulated soft drinks, confectionery, ready meals, breakfast cereals, dairy products and baby food are just some of the products being developed. The main difference between these and their 'non-functional' equivalents seems to be that they have added vitamins and minerals or other chemical compounds. However, many of these foods would not traditionally be recommended as contributing to a 'healthy diet'.

The Japanese Ministry of Health and Welfare has supported the development of these functional foods as a means of achieving a healthier population. Twelve classes of ingredients, such as dietary fibres, oligosaccharides, and various vitamins and minerals, are being considered for approval by the Japanese authorities. If approved, foods containing these will be allowed to be sold using specified health claims.

Similar trends are also emerging in western countries, with expanding markets for breakfast cereals, high-fibre breads and high-energy and isotonic sports drinks. One of the main problems will be in defining these products. In the European Community, the mere presentation of a product as preventing or curing a disease, makes it a drug and subject to separate legislation. It is, therefore, essential that the European Commission clarifies what it accepts as a health claim and how they can be used. The Commission does intend to bring forward proposals for the regulation of health claims but so far (mid-1992) has failed to do so.

(d) Food irradiation

Food irradiation is a preservation technique which has been permitted in the UK since 1991 on a limited number of products, including herbs and spices, vegetables, cereals, fish and shellfish. It has been the focus of heated debate and controversy. It subjects food to doses of ionising radiation. These delay the ripening of fruit; prevent sprouting in vegetables; kill pests; and reduce or eliminate micro-organisms like salmonella and listeria. Irradiation can also be used to replace the potentially carcinogenic chemical fumigation of herbs and spices. A longer shelf life and food free from microbiological contamination are given as its main advantages.

There has been great consumer resistance to its introduction. A survey by Consumers' Association in 1990 found that over one-third of those questioned thought food irradiation should not be permitted (6). The main arguments put forward against it are that:

- not all bacteria and viruses that cause food poisoning will be eliminated by the process and harmful toxins may remain in the food;

- vitamins are lost during the process and again during the extended shelf life;

- old or contaminated food could be disguised or 'cleaned up' and the problem of unhygienic food handling and processing, which contribute to contamination, will not be resolved;

- with no test to determine whether or not foods have been irradiated, too much reliance will be placed on accurate documentation and labelling.

Concerns have also been raised about the safety of the process. However, the Advisory Committee on Novel Foods and Processes in the UK and the World Health Organisation are satisfied that, when correctly applied at recommended levels, it is safe.

By law, any food that has been irradiated must be labelled. This lets consumers make their own choice about whether to buy and consume

183

such products. In the current climate of opinion, it is unlikely that food irradiation will be widely accepted in the forseeable future, whatever its alleged advantages. Indeed, none of the major retailers has yet decided to sell irradiated products.

The food irradiation debate illustrates the problems inherent in a situation where the technology, instead of the consumer, attempts to drive the market. Although the pro-irradiation lobby has tried to sell it on the merits of consumer protection and increasing quality and choice, consumers themselves have not been convinced. (Indeed, some consumers even fear that the food itself can become radioactive.) It also highlights the vital role of food labelling, to enable consumers to make informed decisions.

10.2 The regulation of novel foods

(a) In the United Kingdom

Novel foods and processes, including genetically-modified foods, are assessed by the Advisory Committee on Novel Foods and Processes (ACNFP) before they can come on to the market.

The notification system is voluntary. The prime responsibility for carrying out the required toxicological and nutritional studies lies with the company developing the new food or process. The ACNFP then assesses the adequacy of these studies – reviewing the safety of an ingredient or the process. Another government advisory committee, the Food Advisory Committee, then considers any implications for labelling and makes recommendations, as with the labelling of irradiated foods. (Although additives come under the legal definition of food, they are controlled by separate regulations that list the permitted amounts for each type of additive.)

The ACNFP assesses novel foods and processes using a 'decision-tree' approach, which enables them to be systematically classified and the necessary tests identified according to various levels of perceived risk. For example, for an existing food being processed or used in a new way, it is likely that only a nutritional and a toxicological assessment would be required. For a totally new food or ingredient, like Quorn (made from the fermentation of mycoprotein and used as a meat substitute), the committee would require additional studies: the techniques used in production; the history of human exposure; the extent of potential use; and the history of the organism itself. For a food that contained live genetically-modified organisms, an even wider array of safety studies would be needed.

184

One weakness of the UK system is that notification of the new food and its submission for clearance is voluntary. So it relies on the co-operation of industry. In theory, a company could place new, inadequately labelled products on the market without prior clearance (although there is no evidence to suggest that this has happened). There are no independent safety studies and no provision for nutritional or safety monitoring once the product is on the market.

The system has also been criticised for being unnecessarily secretive, although in recent years this has been less true. Agendas of meetings of the Advisory Committee on Novel Foods and Processes are now published; copies of its reports to ministers are available on request; unpublished toxicological data considered by the committee are deposited with the British Library; and its *Annual Report* summarises the submissions and advice it has given. Both a consumer and an ethics representative also now sit on the ACNFP, although there is still no open consultation with the public.

(b) In Europe

As David Jukes reports in chapter 9, food regulation is increasingly determined in Brussels. The Community already has over three hundred directives/regulations in the food and agricultural products sector.

The European Commission has been developing a proposal for a Council regulation on novel foods and ingredients since 1989 and a formal proposal has been published (7). If the current proposal is adopted, it would harmonise the notification and authorisation procedures for all such products coming on to the EC market. It would put responsibility for deciding whether a new product contains novel ingredients or has been processed in a novel way on the company intending to market it. If the new food or ingredient was classified as novel, according to the criteria set out in the draft regulation, the company would be obliged to carry out a scientific assessment of it.

A two-tier system, with products assessed either at the national or European level, has been suggested by the Commission. A list of 'experts' - qualified independent scientists nominated by member states - would be drawn up by the Commission and would be responsible for assessing the safety data on a new product or process. Some products would only require approval by at least one of these official 'experts' and subsequent notification to the Commission before being placed on the market. Other products considered to present a greater risk (those containing genetically modified organisms, for instance) would have to undergo a more complex, centrally-operated Community authorisation procedure before being placed on the market.

These are welcome developments. Prior evaluation and approval of all novel foods, based on mandatory safety assessment, is long overdue. The current proposal's main weaknesses are that it could rely too heavily on the opinion of only one expert at the initial stages; it does not make clear provisions for labelling, other than on an ad hoc basis; there are no provisions for monitoring the impact of novel foods on the total diet; nor for reviewing their safety once they are on the market.

Section two: Biotechnology

10.3 What is biotechnology?

Biotechnology is a broad term describing a variety of techniques, some still being developed, but many of them used since human beings first began domesticating plants and animals. One useful way of defining the word is to take it in chronological stages (8):

Traditional biotechnology has been practised for thousands of years in baking, brewing and cheese-making through traditional fermentation processes. Similarly, plants and animals have been selectively bred over hundreds of generations to produce varieties more suitable for human needs. Many of our modern domesticated animals and crops have been changed so much that they now bear little resemblance to their wild ancestors. More recently, through selective breeding, the genetic material of plants and animals has been manipulated to control more closely specific characteristics, such as higher yields. These techniques are generally accepted as 'natural' and only thought of as biotechnology by scientists.

A *newer form of biotechnology*, pioneered over the last hundred years and familiar to most of us, is in the medical field. Vaccines and antibiotics, such as penicillin, are produced in the laboratory and use natural micro-organisms to create substances which help the body protect itself against diseases like smallpox, polio and influenza. Although there is a degree of risk with this form of biotechnology, it is now seen to have substantial health benefits and is not generally regarded as 'unnatural'.

The latest developments in biotechnology are the result of spectacular advances in molecular biology, microbiology and genetics since the 1960s and 1970s. They involve a number of techniques, in particular genetic modification or 'engineering'.

Genetic modification is a particularly important and controversial technique of biotechnology. It transfers genetic material from one cell to another, from one species to another or to bacteria or yeasts, in order to produce specific traits in the host organism. This can be achieved by a number of methods, the most important of which is 'recombinant DNA technology'. Since Crick and Watson's pioneering work in the 1950s (9), there have been rapid developments in scientists' understanding of how genetic information is passed from one cell to another, and from one generation to another. Chromosomes, found in the cells of all living organisms, are made up of many tiny units – genes. These instruct our bodies to make proteins and enzymes which are responsible for the characteristics of a particular cell or organism. Genes are, therefore, the units of heredity passed on from one generation to the next.

Genes are made up of DNA (deoxyribose nucleic acid), the molecular basis of heredity. Each molecule has two complementary strands assembled in the form of a spiral staircase – the double helix. Genetic modification enables pieces of DNA to be taken from a plant, animal or micro-organism and transferred into a host organism, where it is incorporated into the DNA of the host.

The next four sections look in detail at genetic modification and the other most recent developments in biotechnology – techniques that raise environmental, economic, social, ethical and consumer concerns.

10.4 The uses of biotechnology

Biotechnology is often described (10,11) as a key technology for the future economic development of the developed and developing worlds in the twenty-first century. The main potential benefits claimed for it fall into three general areas – health care, the environment, and food production and processing.

Health care: one of the earliest achievements was the production of human insulin needed by diabetics, by inserting the gene coding for this hormone into bacteria (12). Genetic modification has also enabled great progress in diagnostic methods and other drug treatments, for example, a genetically-modified vaccine has been produced to protect against hepatitis-B, and the proteins required for blood clotting, such as factor VIII, can be produced – of great benefit to haemophiliacs. Also, by locating individual genes on human chromosomes, it has become possible to identify those which cause specific conditions like cystic fibrosis and muscular dystrophy.

Environmental management: this may be improved through less use of fertilisers, pesticides and other chemicals. Bacteria have been designed to act as 'effluent scavengers', eating up oil spills, sewage waste and chemical pollutants such as polychlorinated biphenyls (PCBs) and dioxin. This could reduce the need for waste disposal by incineration or in landfills, which risk gas escapes or toxic substances leaking into water supplies. There are possible further developments, too, in biodegradable plastics and alternative energy sources (13).

Food production and processing: biotechnology has important implications for agriculture and the food industry, and for the consumers of its products. It raises concerns about its social, economic and environmental consequences, and the extent to which it is ethical to 'interfere' with nature. We return to these issues in section 10.8 onwards. First we look more closely at the practical results of biotechnology on the food on sale today or likely to be on sale tomorrow.

(a) Plant production

Improvement of crop varieties: increases in yield or improvements in specific traits have in the past been achieved by classical breeding methods, which are time-consuming (because they involve many generations), costly and somewhat hit and miss. With genetic modification, it is becoming possible to transfer a desired characteristic in a single generation, without the risk of adding undesirable ones. Examples include breeding new crop varieties suitable for particular environmental conditions, such as better performance on dry or salty land, or for faster growth in northern areas where the growing season is shorter. Similarly, nutritional content may be altered, such as protein levels in wheat or the fatty acid content of vegetable oils.

Resistance to disease, herbicides and pests: some plants have a natural genetic resistance to attacks by local insects or to fungal diseases. The relevant genes can be identified and incorporated into other varieties, thus avoiding the lengthy breeding process. Resistance to three major virus diseases has been achieved in potato plants, and may also be possible in cucumbers, lettuce, tomatoes and tobacco plants (14). This opens up enormous possibilities for controlling viral plant infections.

At present, fields are treated with a variety of different herbicides which kill weeds but must avoid harming the crop. Herbicide resistance would enable crops to be treated with weed killers that otherwise injure or kill them. Resistance to glyphosate has already been achieved in tobacco plants, tomatoes and soya beans (15). The rapid progress reflects the large investment from the agrochemical companies which produce herbicides. They stand to see a return from the sale of the herbicide-resistant crops and the herbicides used upon them. Plants with resistances to herbicides, insects and viruses will probably enter agriculture within the next decade.

The need for chemical pesticides may be reduced by genetic modification. For example, a bacterium is being produced which poisons the caterpillars feeding on the roots of corn, but appears to be harmless to humans, animals and the plant itself.

Nitrogen fixation: the nitrogen that plants require can be applied to the soil in the form of fertiliser, but it is both expensive and environmentally hazardous. Bacteria found in the roots of legumes, such as beans, can take nitrogen from the air and convert or 'fix' it into a form that can be used for plant growth. Genetic modification is now being used in an attempt to alter these bacteria so that they can live in the roots of cereal crops, and provide a ready-made source of fertiliser, thus reducing the need for external application. This technology is still in its early stages (16).

Control of undesirable traits: just as beneficial genes can be inserted into plants, there is scope for eliminating, replacing or masking others. An example is the masking of the gene which makes tomatoes ripen quickly. An extra gene is inserted which nearly, but not completely, cancels out the effect of early softening, thus producing a firmer tomato. This would be a commercial plus, allowing the fruit to be transported, stored and displayed more easily. The same gene is thought to control softening in other fruit, such as peaches, and research in this area has wide implications for the future quality and marketing of fruit.

(b) Animal and meat production

Transgenesis: 'transgenic animals' have an altered genetic structure. The process modifies the reproductive cells to change the genetic structure of the next generation.

With animals, the main technique is to inject DNA into an already fertilised egg. The developing embryo is then transferred into a foster mother. In this way, heritable characteristics are produced in the offspring – for example, inserting a cow's gene into pigs to increase growth rate and reduce fat.

189

Such hybrids are not new. The mule has been with us for centuries. The difference lies in how it is achieved, the potential for the gap to widen between the species involved, and the reproductive capacity of these new transgenic animals.

Another outcome of transgenesis is the production of certain proteins in the milk of sheep or cattle. These include insulin and factors VIII and IX, used in blood clotting, which have important medical uses and are already on the market (17). Transgenic animals can also be produced to provide models of human diseases, like the Oncomouse, a mouse genetically modified to develop cancer.

Embryo transfer: in this form of biotechnology, ordinary cows or ewes are used as surrogate mothers for growing embryos derived from the highest quality breeding stock. Commercial animals give birth to offspring with 'greater genetic worth' than they could produce themselves. The high performance females are treated with hormones to stimulate multiple ovulation. The eggs are then fertilised, either in the mother animal (*in vivo*) or in the test tube (*in vitro*), with sperm from the best available males. The resulting embryos are then transferred to the surrogate mother.

Embryo transfer can increase the average number of daughters from top quality cows from three-and-a-half to over twenty in a lifetime. The technique is widely commercialised for dairy cows, with frozen embryos being much cheaper to transport than livestock.

Nuclear transfer: not to be confused with embryo transfer, this technique produces 'clones', or genetically identical offspring. The complete nucleus of a single cell from an embryo is removed and replaced by another nucleus, extracted from a developing multi-cellular embryo. The animal develops from the transferred nucleus and will be virtually identical to that of the donor. It is now possible to take several nuclei from the cells of an eight- or sixteen-celled embryo and transfer them into de-nucleated cells, to produce several identical offspring from one fertilisation.

In Australia and the UK, five identical sheep have been reared from one embryo by nuclear transfer and may lead the way towards 'super-strains' of farm animals through cloning (18).

Antibodies and vaccines: remarkable progress has been made in the production of subunit-vaccines from genetically-modified viruses and bacteria, in both human and veterinary medicine. Through the insertion of DNA from a disease-producing organism, micro-organisms such as *escherichia coli* are programmed to produce the proteins of the disease-producing organisms; these can stimulate the production of specific antibodies. The proteins can therefore be used as vaccines. Work is well advanced in producing a vaccine for animal gastro-enteritis which can cause large losses among young pigs, and vaccines are being developed against the foot and mouth virus and mastitis in cattle (19). Viruses are also being modified to operate as diagnostic tools for the detection of animal diseases.

Hormone production: the therapeutic use of hormones is a part of everyday veterinary medicine. More controversial is the potential use of hormones for non-therapeutic uses. Steroid hormones are capable of stimulating faster growth, more efficient feed conversion and the speedier 'finishing' of cattle for the market, although they have been prohibited for these purposes within the EC since 1988. There has been controversy over the use of the growth hormone bovine somatotropin (BST), to increase milk yield from cows (20). Although it is currently under a moratorium in the European Community, BST was recently under trial in the UK and the milk produced was added to the general milk supply. Trials of porcine somatotropin in pigs, conducted overseas, have reduced body fat by up to eighty per cent and improved feed efficiency by twenty per cent. Research is also taking place into growth hormones for sheep and chickens. These developments may have significant commercial implications but they also raise important consumer questions.

Fermentation processes: these are also likely to change as a result of genetic modification. It was originally thought that the specific chemical changes brought about during fermentation could only occur in the presence of living organisms. Now, by careful extraction, the agents responsible for promoting chemical changes (enzymes) can be isolated from the parent organism and made to work on their own. Enzymes are used in the production of beer, cheese and starches, and also to extract substances from food. Enzyme technology has contributed to rapid developments in the industry that converts starch to glucose and fructose syrups, and the development of new sweeteners. Mycoprotein (produced from fungi grown by fermentation) is now an accepted food marketed under the brand name Quorn. It was one of the first 'novel' foods to gain clearance from the Advisory Committee on Novel Foods and Processes. Since 1991, three enzymes produced by genetically-modified bacteria have been cleared for use in cheese production, two of which are now on the market. A genetically-modified baker's yeast has also been cleared.

10.5 The biotechnology industry

(a) Research and development

The government's perception of biotechnology as a key for future economic development has made it a high priority for investment. A 1990 report from a government advisory committee said:

> 'Our assessment convinces us that biotechnology remains a topic of immense potential, requiring continued long term investment in the science base.' (21)

This is a fiercely competitive field and concern is often expressed that the UK, and indeed the whole European Community, is falling behind the USA and Japan, both in scientific research and in developing new commercial opportunities (22).

In 1991, there were approximately 800 firms active in biotechnology research in the EC, compared to 1,000 in the USA and 300 in Japan. Most of them are in the pharmaceutical or chemical fields. In 1987, the total public investment in the EC as a whole was 1,630 million ECU, compared to the equivalent of 2,484 million ECU government funding for biotechnology in the USA.

During the 1980s, a large number of research initiatives was established, many with joint funding from government and industry. For example, several LINK programmes (collaborations between industry and academic institutions) were set up in the UK, with the government committing £32.25 million to a wide variety of research projects, with similar financial input from industry. Also in the UK, the Agricultural and Food Research Council alone had a budget of £25 million for biotechnology research for the year 1989/90 (23).

(b) The market

It is difficult to collate data on the current profits and future markets of new biotechnological products. Forecasts vary enormously. In the late 1980s, predictions for the world market by the year 2000 ranged from $9 billion to over $100 billion (24). Nevertheless, there is widespread belief that the sector is set to expand dramatically. A 1991 EC paper said that 'even the most conservative estimate yields a threefold increase in sales' (25).

Part of the difficulty in anticipating the size of future markets lies simply in uncertainties about scientific developments. It is also impossible to predict the economic and social climate in which the infant industry will emerge. In the agricultural and food sectors, for example, it is much harder to foresee which products will be acceptable, or indeed unacceptable, to consumers, than in the health field where the benefits are often more clear cut. The development and direction of regulations, both nationally and internationally, will also affect its expansion.

Returns on the high levels of early investment are only now beginning to be realised, with few companies so far recording profits and most of these in the health care sector (26). Although the agricultural sector is expected to grow rapidly during the 1990s, the profits are less certain. This is due to the long time-scale needed to develop products; public concern about ethical issues and the release of genetically-modified organisms into the environment; and uncertainties about the regulations that will be introduced.

10.6 The regulation of biotechnology

(a) European directives

In April 1991, the European Commission published a document setting out its position on biotechnology within the Community (27). This called for the promotion of the 'beneficial application of biotechnology', while ensuring the safety of man and the environment. However, it clearly stated that it did not intend to place undue burdens on industry.

Many products of biotechnology will not require official assessment and/or authorisation because they are produced through traditional methods (like cheeses, beers and yeasts). Products of genetic modification, however, will be considered on a case-by-case basis.

In 1990, three major directives concerning biotechnology were adopted by the EC. A directive requires member states to incorporate the legislation into their own national laws. This is now being done in the UK where the proposed regulations will extend and replace the existing genetic manipulation regulations 1989 (SI1810).

Directive on the 'contained use' of genetically-modified micro-organisms

This requires all factories and research laboratories working with genetically-modified micro-organisms to be approved, and risks to human health and the environment minimised. In case of an accident, full information must be given to the authorities, which are then responsible for any necessary action.

193

Directive on the deliberate release of genetically-modified organisms into the environment

This requires that prior environmental risk assessments are carried out, and that the competent authorities are informed of any proposed release of live genetically-modified organisms to the environment (including small-scale field trials, large-scale introductions and the marketing of products). Any products involved must be authorised. Experimental releases can be approved by national authorities, whereas marketing a product needs Community approval. Once cleared, a product can circulate freely throughout the Community.

Directive on the protection of workers

This requires that workers are protected against risks from exposure to biological agents in laboratories and factories. The level of protection is related to the degree of potential risk and involves: health and safety precautions by employers; information and training for workers; and notification to the authorities of accidents.

These directives go some way towards protecting the public. Whether or not they achieve adequate protection will, of course, depend on the rigour with which they are implemented by national governments. The existing products of biotechnology, such as new crop varieties and mycoprotein, are covered by existing general food safety legislation. In the UK, as we have seen, all novel foods and processes (including the products of genetic modification) undergo a clearance procedure by the Advisory Committee on Novel Foods and Processes, though still on a voluntary basis. The proposed European Council regulation on novel foods, if adopted, would provide a common procedure, including a mandatory safety assessment, throughout the EC.

But does the regulation of biotechnology take into account the ethical questions it raises? The draft EC regulation on novel foods makes no reference to ethics. It seems they will not be considered within the proposed approval structure. However, the idea of a European ethics committee has been raised and, in early 1992, the European Commission set up a group of advisers consisting of six members considered to be 'eminent and independent figures'. The group has been asked to advise the Commission on the ethical implications of some of the developments in, and applications of, biotechnology. As its first task, it has been asked to look at the potential ethical impact of using growth promoters like BST in agriculture and fisheries.

This development is welcome. But it is still too early to assess whether a group of advisers like this will be effective in taking into account consumer concerns about biotechnological developments and in influencing regulatory decisions.

(b) Patents

Another very important area of legislation is the patent, an intellectual property right. A patent is a right, given to an inventor by the state, to exclude any other parties from commercially exploiting the invention, unless they are granted a licence to do so by the inventor. Patent-holders normally demand the payment of a royalty fee when they grant a licence. In return for this protection, the inventor must publish a full description of the invention.

In biotechnology, as in other fields, the patenting issue provokes intense debate. Researchers have their academic reputations to protect. Industry relies on patents for commercial success. And the ethical questions raised by the concept of 'inventing' and 'owning' life forms (as opposed to owning individual animals, like a pet or farm animal) are of great concern to the wider public.

Commercial success in biotechnology will depend critically on the extent to which inventors and manufacturers can obtain patents for products. Traditionally, it has not been possible to patent plants and animals, on the grounds that they are products of nature, rather than 'inventions' (although intellectual property rights in recognised plant varieties have existed for some time). This principle is now being eroded. In 1980 the US Supreme Court, in the case of Diamond vs Chakrabarty, decided that a genetically-modified bacterium could be patented. This set a precedent for claims on the 'ownership' of living organisms (28). It was followed, in 1988, by the first animal patent – the Oncomouse, a laboratory mouse genetically engineered to develop cancer a few weeks after birth, and used in medical research. So the principle that life forms can be 'invented' and treated as a commodity, was established – a significant ethical leap.

The legal situation in Europe is less clear. The European patent convention, in force since 1977, states that patents cannot be granted on plant or animal varieties nor on essentially biological processes for the production of plants or animals (this does not apply to microbiological processes or their products). In 1989, the European Patent Office (EPO), which is not an official body of the EC, rejected an application from Harvard University for an Oncomouse patent. But in October 1991 it reversed its decision on appeal, thus paving the way for a flood of biotechnology patent applications in Europe (29).

195

The EPO's decision has pre-empted European Commission attempts to harmonise the law on patenting biotechnology in member states. A draft directive, which would allow the patenting of plants, animals and micro-organisms, has been under consideration since 1988. If adopted, it would enable many new genetically-modified crops and animals, together with any subsequent offspring, to be the subject of patents. By providing guidelines on what may or may not be patented, it aims to provide a uniform regime of patent law in Europe to encourage biotechnology.

The EPO's decision to grant a patent for the Oncomouse has caused outrage from animal welfare and other concerned groups and from many Euro-MPs who have criticised the EC proposals for deliberately playing down the 'social, ecological and ethical aspects ... as a tiresome afterthought' (30).

10.7 Consumer attitudes to biotechnology

Compared to the vast resources invested in technical research and product development little attention has been paid to investigating consumers' views on biotechnology. However, the existing evidence suggests that consumer acceptance cannot be guaranteed (31).

This is highlighted by two recent studies.

The spring 1991 Eurobarometer survey (32), which interviewed 12,800 people and was carried out by the European Commission, included a number of questions on biotechnology. The results show that public understanding of it is very low, although there is more awareness about it in the northern European countries than in the southern. (Only one in five respondents claimed to feel capable of answering the questions.)

Only 50 per cent of people thought that biotechnology would improve our way of life over the next twenty years. This was the second lowest score – telecommunications (80 per cent), solar energy (76 per cent), computers (74 per cent) and new materials (63 per cent) were all regarded as more useful.

There was more acceptance for research involving plants (77 per cent) and micro-organisms (86 per cent) than that involving animals (47 per cent) and people thought there were greater risks attached to work with transgenic animals than with plants and micro-organisms. There was consensus about the need for 'government control', with over 90 per cent in favour of control of all research involving genetic modification.

Medical and environmental applications of biotechnology were more likely to be considered worthwhile (96 per cent and 97 per cent respectively). Only 65 per cent agreed that food applications could be useful: the potential risks were seen to be higher.

A detailed study of the factors influencing consumer acceptance of biotechnology specifically in foodstuffs was carried out in 1990 by the Institute for Consumer Research (SWOKA) in the Netherlands (33). There was a generally low level of acceptance for the use of 'genetic engineering' (an average rating of 5.6 on a scale of 38 points). There was little variation in individual reactions to different food products; respondents who rated the acceptance of one product low, or high, tended to rate others similarly.

Consumers' socio-economic status, religion and age made very little difference. Those with a more technological outlook appeared to show greater acceptance of the use of 'genetic engineering' in food production, although those who already knew something about genetic engineering showed lower levels of acceptance.

Attitudes were influenced by the *type* of genetic engineering involved and the *purpose* of the end-product. For example, its use in the reduction of pesticides or for health purposes were more acceptable than for improving the taste or prolonging the shelf life of food.

The amount and type of information about genetic engineering available influenced the level of acceptance. Where foods were presented as new, but with no reference to genetic engineering, they were rated positively; if it was revealed that they had been made using genetic engineering, the acceptance level was lower. If a possible adverse effect was mentioned, the products were rated negatively.

Section three: Consumers and new technologies

10.8 The issues for consumers

Until relatively recently, consumers' concerns about food in the UK centred broadly on such things as price, quality, convenience and appearance, with safety for the most part being taken for granted. Over the last decade this has substantially broadened to cover issues like animal welfare, the use of pesticides and veterinary drugs, the environmental impact of production methods and new techniques of processing and preservation.

The food industry welcomes the opportunities that new products and processes, including biotechnology, offer. The benefits for consumers are less obvious. Here we highlight some issues of consumer concern – safety, information, choice, labelling, economic/social and ethical factors. In an area where both the technology and the implications of expanding that technology are still in their infancies, these issues need a wide airing and an informed public debate.

(a) Safety

Consumers must be satisfied that any new product or process is safe. This is particularly true for food. New technologies like irradiation and biotechnology are still little understood by the public and are perceived as potentially dangerous.

The novel foods assessment procedure in Britain, which identifies the type and number of safety tests and the information required for different applications, ought to reassure consumers of the rigour of the system. Its weakness, as we have seen (section 10.2), is that it is not statutory but is carried out voluntarily. The proposed new EC regulation, however, would require mandatory safety assessments and notification/authorisation of all novel foods and ingredients.

There are concerns, too, about the risks of releasing genetically-modified organisms into the environment. Although controlled trials are carried out, the delicate complexity of ecosystems makes it impossible to predict every eventuality. Past experience of disastrous ecological consequences, such as the release of the rabbit into Australia or the rat into New Zealand, make some people concerned that the widespread introduction of genetically-modified organisms could cause ecological havoc.

A recent north American study (34) found that foreign genes introduced into crops pollinated by insects – in this case radishes – can quickly spread into wild varieties up to a kilometre away. This has increased fears that weeds will cross-breed with genetically-modified crops, inheriting traits such as resistance to drought, frost, pesticides, and herbicides. Given the large number of crops pollinated by insects, this has serious implications.

(b) Information about technologies and policies

As every marketing manager knows, the type of information and the way it is presented is a key to the consumer's reaction to a new product. Biotechnology is claimed to have the power to improve the environment, the animals and plants used in agriculture, our health and the quality of the food we eat. Those involved in the research and marketing of its products have a great interest in its success. Only time will tell whether their claims can be substantiated.

Meanwhile, it is important that the debate is opened up to the public – the consumers of the end-product. There is still a vast gulf between scientists' and industry's knowledge and understanding on the one hand and consumers' on the other. According to the Eurobarometer survey in 1991, the media – with its tendency to sensationalise – is the public's main source of information about novel foods and biotechnology. Technical reports use scientific language and jargon incomprehensible to non-specialists (35). At present, people place much more confidence in consumer and environmental groups as sources of reliable information on biotechnology, than they do in public authorities (36). With more openness and dialogue between government, industry *and* consumers, greater understanding and trust could be established.

The decision-making processes in many areas of UK government policy have traditionally been secretive. For example, the government's food and other advisory committees of independent experts – mostly scientists – have been completely closed to the public. However, there have been improvements. Consumer representatives have been appointed to the Food Advisory Committee since it was set up in 1983 and, more recently, to the Advisory Committee on Novel Foods and Processes. Although the papers discussed at meetings remain confidential, agendas, notes of the meetings and annual reports are now published. These improvements are welcome. However, there is a need for even greater openness if consumers are to be in a position to influence the direction of developments and have confidence in the policy process.

(c) Choice

The growing numbers of novel foods and processes coming onto the market are going to have a profound effect on overall choice. In many respects, choice will be widened. Low-calorie foods made with intense sweeteners or fat replacers are, for example, welcomed by people attempting to lose weight (whether or not they have any real impact in achieving this). Similarly, some of the new 'health-enhancing' products – such as bioyoghurts or high-fibre bread – undoubtedly increase consumer choice.

199

But is there also a risk that choice may be narrowed? Will it become difficult to buy certain foods, such as soft drinks which have *not* been sweetened using artificial sweeteners or tomatoes *not* genetically modified to delay softening?

Will consumers know whether certain products, such as fruit and vegetables, oils, flours, meat, cheese and (if the ban on BST is lifted) milk, have been genetically modified? Will they be able to avoid them if they wish to? Without some form of labelling, it may not be possible to know that they have been produced in this way, and it is not clear how choice will be ensured.

(d) Labelling

Much of the debate about consumer choice comes down to the availability of information, on food labels and elsewhere. Do consumers have enough information to make informed purchasing decisions and is this information clear, accurate, useable and not misleading? As more and more foods are sold with implicit health claims on the label, it is vital that these are regulated to protect consumers from being misled.

Consumers increasingly want to know not just what is in their food, but how it is produced. The Food Advisory Committee's advice to ministers that irradiated foods should be labelled (37) was therefore a welcome decision - not least because production processes do not normally have to be labelled.

More recently the Food Advisory Committee has recommended that consumers need clear, informative labelling in order to make decisions about buying genetically-modified products. It has issued for comment its own guidelines on categories of foods and food ingredients from genetically-modified sources. Under these guidelines, two of the four categories would have to be labelled '(contains) products of gene technology' (38). These are foods or food ingredients which are:

● novel products of genetically-modified organisms which differ from conventional products;

● food derived from an organism which has been modified to contain one or more genes from sources outside its own species.

The two other categories - 'nature identical' products of genetically-modified organisms and food from genetically-modified organisms containing genes from the same species - would not have to be labelled. Whether this system will be accepted by the government and be acceptable to consumers will be of keen interest and debate.

A key problem is the complexity of the technology itself and how it can be categorised for labelling purposes. For example, how far back in the food chain should labelling apply? Should honey which contains pollen from genetically-modified plants be labelled? As more and more foods are produced using this technology, it may become impossible to distinguish between those which have and those which have not. Moreover, food labelling is controlled by the European Council Directive 79/112 and the UK could not set labelling criteria which did not comply with it.

The Food Advisory Committee's guidelines are a step forward, in that they recognise the essential role of information in upholding the principle of consumer choice and recognise the need for some form of labelling. However, the situation concerning the labelling of these products in the EC is still unclear. There must be a much wider information campaign, which addresses consumers' genuine concerns, if 'gene technology' is not to suffer the same public rejection as irradiation.

(e) Economic and social issues

Biotechnology has important social and economic implications for the agricultural economies of both of the developed and developing worlds. For example, the genetically-modified growth hormone BST, administered to cows can increase milk production by between ten and forty per cent. The arguments for BST are based, therefore, on its ability to improve efficiency of production. However, BST is currently under a moratorium in the EC, partly as a result of concerns about the impact on the common agricultural policy. European consumer organisations have also raised concerns about the safety of BST; the implications it has for animal welfare; the risk of environmental degradation resulting from intensification of production; and its economic impact on small dairy farmers.

Biotechnology, its supporters claim, will increase food production in terms of higher yields and improved nutritional quality in crops, and help to resolve the problems of hunger in the developing world. Similar claims were made for high-yielding rice and wheat varieties in the 1960s. Experience now shows that although there were some benefits, the 'green revolution' also exacerbated inequalities between rich and poor producers (39). The agrochemical multinational firms, which profited from the green revolution by supplying their fertilisers and pesticides, have seen that genetically-modified strains could by-pass the need for their products. They have diversified into seed production, thus raising the possibility of the development of multi-product cartels.

One of the greatest threats to developing countries is the replacement of traditional commodities by laboratory-produced ones. In Madagascar, for example, the livelihood of seventy thousand vanilla farmers is threatened by the production of a natural vanilla flavour using laboratory techniques. Elsewhere, high fructose corn syrup, produced from maize starch, is now being used as a cheap replacement for cane sugar, a vital source of income for several developing countries (40).

The development of super-strains may also lead to further losses of traditional varieties and less diversity in plant genetic material in the environment. This diversity is crucial to ensuring the stability of the food supply: over-concentration on a few varieties can lead to vulnerability to disease. Indeed, it is this very diversity on which the biotechnology industry is based.

It is likely that many new strains of food crops will be modified so that they are sterile, partly to prevent their spreading to other species and upsetting the local ecological balance. However, this means that small farmers, if they wish to invest in these varieties, will no longer be able to retain some of each year's crop as seed for the following year. They would have to buy new, patented seed annually. Many peasant farmers and their families in the developing world, surviving on narrow margins, could have to choose between incurring the costs associated with the new strains or facing competition from them.

(f) Ethical issues

Ethical concerns about genetic modification could emerge as the most important debate in terms of public acceptance.

Some have argued that it is 'interfering' with nature and could be the first step on a path towards eugenics programmes, whereby attempts are made to 'improve' the human race through genetic alterations. Whether or not this fear is justified, genetic modification undoubtedly involves value judgements about what are 'desirable' or 'undesirable' uses of genes (41). Moreover, it is not clear who will ultimately benefit – or lose – from the predicted developments, nor who is being (or should be) consulted about the direction of scientific research and its applications.

Many people may reject genetic modification on moral and/or religious grounds. In the Eurobarometer survey, 20 per cent of respondents found the genetic modification of animals totally unacceptable on moral grounds; while a further 28 per cent felt it should be considered on a case-by-case basis.

The question of whether it is ethical to patent a life form raises specific concerns about the 'ownership' of life, and whether we can reduce life to 'just DNA' as if it were any other commodity. A patent on an animal treats it as an invention rather than as an independent being, and raises the prospect of ownership not just of individual animals, like pets and farm animals, but of the 'design' of whole sub-species.

The impact of genetic modification on the welfare of animals brings other concerns. The potential use of growth hormones and mice engineered to develop cancer are just two examples. It is not possible to predict precisely the effects of inserting genes into animals: the whole process could encourage more animal experiments, at a time when growing numbers of people object to this.

These ethical concerns need to be openly debated. The European Commission's new group of advisers on bio-ethics (described in section 10.6), which will consider the implications of biotechnological developments, is an important step forward and could play a significant part in this process. In setting up the group, the Commission has at least recognised the need for greater dialogue. The actual influence of the group remains to be seen. But it could make a useful input into the new authorisation procedures set out in the proposed EC regulation on novel foods and ingredients, in addition to bringing the whole ethical debate on genetic modification into sharper public focus.

References to chapter 10

1. Advisory Committee on Novel Foods and Processes, *Guidelines on the Assessment of Novel Foods and Processes,* HMSO, 1991.

2. Commission of the European Communities, *Proposal for a Council Directive on Sweeteners in Foodstuffs,* COM(91) 195 final, 1991.

3. S. Dibb, 'Can diet products help you slim?' *Food Magazine,* 14 (2) July/September, 1991.

4. 'No Fat Foods', *Which? Way to Health,* Consumers' Association, June 1991.

5. PA Consulting Group, *Functional Foods: a new global added value market?,* 1991.

6. A. Foster, 'Consumer attitudes to irradiation', *Food Control,* 2 (1), January 1991.

7. Commission of the European Communities, *Proposal for a Council Regulation on Novel Foods and Novel Food Ingredients,* COM(92)295 final – SYN426, 1992.

8. E.L. Roberts, *The Public and Biotechnology: a discussion document*, European Foundation for the Improvement of Living and Working Conditions, 1989.

9. J.D. Watson, *The Double Helix*, Weidenfeld and Nicholson, 1968.

10. Advisory Council on Science and Technology, *Developments in Biotechnology*, HMSO, 1990.

11. Commission of the European Communities, *Promoting the Competitive Environment for the Industrial Activities Based on Biotechnology within the Community*, Commission Communication to Parliament and the Council, SEC (91) 629, 1991.

12. J. Katz and D.B. Sattelle, *Biotechnology in Focus*, Hobsons Publishing, 1988.

13. D.B. Sattelle, *Biotechnology in Perspective*, Hobsons Publishing, 1988.

14. Agricultural and Food Research Council, *Recent Advances in Plant and Microbial Biotechnology*, AFRC (no date).

15. Advisory Council on Science and Technology, see reference 10.

16. Agricultural and Food Research Council, see reference 14.

17. Advisory Council on Science and Technology, see reference 10.

18. J. Katz and D.B Satelle, see reference 12.

19. Advisory Council on Science and Technology, see reference 10.

20. Advisory Council on Science and Technology, see reference 10.

21. Advisory Council on Science and Technology, see reference 10.

22. Commission of the EC, see reference 11.

23. Advisory Council on Science and Technology, see reference 10.

24. Advisory Council on Science and Technology, see reference 10.

25. Commission of the EC, see reference 11.

26. M. Crawford, 'Wall Street takes stock of biotechnology', *New Scientist*, 23 November 1991.

27. Commission of the EC, see reference 11.

28. Patent Concern, *Patenting of Plants and Animals*, Genetics Forum, 1991.

29. T. Wilkie, 'Patent for mouse upsets moves to EC harmony', *Independent*, 16 October 1991.

30. D. Mackenzie, 'Europe rethinks patent on the Harvard mouse', *New Scientist*, 19 October 1991.

31. T. Hoban and J. Burkhardt, 'Determinants of public acceptance in meat and milk production: North America', *Biotechnology for Control of Growth and Production Quality in Meat Production: implications and acceptability*. International Symposium, Washington, 5-7 December 1991, pp. 229-244.

32. Commission of the European Communities, *Highlights of the Preliminary Results of the Spring 1991 Eurobarometer,* DG XII, Concertation Unit for Biotechnology in Europe, 1991.

33. A.M. Hamstra, *Biotechnology in Foodstuffs: towards a model of consumer acceptance,* SWOKA, the Netherlands, 1991.

34. A. Coglan, 'Will altered crops run wild in the country?', *New Scientist,* 21 March 1992.

35. R. Straughan, *The Genetic Manipulation of Plants,Animals and Microbes: the social and ethical issues for consumers,* National Consumer Council, 1989.

36. Commission of the EC, see reference 32.

37. Advisory Committee on Irradiated and Novel Foods, Report on the Safety and Wholesomeness of Irradiated Foods, *Appendix F,* HMSO, 1986.

38. Food Advisory Committee, *Guidelines for the Labelling of Foods Produced Using Genetic Modification,* Ministry of Agriculture, Fisheries and Food, October 1990.

39. G.R. Conway and E.B. Barbier, *After the Green Revolution: sustainable agriculture for development,* Earthscan Publications, 1990.

40. Genetics Forum, 'Genetic Engineering', 1990.

41. R. Straughan, see reference 35.

Printed in the United Kingdom for HMSO
Dd 293664, C30 10/92